Ice Cream Camelot

B.J. Neblett

Brighton Publishing LLC
435 N. Harris Drive
Mesa, AZ 85203

ICE CREAM CAMELOT

B.J. NEBLETT

BRIGHTON PUBLISHING LLC
435 N. HARRIS DRIVE
MESA, AZ 85203
WWW.BRIGHTONPUBLISHING.COM

ISBN: 978-1-62183-093-1

ISBN 10: 1-62183-093-4

First Edition

Cover Design: Emily Gussin and Tom Rodriguez

Dedication

For Mom and Dad and my sister Mary
For my beloved Aunt Mary
For Chris
And especially for Amy

"Let us never negotiate out of fear. But let us never fear to negotiate."

John Fitzgerald Kennedy

"There is no such thing as an empty space or an empty time. There is always something to see, something to hear."

John Cage

"Life's a bitch, Daddy-o…"

Christopher Murphy

Acknowledgments

I'd sincerely like to thank the following people without whose help this book would never have become a reality.

Emily Gussin for her wonderful cover art work, and especially for her many hours of thoughts and feedback during the writing process, and for playing a great second base.

Lisa Battaglia for her patience, and support.

Rita Bresnahan of the Ballard Writers Collective for her constant nagging and the wonderful profile she did of me.

The entire Ballard Writers Collective for their help and support.

Jenna Solie for the great web and blog sites and her continued help and support.

My entire softball team for putting up with my craziness and wild mood swings while I was writing.

Don and Kathie McGuire and the entire staff at Brighton Publishing for their help and support and mostly for believing in me.

Everyone who has made my first novel, *Elysian Dreams,* a success. Hang in there, the sequel is on the way.

And of course, to my God and Creator for the crazy life and the wonderful talents he bestowed upon me.

ᥱ᠊ᤊChapter Oneᥱᤌ

When you are a boy of eleven you know everything: everything you need to know, everything you want to know, and a lot of stuff you don't care about. The latter comes mostly from school and parents. The other stuff, the stuff much more important to the boy of eleven, comes from the street, from the guys you hang with—from friends. It comes from comic books and older brothers' *Playboy* magazines; from JD Salinger and William Golding and Ray Bradbury; from Mickey Spillane under the covers with a flashlight; from movies and TV; and from just being eleven.

At eleven, a boy's vision is a panoramic three hundred and sixty degrees. His mind is a sponge, his understanding instant. He loves and hates with the same over-abundance of enthusiasm. And he can switch between the two in less time than it takes to lose a prized Warren Spahn or Joe Oliver baseball card in a heated game of Match.

His world may stretch from the corner drugstore to the local hangout to the junior high; from the neighborhood pool to deep inside the woods he's not suppose to enter, to the spooky old house that gets egged each Mischief Night. But to the eleven year old, this world includes the dusty frontier streets of Dodge City and the reddish, rusty surface of Mars. He covers his territory on his trusty two-wheeler that is at once a painted appaloosa or a thundering Indy race car.

The eleven-year-old boy lives for the moment and dreams of the future. Life is simple at eleven. Life is black and white. Life is good. Life is uncomplicated for the eleven-year-old boy.

Except for when it comes to the eleven-year-old girl. Then logic short circuits and the world becomes a melting ice cream cone of twenty-seven flavors, an impossible choice between apple pie and chocolate cake, between Roger Maris and Willie Mays.

This condition can be directly traced to a simply complex source: hormones. When freshly hatched hormones meet eleven-year-old logic, they beget a love child named confusion.

The eleven-year-old boy can figure out and understand anything; how to take apart his sister's bicycle, what makes his mom crazy, the bare minimum it takes to appease his teacher, how to sneak into a Saturday matinee, where to find the best returnable bottles and shortcuts to just about anywhere.

He also knows how to make the entire fifth-grade class laugh out loud and how to strike out the school bully, thus humiliating him. These ploys are always good for impressing the eleven-year-old girl. But he doesn't understand why he wants to impress her, only that he wants to—has to—*needs to*—impress her.

All of this is true. I know. I was an eleven-year-old boy. I lived in Camelot and ate the ice cream before it all melted all twenty-seven flavors.

The lightly freckled, eleven-year-old object of my personal confusion appeared on the first day of school in 1961.

For some reason school always started on a Wednesday. Not on a Monday as logic might dictate, but on a Wednesday.

My eyes opened involuntarily to the sound of water running. Then off. Then running…

Off.

Running…

Off.

Dad was in the bathroom, shaving.

Men on TV rinsed their Gillette safety razors in the murky water pooling in the sink. My Uncle Jimmy used an electric razor: *Close as a blade, twice as comfortable.*

Not my dad. Seven days a week—an hour later on Sunday—it was *push, pull, click, lock.* Then shave… rinse… shave… rinse. Water running… Water off.

Running…

Off.

There was a slot in the back of the medicine cabinet where Dad ejected the used razor blades, *push, pull, click, lock.*

"Where do the razor blades go?"

"Down inside the wall."

Running…

Off.

"What happens when the wall gets filled up?"

Dad gave me an incredulous look. Another question unanswered. Parents do that sometimes, give their kids *the look* and don't answer. They want them to figure it out for themselves. Like the one about the first day of school.

"Why Wednesday?"

Of all the adults I asked over the years, not one could give me a satisfactory answer. Some gave me the look.

"Why Wednesday?"

There was something about Labor Day and vacations and the school year. But then why do some schools begin *before* Labor Day?

I never figured it out for myself. But whatever the reason, it seemed to fit, seemed right. Like Thanksgiving always being on Thursday, only of course without the giving thanks—or the cranberries.

Push, pull, click, lock...

If I hurried, I could be next in the bathroom, before my sister. Mary, being two years older, had the larger bedroom, right next to the bathroom. I slept in there one time when my room was being painted. The toilet kept running and kept me awake until dad got up and went in and hit the handle. When my sister gets married in 1969 I'll move into her room.

Today is a Wednesday, not a hurrying day. Mondays are for hurrying, if you are the hurrying type. Some people are. I'm not.

You see, there is a natural order about things: peanut butter sandwiches are made with grape jelly, not strawberry. The toilet paper roll can go either way, over or under. School starts on Wednesday. You rush on Monday, maybe Tuesday morning, not Wednesday. Someday the wall will get filled up with used razor blades.

Grownups don't seem to understand these things, at least not parents. Or they have forgotten, or don't care. It's a shame—being grown up seems to take something from a person.

No more water running.

Dad left the bathroom and headed downstairs. He switched on the white plastic Silvertone kitchen table radio. Everything in 1961 was made of plastic.

"WIP news time 5:46 a.m."

He'll cook two fried eggs in butter, three pieces of bacon, juice, coffee, milk, and two slices of toast with butter. The broiler drawer on the gas oven squealed like one of grandpa's piglets. It's the same thing every morning.

Squeal!

In a couple of years dad will suffer a mild heart attack. He'll change his eating habits a little. And he'll start noticing some things again. When I return home from the Army in 1972, my parents will still be making toast in the gas oven's broiler.

Squeal!

Maybe if they had bought a toaster they would have stayed married.

I could hear my sister in the bathroom. Mary's the hurrying type most of the time. She'll make a good parent. She already has the look.

It was too early to get up. Jerry Stevens hadn't even come on yet. The transistor radio under my pillow was still switched on. I must have fallen asleep with it on again. Good thing I had a spare nine volt.

The radio was a surprise gift from my parents last Christmas. My sister got one, too. Hers was red, mine black plastic with silver trim and white dials, in a soft leather case. It was about the size of a pack of cigarettes, king size.

One night I came home from hanging out with the guys. Hanging out with the guys is important in an eleven-year-old boy's life: the street corner or vacant lot or playground is his society, his clique, his water cooler. It's an integral part of how a boy of eleven knows everything. The guys I hung out with were mostly older.

Arriving home, my mom met me at the door. I had a pack of Salem cigarettes in the breast pocket of my denim jacket.

Mom pointed to the obvious bulge. "What's that?"

"My radio."

The black transistor radio with the built-in antenna became my prized possession. From the Christmas I received it in 1960, it never left me. It changed my life in several ways. I still have it.

The radio gave the time—one minute till six—then a legal ID. Those are the ones with the station's call letters and transmitter location: every hour at the top of the hour—FCC regulations. My mind was set on being a radio DJ. *Spin all the hits—another Alan Freed.*

"WIBG radio 99, Lafayette Hills—Philadelphia, a Storer Broadcasting Company."

It was news time. I switched off my radio and slipped it from the leather case to install a fresh battery. It wasn't that I didn't care about the news; unlike most kids my age, I often listened.

One winter morning in 1959 the smell of Dad's breakfast was too strong. If you joined him he'd cook for you, as long as you didn't talk too much, so he could listen to the news. Dad didn't seem to know or care anything about music. I came downstairs hoping he was still frying bacon. Peggy Sue flowed out of the white plastic table radio. Dad was listening to rock'n'roll?

The song faded after a few seconds. The popular La Bamba segued in; then the music dissolved. "JP Richardson, known as the Big Bopper, Ritchie Valens, and Buddy Holly, dead in an Iowa plane crash. This is 610, WIP."

I was very aware of rock-n-roll and familiar with Buddy Holly. My aunt Mary often looked after me till she died of breast cancer at a very young age. Mom's kid sister never married. She smoked, worked in night clubs, and dated a cool guy named Dominick who carried a pistol, drove a big black Buick, and was connected. She loved him and loved music. I loved her. I can still see her influences on me today.

It was from my aunt that I learned about blues, jazz, bop, R&B, and, most of all, about rock 'n' roll. My sister and I were already collecting 45's. Wherever we went there was music: on the radio; the juke box; the record player; in Dominick's car. It was music that my aunt loved, music that spoke to me, somehow made me feel special.

I remember being at my grandmother's, in front of her burly Dumont TV, watching *Bandstand*. This was when rock 'n' roll was uncorrupted by big money, before the network took the show national. Aunt Mary would pull me up off the floor to dance along with the kids on the flickering black-and-white screen.

6

After my aunt's death, my sister and I continued to tune in Dick Clark and *American Bandstand*. She liked to watch the dancers and see the guest stars. For me it was always the music.

My aunt provided the first piece of the puzzle that was my enigmatic life: music. My transistor radio was the key.

I think that February morning in 1959 was the first time I made a conscious effort to listen to the news. That evening my sister and I ate supper on the folding plastic TV trays in the den. John Facenda, Channel Ten's stoic anchor, gave the news in his classic, baritone, authoritative announcer's voice: a fire in west Philly, a shooting, an accident on the Schuylkill Expressway tying up the morning commute, Castro in Cuba.

Then there were haunting images of a private plane, what was left of it, smashed and tangled, up-ended against a barbed-wire fence. Three indistinguishable bodies lay scattered in the fresh snow, like discarded rags, the pilot dead in the cockpit.

The *Evening Bulletin* carried a front-page headline: Rock Stars Die in Plane Crash, and a half-page article with more pictures inside. My sister kept the newspaper clipping taped to her bedroom mirror till she graduated from high school.

I remember the news of the three young musicians' deaths making me feel bad, empty. Aunt Mary had just recently passed away. The deaths of Holly, Valens, and the Bopper made me feel as I did when my aunt died. But I didn't understand why.

I found myself listening to the news in the morning with Dad sometimes. I didn't always know what I was hearing. Often I'd ask questions about what was being said. Dad would give me the look, not wishing to be disturbed. But later, after dinner, he'd point out an article in the *Bulletin* that pertained to my earlier question.

I learned to read the newspaper that way. I learned about the world, about war and crime, about the race for space and struggles going on in Cuba and some place called Southeast Asia, and about something called integration and segregation. Dad taught me many things this way, with the look and then helping me to figure it out for myself. But my young brain managed to adopt its own kind of twisted isolationist logic. I didn't know anyone whose name appeared in the newspaper or on TV, not personally anyway. The victims of crimes and accidents, those who lived in other countries, even other states, weren't important. They weren't connected to me, my family, or my friends. Therefore, their lives couldn't have an impact on my own. I came to refer to them in my mind as background people. Things happened to them, not to me. Yet my aunt was gone, as were my mom's dad and mom. And the tragic plane crash in Iowa stirred new, even more confused feelings inside of me, as did the titillating sounds and images flowing from my radio.

WIBG—Wibbage—didn't do much news, mostly in the morning, and just enough to keep the FCC happy. What little they gave was short, concise, and usually of interest to me. I liked that. Mostly they just played the hits along with the "oldies," a term newly coined by LA DJ Art Laboe. It was perfect. Not only did my little radio keep me up with all the hits, it filled me in on the great rock 'n' roll I may have missed.

But as the 1960 campaigns and presidential election rolled around, I became fascinated by the grim, determined images on the nightly news. The interviews, the speeches, the promises, the accusations and counter charges, and the raucous, chaotic conventions with their balloons and banner waving and frantic calls to order, gavel hammering away, held my attention. Every evening the two icons—the elder, unshaven establishment, and the young, clean-cut, charismatic hopeful—debated the economy, world trade, isolationism, communism, and other topics new to me right there in my den. In the pre-Dallas fall of 1960 I was actually able to shake the hands of both Kennedy and Nixon, as each motored in turn through my welcoming little town.

The background people were beginning to spill over into my safe, comfortable, innocent existence.

The news, local and national, gradually became part of my young life. In the rapidly changing '60s, it was hard to avoid. With

8

true parental logic, my parents complained that if I could watch the news and read the newspaper, why couldn't I do my homework and do better in school?

I didn't give them the look. The answer was simple and clear: school was boring.

⟪Chapter Two⟫

Wednesday, September 6, 1961. While I was settling into the routine of fifth grade part two, the first Americans to enlist in the newly formed Peace Corps were settling into an uneasy routine in West Africa. Drawing on campaign fodder, as one of his first official acts of office, the country's youngest elected president signed executive order 10924, creating the civilian missionary-type program. By fall, volunteers were in Ghana and Tanzania to "promote world peace and friendship..." Democratic and Republican detractors alike were quick to proclaim that the service organization would become a safe haven for draft dodgers. However, the Peace Corps would prove to be just the first of many stunning victories, as well as agonizing defeats, for the short-lived presidency.

With nearly everything against him, John F. Kennedy earned the highest office in the nation through a tough-fought, nose-to-nose campaign. Young, Catholic, and Democrat were not the three best things to be if you were a politician in 1960. Running against Richard M. Nixon, the vice president of an enormously popular president was considered political suicide. Throughout the 1950s, Americans enjoyed peace and an unprecedented prosperity. Establishment America looked to the new decade with the same confidence and optimism that had marked the Eisenhower '50s.

John Fitzgerald Kennedy was born May 29, 1917, in Brookline, Massachusetts. He was the second of nine children in a family of self-made Irish immigrants. From the time of his arrival in America, it was patriarch Joseph P. Kennedy's dream that one of his children would one day become leader of his adopted country. To that end, Joe senior soon found himself immersed in the heated, sometimes violent, political arena of nineteenth-century Boston. By the time his first son Joseph Patrick arrived, the family had amassed the wealth, respect, and clout to significantly influence the political direction of the state.

The eldest Kennedy son was attending Harvard Law School and being groomed for a political career when World War II intervened. Receiving his commission as an aviator in the U.S. Navy, he soon found himself stationed in Britain, flying land-based PB4Y Liberator bombers on anti-submarine patrols. On August 12, 1944, Joe Jr. was killed while flying a top-secret test mission near Suffolk, England.

Following the war, Joseph's number two son, John Fitzgerald, was poised to embark on his own career in politics. John was also a veteran of WWII and a naval hero himself, having survived dangerous PT boat duty in the South Pacific. In November 1946 he handily won election to the House of Representatives, retaining his seat for 1950. In 1952 the young upstart Democrat switched to the Senate, defeating popular Republican incumbent Henry Cabot Lodge, Jr., by more than 70,000 votes. The same election saw Republican Dwight D. Eisenhower carry the state of Massachusetts to the presidency. As Democrats in the heavily Republican Commonwealth, the Kennedy family power and influence had been clearly established.

Dick Clark's *Bandstand* wasn't the only thing to catch my eye during the '50s. By the time of the 1956 national conventions, the upstart Du Mont Network was essentially out of business. But the three remaining TV networks—ABC, NBC and CBS—went all out to cover both the Republican and Democratic presidential conventions. For some reason, at the tender age of six, I became fascinated with the proceedings. I didn't really have a choice. Sally Starr Theatre, the Honeymooners, Superman, Jack Benny, and Uncle Miltie Berle had to take a back seat as my politically correct father dutifully tuned in the raucous happenings. The results from San Francisco may have been as predictable as Cadillac's tail fins, with Eisenhower once again going up against repeat candidate Adlai Stevenson. However, the Chicago gathering was the perfect platform to showcase the Democrats' rising star, Senator John Kennedy. Kennedy narrowly missed receiving the party's nod as vice presidential candidate during a call for a free vote. Ironically, perhaps the biggest winners of the conventions were two unknown NBC reporters, Chet Huntley and David Brinkley. The pair proved so popular at their assignment that they soon found themselves co-anchoring the network's nightly news.

As the iconic Ike began his second term and the country began the somewhat mundane routine of suburban American life, Kennedy retreated to rebuild his campaign. The astute Kennedy would keep himself busy and in the public eye throughout the remainder of the 1950s. In 1956 he published a best seller, *Profiles in Courage,* which would receive the Pulitzer Prize for biography in 1957. Kennedy also became a major political force in the passing of 1957's Civil Rights Bill. The upstart senator stated publicly that he fully accepted and supported a controversial U.S. Supreme Court decision.

The 1954 ruling, Brown vs. Board of Education of Topeka, established that "separate public schools for black and white students was unconstitutional." By aligning with those who favored desegregation, Kennedy place himself squarely in the middle of the growing and volatile issue of civil rights. The controversy would carry over well into and beyond the 1960 presidential elections. But the wily politician knew exactly how and when to choose his battles. In 1958 the now familiar and wildly popular senator was re-elected by more than 874,000 votes. The same election saw Eisenhower's Republican Party lose a record sixteen Senate and forty-eight House seats. The Democrats' modest edge became an insurmountable majority. The stage was set for a new decade and a new leadership.

In the late '50s westerns were the rage on TV's vast wasteland, and no self-respecting kid of the times would be caught dead without his six-shooter. Even the charismatic Kennedy took time to pose for a publicity shot wearing a coonskin cap.

Christmas 1957 brought a lot of snow and some very cool cowboy goodies. Dominick, my Aunt Mary's ever-present paramour, surprised me with a full set of Western duds, including chaps, spurs, ten-gallon hat, and a set of cap-firing, pearl-handled six shooters.

Dominick's quiet but forceful presence in my life was a mixed blessing. His subtle influence had an unspoken but definite and lasting mark on my life. I loved my aunt and greatly admired Dominick, wishing to emulate his suave but tough persona. Later, Kennedy's tough-as-nails TV stance on Castro and communism would remind me of Dominick's sometimes harsh street dealings. As a wide-eyed, impressionable youngster of the '50s, I often sat in silent witness from the back seat of the big black Buick, as Dominick dealt out mob-ordered street justice. Violence, be it on the city's streets or confined to the TV screen, both news and otherwise, was a daily part of my young life.

One Sunday afternoon, Dominick, Aunt Mary, and I piled into his Buick sedan and headed for a park near 2nd and Dickenson Streets on the boarder of Philly's Little Italy. While Dominick played bocce and my aunt looked on, mingling with the other women, I made my way to the playground and the sandbox, pail and shovel in hand. As usual, the local bully took sadistic pleasure in pushing me around, kicking sand in my face and trampling my carefully constructed castles. I was about six at the time, small and without many friends or muscles. But I did have a plan. When it came time to leave I purposely left my prized pail and shovel behind.

It wasn't unusual for Dom to keep his .38 in the Buick's glove box. But he'd often slip a light, compact Beretta into one of my pockets. At the time, it was a common practice for hoods to have their girlfriends or kids carry the goods for safe keeping. Returning to the car that particular afternoon, I waited for Dominick to tuck the lethal weapon into the inside pocket of the front flap of my overalls. Putting my hastily thought out plan into action, I told my aunt I had forgotten my pail and shovel, and I darted for the sandbox. Coming up to my tormenter from behind, I tapped him on the shoulder. As the unsuspecting boy turned, I deftly slipped the Beretta from its hiding place and swung blindly. The pistol glanced across the other's chin, knocking him into the sand just as I had witnessed Dominick do on occasion.

Satisfied with the stunned figure at my feet, I quickly replaced the weapon, pick up my pail and shovel, and calmly and proudly returned to Dominick and my aunt. For all I know I could have killed the poor boy. The incident went unnoticed and unreported. Such were the times and surroundings of my early youth.

By 1960 it was becoming increasingly evident that the order of the day would be *change*. No matter how desperately Americans longed to cling to the peace and sameness of the past decade, the world was in flux. The Russians were in space, Castro was in Cuba, and civil rights and integration were quickly becoming the catch words of a new era. In addition, another war lurked just around the next corner. Even my life had taken some drastic and unexpected changes. My beloved aunt had passed on, the family had moved to the suburbs, and I was spending less and less time running the streets of South Philly. I never saw Dominick again. A generation of backyard barbecues and bomb shelters had been born out of old fears and new threats, both real and imagined. This new, younger generation was ready for a change in the guard, and John Fitzgerald Kennedy was their choice, describing himself as a man "born in this century," keen to explore "the New Frontier."

With the limited understanding of my age, I followed the 1960 campaigns, proudly displaying a Kennedy/Johnson button on my school jacket, much to my conservative Republican father's dismay. Try as I may I didn't fully understand the mechanics and methods of the political scene, including the newly popular catch phrase "racial equality." Here ten-year-old reason faltered.

Growing up in ethnically diverse and divided South Philadelphia, I witnessed firsthand the real and imagined boundaries that separated Italians from Irish, Germans from Polish, the poor from the wealthy, and black from white. Through mute acceptance, my parents and teachers alike instilled in me the belief that this division was normal. My background people were neatly and logically ordered. Thanks to TV news, I also witnessed the heart rending, often violent struggles for racial equality, especially in the South. The simplistic logic that all men were created equal seemed to me a no-brainer. We were taught it in school, preached it in church, and lectured on it in the news. And yet the girls sat behind the boys; wives were subservient to their husbands; and blacks lived separate from whites. I had always been taught to treat everyone with equal respect. But it never occurred to my young mind that everyone I came into contact with was of the same race. I sympathized with the struggles of black Americans and witnessed the inequality of my own existence, never once equating the two.

What I did understand was that young Americans all across the country were drawn in by the Kennedy charm and magnetism. The rhetoric was too loud, the momentum too strong, and the bandwagon too exciting to resist.

Following the conventions, the fall campaigns kicked into high gear. This time my *Twilight Zone* and *Ozzie and Harriet* and *Untouchables* were preempted by terse political updates and tense political debates. All the while the country grew more divided: the segregationists vs. the integrationists, the established vs. the new order, the right vs. the left, the young vs. the old. Lines were tightly drawn and Election Day found the dissimilar pair in a dead heat.

Tuesday, November 8, 1960, brought confusing and conflicting news feeds:

"Uncertain Election Results Favor Kennedy"

"Fighting Erupts in South Vietnam"

In Hyannis Port, Mass., Sen. John F. Kennedy watched his early lead over Vice President Nixon narrow as the evening progressed and refused to claim victory before Nixon conceded defeat.

Nixon watched the returns come in at his suite in the Ambassador Hotel in Los Angeles and later "virtually concedes," according to a report written to appear the next day.

In California, with 32 electoral votes, Kennedy maintained a lead over Nixon. Nixon, however, remained confident of winning his home state once absentee ballots were counted.

In Illinois, Kennedy maintained a slim lead.

Despite the uncertain returns, *New York Times* reporter James Reston prepared a story for tomorrow's edition of his paper saying it appeared Kennedy had won election.

Another story prepared for the next day's paper said, "... in the final hours of Election Day we do not collectively know what we have decided."

The agonizing election night dragged on into the next day without a clear winner. Finally, 43-year-old Kennedy was declared the victor in one of the closest presidential elections of the 20th century. Kennedy managed to carry the popular vote over Nixon by just two-tenths of one percent. In the Electoral College he won 303 votes to his opponent's 219. And in a portentous sign of troubled times to come, fourteen electors from Mississippi and Alabama refused to support Kennedy because of his support for the civil rights movement.

Friday, January 20, 1961, I sat in my desk at St. Pius X Grade School, watching with the rest of my class as Kennedy was inaugurated the thirty-fifth president of the United States. During his acceptance speech, the compelling leader boldly stated that we were "on the edge of a new frontier," letting "the word go forth from this time and place, to friend and foe alike, that the torch has been passed to a new generation of Americans..."

Feeling a part of that new generation, I had unwittingly found an idol and hero.

My bed was cozy and my sister Mary was still in the bathroom. Jerry Stevens came on the radio: "Six to ten in the a.m. with music to get your day rockin'."

After him it would be old Bill Wright senior. Housewives liked him, including my mom. How many wives spent their afternoons cleaning house to the jungle rhythms of rock 'n' roll the world will never know. Then from two to six p.m.: *The Rockin 'Bird Flies!*—Joe Niagara.

Joe had been doing afternoon drive at Wibbage since the station went 24-hour rock 'n' roll. In the '50s, media maverick Todd Storz noticed kids would play the same songs over and over. Like the records on the jukebox, the more Storz watched the more he became intrigued. It wasn't long before Storz was experimenting with music rotation at one of his radio stations. Soon Frank Sinatra and Doris Day and Nat King Cole were rotating as regularly as the inevitable commercial spot. The Top 40 format was born.

Adults may have enjoyed their regular doses of big bands and swing, but when rock 'n' roll met Top 40 all bets were off. WIBG became the first station in the country to play non-stop rock 'n' roll, following the new and highly successful format, tweaking and adjusting it for different times of the day and night. A revolution was born. I don't remember the event but it caused uproar. It was still being talked about and discussed by concerned parents and civic groups.

By 1961 there were a lot of rock 'n' roll stations, but Joe Niagara was the number one DJ in the country. And WIBG was the number one station. The recent payola scandals and resulting congressional investigation had managed to expose if not remove much of the corruption and double dealing within the broadcast industry. But DJs still held court and radio stations still held clout. And the fickle, intangible commodity known as the hit record could still be manipulated, to a certain profitable extent. Radio was big business, and rock 'n' roll was quickly becoming bigger business. And everyone wanted a slice of the pie. As a result, the industry began keeping close tabs on the latest fads and trends and dances to wiggle out of the City of Brotherly Love. And if it didn't get played on Wibbage, it didn't get played.

Joe Niagara, along with fellow Wibbage DJ Hy Lit, became early mentors of mine. Today, the iconic pair, plus Jerry Blavat, another famous and infamous Philly DJ, are enshrined in Cleveland's Rock 'n' Roll Hall of Fame. Those three disembodied influential voices, emanating from my plastic transistor radio, set me on my chosen career path. I have been honored to be able to call all three men my friends. In the 1970s I would get to share on-air time at radio stations with both Hy Lit and Joe Niagara. Life was good.

Jerry Stevens and the Wibbage hit survey kept me company for the next hour while I pretended to be getting up. Mom hollered from her bedroom. "Hey. Did you forget? It's the first day of school."

Yeah, like I could forget.

What kept my parents happily married during the '50s and '60s must have been true love, or the kids, or desperation… or more likely a combination of all three and a lot more. My father, the very conservative, stoic head of the family, was a poster boy for all the Madison Avenue, Dr. Spock, Anne Landers psycho-babble of the nuclear '50s family: Men were the bread winners; wives stayed home and took care of the house (and their husbands); kids respected authority; and the suburbanite family was safely isolated from the world and its problems. In reality, my clan was the poster family for dysfunction, including a well-meaning but clueless father, an overachieving daughter, a delinquent son, and a fun-loving, flighty, overbearing, over-loving mother. I couldn't have had a better childhood if I had it scripted.

Mother Rose Neblett's ambition in life was to be an actress. Since high school, Mom acted, worked, and volunteered in anything that might bring her attention and fame. I'm sure she married Dad mainly because in the '40s it was expected of good, dutiful Italian daughters, my rebellious, fun-loving aunt notwithstanding. Don't get me wrong, I'm sure she loved Dad very much. And he loved her. He just didn't get her. I can't remember a school function or variety show that didn't include Mom's talents. Meeting local friends who did quite well as part-time models led her to print and advertising work. Many times I would climb aboard a SEPTA bus only to find myself face to face with the bigger-than-life face of my own mother, hawking pasta or health insurance or a local bank. At various times, Mom was a full-time spokesperson for products as diverse as Blue Cross of Pennsylvania, PNB National Bank, a local pizza shop, and 7UP. Her 4'10" Italian frame and natural comedic air lent themselves to character parts, and soon she was appearing regularly on the Mike Douglas television program and doing little theatre. This led to becoming a member in AFTRA and the screen actors' guild, which in turn led to an agent, voice-overs, more TV work, and even movie roles.

Mom loved the stage and acting and reveled in the attention and modest fame afforded to even a bit player. Dad remained silently proud of his errant wife, saving his compliments for the well-prepared Swanson TV dinner awaiting his return from work. I had a ringside seat at a sit-com that was better than anything the networks could conjure up. Yet, through all the movies and head shots and tryouts and rehearsals and plays and TV and movie shoots and trips to New York, I can honestly say my sister and I never felt neglected. Mom was always there for the family. As for my loving, conservative father with the *Father Knows Best* complex, she drove him nuts.

I switched off my transistor, pulling myself out of bed. The ubiquitous blue tie and white shirt lay neatly across my desk chair, not a welcoming sight on the first Wednesday of school. St. Pius X Catholic Grade School had a dress code. Girls wore navy blue jumpers over a white button-up blouse and blue and white saddle shoes. Like many things in the '50s and '60s, the boys had it easier: slacks and suit or sports jacket with an ugly blue tie. School colors were blue and gold. In nine years at St. Pius I never saw anything gold.

Dominick's life style, to mention nothing of his ubiquitous gun tucked neatly into the waistband of his seersucker slacks, continued to influence me. During the heyday of the TV private eye, Butch Bartley and I used to wear our very real-looking toy .38s to school under our jackets. Butch had an *Untouchables*-style shoulder holster. Mine was the kind that clipped to my belt, just like Dominick's. I still wore mine sometimes.

Toys were a lot different in 1961. Before consumer groups and law suits and warning labels—before parents got lazy, or forgot, about teaching their children right from wrong. It was a time when common sense was in fashion.

My chrome plastic .38 is a perfect example. It was the same size and shape, and looked and worked exactly like the real thing. The cylinder swung out to the side. It came with hard plastic, hollow cartridges. You placed a Greenie Stickum Cap on the rear of the cartridge over the hole, and then slipped a soft plastic slug over the other end. Six bullets were then loaded into the cylinder. When you pulled the trigger the hammer came back, the cylinder rotated, and the hammer snapped in place, setting off the cap. The resulting explosion sent the none-too-soft slug hurling far across the room— just like the real thing.

It didn't take a genius, just a ten-year-old boy, to figure out using two caps would propel the slugs a lot further and faster. Against bare flesh they left a stinging welt. I knew from experience playing G-Man and bootlegger.

Believe it or not, on a dare, I once placed the barrel to my temple and pulled the trigger. It hurt like hell. And the double cap explosion left a ringing in my ear that lasted an hour.

Kids do things like that sometimes.

I also had a wooden musket that replicated the real thing. It used the redoubtable green caps with the sticky backs as well. Using baby powder not only added to the realism of powering and loading, it also helped the cork mini-ball sail far across my considerable back yard.

Such were the toys of my youth, some potentially dangerous, others not obviously so. And the only warning labels came from the mouths of parents.

The bathroom's yellow, black, and white patterned tile floor was cold beneath my bare feet. My sister was back in her bedroom, probably hurrying around. I sat on the grey plastic toilet seat and noticed the empty toilet paper dispenser. Mary had left a fresh roll on the sink. Snatching off the cardboard tube, I replaced it with the new roll. The tissue hung down from the backside of the wall-mounted dispenser.

Perfect.

Dad would hate it.

Push, pull, click, lock…

Until today, summer had been in full effect. The Delaware Valley, along with the rest of the country, had baked for three long months. Temperatures topped out in the mid to upper nineties, with plenty of humidity. Just the way I liked it. As the country sweltered over the summer of '61, the standard greeting became, "Hot enough for you?" Consequently, the standard reply became, "Remember last winter when you wished you were warm?" Grownups can be weird.

The extreme heat didn't bother me nearly as much as did the bitter cold. Except for when it came to school and the stuffy, stifling classrooms. And the proximity of our house to the school made winters even worse.

Dad retired from the Navy in '54. He landed a good job as chief electrician at Wyeth Medical Research Labs in Radnor. In early 1956 the search for a house commenced. We were leaving south Philly. I'd still spend most of my time there, but in just a few short years, with my Aunt Mary and Grandma D'Nato gone, trips to my beloved city streets would eventually be reduced to the requisite holiday visits with friends and yearly trips to the cemetery.

Sundays became house hunting time. The family would pile into our beat-up brown Ford and head for suburbia. We would spend the day at new developments—the word "subdivision" hadn't yet come into vogue. Most of these developments were little more than a series of blacktop streets running past countless tracts of dirt marked with wooden stakes driven into the ground—future new home sites. Sample homes were brightly lit and gaily furnished, with lush expanses of shimmering green lawns. Perfect for the young baby boomer family, with their median income, GI Bill financing, back yard barbecue, and 2.6 kids. I never quite understood that statistic. But there were plenty of times when I felt like six-tenths of a kid.

Let me amend that statement to read sample *home*. One model was all that was needed and all that was usually offered. All were identical. You had your choice of six exterior colors. That is, unless your future neighbor picked that color first.

There used to be a song about little boxes:

Little boxes on a hillside,

Little boxes just the same.

And they're all made out of ticky-tacky,

And they all look just the same.

It was to one of these little boxes in a development twelve miles west of Philadelphia called Lawrence Park that the Neblett family emigrated in the sticky, pre-air-conditioned summer of 1956. I asked who Lawrence was to have a road, a development, and a whole shopping center named after him. I got the look.

Our house was brown and white, a split level, three bedroom, one and a half bath, one car garage affair, not made of ticky-tacky, but of wood and some brick. It occupied a generous sized lot with a spacious back yard on North Central Boulevard, the last street of the initial build out. Eventually there would be a South Central Boulevard and a public grade school, a swim club, a playground, two ball fields, a small wooded area for me to explore, large woods for me to get into trouble in, and more streets with additional split levels.

And they all looked just the same.

That year I learned an abiding lesson about poor, struggling private Catholic schools and my father's dry, witty way of teaching life lessons. Anyone who has ever suffered through a parental lecture about walking five miles through rain and snow to school, please take note.

Newly built St. Pius X Catholic Grade School sat on Lawrence Road at the entrance to our development. The overcrowded school served a broad area and dictated anyone living within one mile would have to walk or car pool. Our little box sat just within the one mile limit.

Thanks, Dad.

To make matters worse, Lawrence Park was built in an area of gracefully rolling hills. The steep streets made for great sledding and exciting bicycle and wagon riding. They left much to be desired when it came to walking.

My daily trek to school took the following path: out the front door and across the street, then up Cornwall Drive, easily the steepest street in the development. The kids called it the widow maker as they raced down on their Flexible Flyers at breakneck speeds. The apex of Cornwall Hill terminated at Hastings Boulevard, forming a T. A right turn and I began my long descent down to Sussex Boulevard. Here my journey turned left and the landscape mercifully began to level out a little. It was then a short hike to Lawrence Road, where I again turned left, walked a short distance, and came face to face with Sam the school crossing guard.

For a number of years, those who walked to school were also required to walk home for lunch. Someday I will sit down and figure the mileage I logged in nearly a decade of walking, sometimes four times a day, uphill both ways. Riding my bike helped, except of course when it rained or snowed. And before you ask, no, my mother never drove.

I've since come to believe there is a slight sadistic streak hidden deep inside my father. To this day I can picture him pointing to the realtor's map, indicating the yet to be built brown house on North Central Boulevard, just under one mile from my future school, a knowing grin showing on his face.

If summers in the Philadelphia area could be hot, winters were cold and snowy and miserable. The past winter was proof positive. Growing up in the Northeast, I was used to the cold; I just didn't like it much. Especially the snow shoveling.

Since I was the only male heir, naturally the tasks of mowing the lawn and shoveling snow fell on my young shoulders. The sidewalk and driveway were to be clear of ice and snow by the time my dad turned into the driveway at 5 p.m. Figuring it might help me to enjoy the chore more, Dad gave me some sage advice: think of it as play time. Make a game out of it! And so I did.

Along with the usual snowmen and occasional snow fort, as I shoveled I'd pile some of the snow at the end of the driveway. By the time I finished I'd have a nice wall—maybe six inches thick and about two or three feet high—of lightly packed snow. Five o' clock, right on schedule, our green '57 Plymouth would appear rolling down Cornwall Hill, the connecting street to ours. Dad, seeing my handiwork, would set himself and speed up. A quick right on North Central Boulevard, then a fast left into our driveway, and the sturdy Plymouth would easily breech my blockade and roll to a stop in front of the garage.

Dad would emerge victorious, grinning, and bark, "Finish shoveling up the remains before you come inside!"

Remains, huh?

Over the holidays of 1960, the East Coast was buried under record-breaking snows. Drifts of five and six feet or more were common. Accumulations of eighteen to twenty-four inches hit some areas. During the school holidays the aluminum snow shovel and I became intimate friends.

Finishing up late one afternoon, I surveyed my handiwork. Cold and exhausted, I had built my wall well. Then scenes of last year's fiasco filled my mind. The green monster had handily dispatched three hours worth of work. I considered making my wall thicker, higher. That was too much work. My ten-year-old brain had a better idea.

Dragging the hose around and attaching it to the front spigot, I gently watered my creation. Within seconds the wall glistened with what I thought was a thin layer of ice.

Perfect.

I returned the hose just in time. Dad's green tank appeared, and then gained speed.

Closer…

Right turn…

Left turn…

Big wide grin…

Something told me this was not a good idea.

KER-THUNK!

The old car slowed, hesitated, shuddered, and then emerged victorious.

Well, almost.

One headlight was shattered. The massive bumper was upturned on one end, and the grill work no longer smiled. Neither did my dad.

I took off at a run.

There was a deep snow fort in the corner of my back yard where Chris Murphy and I had tunneled into a drift. I dove in head first and scrambled to the far side. My heart boomed like a howitzer.

Boom!

Despite the cold I started to sweat.

Boom!

When you are ten, your short life passes in front of you rather quickly.

Boom!

It wasn't my heart.

Boom!

The earth shook.

Boom!

My father mumbled something and the snow fort came down around my ears. It took me fifteen minutes to work up the courage to move, another twenty minutes to dig myself out, and months of shoveling and mowing to pay off the damages. Thank God it happened *after* Christmas!

⨎Chapter Three⨎

I'm sure Kennedy never had to walk to school. Thanks to Eisenhower, in the mid-twentieth century, walking was probably the last thing on any American's mind. During the Second World War, as commander of the Allied expeditionary forces in Europe, the future president witnessed firsthand the necessity and advantages of a well-planned highway system. The Autobahn was the pride of Nazi Germany and would soon become the archetype for super highways throughout the world. During his presidency, Eisenhower pushed through bills establishing a national highway system, under the guise of national security. Real or imagined, by 1960, national security was on the minds of every American.

On October 4, 1957, Russia placed the first satellite, *Sputnik,* in orbit around the earth. The headline news caught a complacent world, confident in the belief that communism was securely contained behind brick and barbed wire, completely by surprise. That stunning success was followed in quick succession by *Sputnik II* in November, which carried Laika the dog, the world's first space traveler, and *Lunik I,* which passed by the moon in January 1959. By October of '59 Russian scientists were routinely photographing the dark side of the moon. Meanwhile, America's first rockets were routinely blowing up on the launch pad at Vandenberg Air Force Base. It seemed even the heavens were no longer safe from the communist threat.

The United States did managed to get the Explorer I and Vanguard satellites into shaky, tentative orbits in 1958. Next, on April 9, 1959, the recently formed National Aeronautics and Space Administration announced the selection of its first astronauts. It was upon the shoulders of these seven daring young men, known as the Mercury 7, which rested the hopes of a successful U.S. space program. But these events were soon overshadowed by more Russian launches, culminating in Yuri Gagarin's becoming the first human in space aboard the *Vostok I* on April 12, 1961. Then finally our country had its own space hero in Alan Shepard, as his *Freedom 7* capsule reached sub-orbital flight on May 5 of the same year. The race for space was on, and we were trailing in a pathetic, distant second place.

Just twenty days after Shepard's historic flight, President John F. Kennedy spoke to a joint session of Congress, America, and the world. His impassioned speech was uncannily reminiscent of George Pal's 1950s space opera *Destination Moon.* It directly addressed America's part in the growing space race, stopping just short of admitting the very real possibilities of an attack from outer space by a foreign power:

"I believe that this nation should commit itself to achieving the goal, before the decade is out, of landing a man on the moon and returning him safely to the earth."

If Eisenhower could build a highway across America, Kennedy would build one to the moon.

Space and all things not of this earth became my second passion behind music and radio. I followed the space race diligently on my transistor and in the newspapers. The nightly TV news was full of the latest developments from Vandenberg and the recently established Cape Canaveral. Posters and sky maps dotted my bedroom walls, along with pictures of the Mercury Seven. Even St. Pius X Grade School interrupted its classes to allow us to watch the historic flights of Shepard, Gus Grissom, and John Glen, America's first astronaut to orbit the earth. As the race for space galvanized the country, it served a second, equally important purpose. Like the rest of the country, my attention was diverted from the more pressing issues closer to home.

Kennedy had inherited a building pressure cooker from his predecessor, a pressure cooker rapidly boiling out of control just 90 miles off the Florida coast.

In 1950, Fulgencio Batista overthrew the Cuban government of Carlos Prio Socarrás. Batista quickly smoothed over his coup by inviting American business interests into the island country. It wasn't long before large American-owned oil refineries and sprawling sugar plantations dotted the Cuban countryside, while fashionable American casinos and hotels lined the sugar-white beaches. Havana became the play toy of the rich, wealthy, and powerful, including senators and congressmen on expense-paid fact-finding junkets. American tourists enjoyed the gambling and night life, American businesses enjoyed record profits, and the corrupt Batista enjoyed growing rich and powerful. Meanwhile, the Cuban population languished in escalating poverty.

Fidel Alejandro Castro Ruz, the illegitimate son of a wealthy farmer, became involved in leftist politics while studying law at the University of Havana. After involving himself in armed rebellions against the governments of the Dominican Republic and Colombia, he led an attack against his homeland and Batista. The rebellion failed and Castro was imprisoned.

By 1954, a now free Fidel Castro and his brother Raul had set up a revolutionary movement operating out of Mexico called the 26th of July. This time Castro marshaled a sizeable army, training and arming his rebels. They kept constant pressure on the corrupt Batista regime through well-organized propaganda and guerilla attacks, retreating back into the safety of Cuba's Sierra Maestra Mountains. Bastia finally fled the island on January 1, 1959. By February Castro had set himself up as Cuban Premier.

It's interesting to speculate what the future might have brought if America had chosen to recognize and aid the struggling government of Fidel Castro: a new ally, or perhaps a new state. But the powers in Washington and their very strong and noisy lobbyists didn't see it that way. Military, political, business, and civilian advisors, most with personal agendas, urged Eisenhower to take harsh action against the government of Castro.

Meanwhile, Fidel Castro traveled to New York City, addressing a full session of the United Nations on September 26, 1960. He took the U.S. to task, complaining against U.S. policy toward his country and interference in their internal affairs. Castro brought to light, and to the world, the dirty little secrets of how "this poor and underdeveloped Caribbean country, with 600,000 unemployed, was contributing greatly to the economic development of the most highly industrialized country in the world," citing "the hundreds of millions of dollars that were extracted from the treasury of the country by the corrupt officials of the tyranny and were later deposited in United States or European banks."

Castro had his facts correct, and the logic of his words gained him sympathy from many countries. All the while Castro was being drawn closer to communism, mainly out of necessity.

Eisenhower, desirous of a quiet final year in office, placed the whole matter on the back burner, publicly adopting a wait and see posture. This angered the quick-tempered Castro, who promptly confiscated more than one billion dollars of American property in Cuba, kicked out the U.S. businessmen, and nationalized the American business interests. On January 3, 1961, as one of his last official acts as president, Dwight Eisenhower broke off diplomatic relations with Cuba. The outgoing president had nothing to lose.

Castro continued to plead to America and other countries for financial and economic help. Finally, in desperation, the bearded leader turned to Russia and Premier Khrushchev, allying himself with the Communist Bloc. His government executed more than 1,000 former members of Batista's regime and those who disagreed with his leading Cuba into communism. The entire political mess landed directly in the lap of the newly inaugurated Kennedy.

In the spring of 1961, the attention of America and the rest of the world lay in space. On April 17, relying on flawed, outdated, and biased intelligence left over from the Eisenhower administration, President Kennedy initiated the Bay of Pigs. Trained by the CIA, 1,500 anti-Castro Cubans invaded their own homeland. The poorly organized coup collapsed within a few days because of inadequate supplies, lack of air support, and overwhelming opposing forces.

A week later, an embarrassed and angry Kennedy faced the American people and accepted full responsibility for the failed attack. Dad, along with the rest of the country, sat glued to the flickering TV set, shaking his head, frustration darkening his stern face, the unspoken words echoing the nation's sentiment: Kennedy was just too young and too inexperienced. My hero had suffered a costly setback to his early administration. However, it wasn't long before the collective American attention was once again diverted. This time the country's interests were divided between the race for space and the race to break Babe Ruth's iconic record.

Sometimes fate can be ironic if not downright cruel. I had always been a huge baseball fan, following my tragic Phillies with a fatalistic verve. I played some little league and a lot of sandlot ball. But I never fully pursued my passion for America's game, preferring to hang out, smoke, and follow a path leading to juvenile delinquency. In tenth grade I was capable of hurling an eighty-one-mile-an-hour fastball with deadly accuracy. But I preferred cars and drinking and trouble making over organized sports. It wasn't long before the coach had had enough, kicking me off the team. A possible career in the Major Leagues was stillborn. The fact that Cuban Premier Fidel Castro played organized ball and had once tried out for the Baltimore Orioles didn't escape me.

Baseball was in my blood, and one of the few things my dad and I shared. He couldn't throw a curve or hit a fastball, and we rarely played catch. But we did watch the games on TV. And I managed to talk him into taking us a few times to Connie Mack Stadium to watch the Phillies lose one heartbreaker after another. Even a revamped team of talented rookies and future All Stars including Robin Roberts, Tony Taylor, Johnny Callison and Art Mahaffey couldn't stave off the declining fortunes of the ball club. By August the Phillies had lost a record twenty-three games in a row.

But headlines, sports and otherwise, the summer of 1961 were focused on two players from the New York Yankee organization. Roger Maris and Mickey Mantle were locked in a dead even struggle to be the first player to hit 60 home runs in one season. No one had come close to achieving that seemingly unattainable mark since the inimitable Babe Ruth had accomplished the feat three decades earlier. My pride and joy was an oversized Roger Maris signature model Louisville Slugger that Dad bought for me mid-season, and I followed the rest of the country in rooting for the underdog. Odds, logic, and the press favored the popular Mickey Mantle to break the Babe's record. The space race, the Berlin Wall, Cuba, and growing troubles in Southeast Asia took a back seat to the drama being played out on the diamond. During several afternoon televised press conferences, President Kennedy took time out to ask whether "those boys from New York had hit another one." I'm sure Boston Red Sox fans forgave him.

At times the elusive mark seemed as distant as the moon, as both Maris and Mantle fell victim to batting slumps. Mickey Mantle remained cool and collected, at least on the outside, doing his best to duck the demanding press. But the young Roger Maris admitted that the publicity and pressure of the contest brought him close to a nervous breakdown. Cast as the villain in a surreal play, Maris lost sleep as well as his hair from the berating of fans and press alike who were unwilling to see their beloved Babe's record broken.

On October 1, 1961, in the fourth inning of the last game of the regular season, before a standing-room-only, home-town crowd, Maris punched his sixty-first home run off Boston right-hander Tracy Stallard. The record-breaking shot became a mixed blessing to the shy slugger. In a 1980 public statement, a rightfully bitter Roger Maris told reporters, "They acted as though I was doing something wrong, poisoning the record books or something. Do you know what I have to show for sixty-one home runs? Nothing. Exactly nothing."

Meanwhile, half a world away, secret dealings in the Kremlin were conspiring to bring the entire world to the brink of destruction.

7:15 a.m. on Wednesday, September 6, 1961—the first day of school. The sun played hooky and battleship clouds threatened to unload a salvo of rain.

"Why Wednesday?"

"What?" Mom called from upstairs.

"Nothing."

"Don't forget your school bag. And leave the radio home!"

Thinking back, it's hard to remember any first Wednesday of grade school that wasn't overcast. Perhaps the clouds loomed mostly in my mind as I once again faced the nine-month daily trudge. Ignoring my mom and my green army surplus school bag—required attire for any 1960s grade-school boy—I adjusted the volume on my transistor and headed out. Who needed a school bag on the first Wednesday?

The smooth sounds of Motown's Marvelettes spilled from the three-inch speaker, Gladys Horton pleading for the postman to "...deliver de letter de sooner de better." Barry Gordy's Detroit-based Motown Records was quickly becoming the new doo-wop. With the simplistic formula of straightforward lyrics, bluesy repetitive four-chord melodies, and an infectious hook, Gordy deftly blended rock 'n' roll with urban rhythm and blues in what would soon come to be known as Soul Music. When "Please Mr. Postman," the Marvelettes' paean to the postal service, reached the summit of the Billboard Top 40 Charts, the upstart label's future was secured.

Transistor firmly in hand, I started the climb up Cornwall hill. Why I left my bicycle home that day I don't recall. Maybe it was because of the threatening skies. Or maybe I was in no hurry for what lay ahead.

This year should be a breeze. After all, it was my second go 'round at the fifth grade. At the same time I would be starting with a new class. All of my friends had moved on.

The summer had passed normally enough. I had returned home on the last school day in June to a sympathetic mother and a caring, comforting sister. Dad was his usual silent monument of a parent, granting me a curt, knowing nod and understanding half-smile as he arrived home from work. But Butch Bartley, once my best friend, seemed distant and less friendly. As the weeks passed we saw little of each other. However, Chris Murphy and Ben Masters and I still played around together. And the Hounds, the club we had formed in Chris's back yard playhouse, were still terrorizing his neighborhood. That significant summer I found myself trapped between blameless boyhood pleasures and more mature escapades.

I never really had a large circle of friends. I was a small kid, and shy. The first half of my grade-school career I was pretty much a loner. And a punching bag for a few bullies. Clark Gilman was the worst of the lot.

Clark was a skinny kid with ugly freckles and wild red hair that matched his disposition. He'd wait for me after school at the top of Hastings Boulevard. A typical bully, Clark would jump out from behind a bush and knock me down, then start kicking and swinging wildly.

The previous year, my first go at fifth grade, I had finally begun to feel comfortable with myself. This was accomplished not at school, but by ditching and spending time riding the West Chester Pike bus, or wandering for hours through a local junkyard. It gave me time to think about things other than school, and teachers, and mowing the lawn, and shoveling snow, and brushing my teeth, and being a good boy. I could think about things important to me, things important to a ten year old. Like going to the moon, and being a radio DJ, and why Wednesday, and planes that fell out of the sky killing people. But mostly I had time to think about people: about grownups, kids, parents, bullies, and my aunt who I missed; about my life, and yes, even about girls.

I lost a year to those days of contemplation. But I found something much more valuable. I began to find myself.

One day after school my hours of thinking began to pay off in a most unexpected manner. Clark Gilman jumped me and knocked me down. I saw his dirty, scuffed Buster Brown shoe swing back. It connected with a thud to my right side. I didn't feel a thing.

I could sense hot blood racing inside of me. I wasn't mad exactly. Rather, a strange calm seemed to be the message coursing through my veins. Dominick's trademarked self-assurance flashed through my mind. I had never witnessed the streetwise Dominick backing down or showing fear of anything. Memories of his coolness buoyed my confidence. If Clark Gilman was going to hurt me, so be it. But nothing said I had to just lie there and take it.

I jumped up.

By any scoring I lost that fight. But the bully left with a bloody nose—it may have been broken—and he never bothered me again.

It would take quite some time to get through my hard head that confidence was a two-edged sword, one forged in responsibility.

"New faces, new experiences, new friends to make," my father reassured me a few days before first Wednesday.

Thanks for the encouraging words, Dad. Parents just didn't get it. Not any parents I knew anyway.

When you're repeating a grade the new faces all stare at you. And the new experiences usually amount to enduring ridicule, defending yourself, and explaining what you are doing there. You don't make friends; you have to earn them. Not an easy task for a shy introvert. I was a baby with a basketball, not quite sure how to handle my slowly emerging confidence.

The staccato drum intro of "Rock Around the Clock" ripped from my radio. All six tiny transistors inside the plastic case in my hand pulsated to the infectious beat as Bill Haley counted down: *"One, two, three o' clock, four o' clock rock..."*

35

Vivid images of Vic Morrow and his gang of juvenile delinquents trashing the teacher's beloved record collection in *Blackboard Jungle* sprang to mind.

"Five, six, seven o' clock, eight o' clock rock..."

What a waste, I remembered thinking—all those cool 78s. I had sat through two screenings of the iconic and disturbing flick at the 69th Street Terminal Theatre the previous year while ditching school. It was easy. At the corner of Sussex Boulevard and Lawrence Road, thirty yards from Sam the school crossing guard, the SEPTA bus stopped. For fifteen cents you could ride the public transportation all the way down West Chester Pike to the shopping district at 69th Street.

The oldie but goodie on my radio made me smile. There were some consolations to repeating. I'd be older than the other kids. And failing a grade added to the mystery and mystique of my carefully cultivated bad boy image. Skipping school and getting into trouble was what caused me to flunk last year. But I wasn't a juvenile delinquent.

Not yet.

I felt the knife bounce in my back pocket. It was like the one Vic Morrow used in *Blackboard Jungle*. It wasn't a switchblade. But the blade did lock into position.

Push, pull, click, lock...

The thin Black Panther knife with the sharp, five-inch stainless blade came from the back page of a Green Lantern comic book, the same mail order house that sold x-ray specs and trick gum and sea monkeys. When I asked Dad to order it, his only concern was what I planned to do with the outlaw blade. He contented himself with the universal young boy reply, "Stuff," adding a terse recounting of a knife he had owned as a boy. He also told me not to tell Mom.

For well over a year the knife rode comfortably in my back pocket, part of my newly gained confidence. A year or so later I would cut a boy's arm pretty badly in a West Side Story influenced knife fight. I don't even remember his name or what the fight was about. He went home telling his parents he'd hurt himself playing. The real story spread, as did my reputation.

But the incident shook me. I soon abandoned the locking blade in favor of a pocket knife. Over the ensuing years the new knife's bottle and can openers saw the most action, as I began finding my confidence in increasing amounts of beer and liquor.

In the strict pecking order of grammar school, all of this put me at the top of the food chain: a reluctant, confused king of my class.

Overhead, two angry ships collided with a thunderous roar. I adjusted the breeze-turned collar of my new tweed jacket. No doubt feeling guilty about my having to repeat fifth grade, my parents had uncharacteristically splurged. They bought me tons of new clothes for play and for school. I even managed to catch them in a weak moment and talk them into finally buying me a pair of matador boots. The black, side zippered, over-the-ankle boots were the mark of a true hipster and greaser. Hell, even DJ Joe Niagara wore them. Now, so did I as I topped the hill and turned onto Hastings Boulevard.

Our next-door neighbor, Mrs. Dunlap, was a green blur in her '57 Olds tank. Now there was one cool ride. A fleeting thought of ditching and heading over to visit my twisted metal friends in the junkyard buzzed my mind. No… not on the first Wednesday, that's how I'd gotten into trouble last year.

I thought about Chris and Ben and other friends who were moving on. We still remained close. Their friendship would provide a connection to the sixth grade. Over the past year or so, partly due to my smoking and increased trouble making, I had been officially accepted by many of my sister's friends. I hung out with them at night at the public grade school just up the street from my house. We would smoke, even drink some, tell stories, clown around, and get into some mischief. A few of us even took to singing old doo-wop tunes while passing a bottle of Thunderbird wine. The older guys liked that I knew the words to all the songs and could easily hit many of the high falsetto parts in "Little Darling," and "There's a Moon Out Tonight," and "Hushabye," and Dion and the Belmont's "I Wonder Why." White doo-wop was just coming on the scene, and Larry Cartelli and Allan Sarafino and Donald Rondo and Timmy and Johnny Mancuso and I actually sounded pretty good for a while.

Most of the older guys I hung out with were greased-back Romeos, befriending me as a possible way to win my sister's affections. I didn't care. I was accepted and enjoying myself and growing and learning, if mostly the wrong things. Their friendship boosted my confidence and provided me an in with the eighth graders. That alone kicked my bad boy image up several notches.

While my recently found friends may have been good for my ego, they were possibly the worst thing for my behavioral problems. I'm not going to cop out here and lay all of my troubles at the feet of older influences, just many of them. I was quite capable of getting myself into trouble and did so with increasing frequency. But my eighth- and ninth-grade buddies were a gateway to some seriously bad behavior. Not the least of these was drinking.

Jerry Stevens read a Clearasil spot and then talked up the next song: "One of South Philly's very own, with a former top ten tune in Wibbage land, he'll be joining me this Friday night for the big St. Anne back-to-school hop. Here's the fabulous Fabian, on the big 99!"

Fabian Forte, or just simply Fabian, was one of the new generation of rock 'n' rollers. In an article about teenagers and rock 'n' roll, *Life* magazine had dubbed Ricky Nelson a "teen idol." The moniker stuck and was soon applied to a host of teen and twenty-something singers. In a bit of fair play turnabout, Nelson recorded "Teenage Idol," a 1962 hit for the young heartthrob.

These performers, usually teens themselves, had managers, handlers, A and R men, song writers, and agents. Some of them lacked the talent to warrant all the attention. But their unabashed good looks and innocuous songs sold records, begat swooning fan clubs, and brought serious money to the labels. Singers like Fabian; Bobby Rydell and Connie Francis; Paul Anka; Frankie Avalon and Brenda Lee; Jimmy Clanton and Bobby Vee—they made rock 'n' roll safe, with music as plastic as the discs on which they were pressed. Despite some of the inane lyrics, their arrival on the scene around 1958–59 was a fortuitous one. By making rock 'n' roll more palatable to adults, they actually helped save the music from self-destruction. And in 1959 rock 'n' roll needed all the help it could muster.

Buddy Holly, Ritchie Valens, Eddie Cochran, Johnny Ace, and the Bopper were dead. Elvis was in the army. Chuck Berry was in jail on a Mann Act. After marrying his 13-year-old cousin, Jerry Lee Lewis couldn't beg a booking or air play. DJ Alan Freed, the man greatly instrumental in getting it all started, was under investigation in the Payola Scandals and taken off the air. Even clean-cut Dick Clark felt the pressure as he testified before the Congressional Sub-Committee Payola Hearings. To save his career, and at the direction of his network, ABC, Clark divested himself of ownership in music-related businesses, including stakes in some thirty-three different record labels. Many other top names in radio and the record industry would fall before the purge abated. Smug parents, school officials, and city fathers sat back, sighed a collective *we told you so*, and waited for the end. Many are still waiting.

Rock 'n' roll was ailing, not dead. A handful of clean-cut kids from the city streets to the heartland, from the Deep South to the deep tans of the West Coast beaches, breathed fresh air into the smoke- and smog-afflicted lungs of rock 'n' roll.

Although more pop-oriented, with less-suggestive lyrics and toned-down rhythms, their music wasn't bad. Many teens accepted the new sound as just another facet of the ever evolving face of rock 'n' roll. But while they lip-synced benign lyrics on *American Bandstand* and *The Ed Sullivan Show*, kids across the country, the real rock 'n' rollers, the real greasers, continued to listen and dance to Jackie Wilson and Little Richard and Jerry Lee and the Coasters and the Drifters and Dion and the Chantels. Our radios were tuned to Wibbage and WHAT and XPRS and WLS and KNUZ and KMOX and CKLW. We grooved to the easily identifiable platter patter of Hy Lit and Jerry Blavat, Jack Carney and Porky Chedwick, Paul Berlin, Jim Lowe, Mother Mabel, Motor Mouth, Dr. Don, Danny Holiday and Art LaBoe. These DJs played the real rock 'n' roll, what many adults maliciously termed "race music."

In the end, after all the hype and publicity and controversy and drama, no matter how you sliced it—bop, pop, doo-wop, rhythm and blues, rockabilly, teen sounds, or just plain crap—in 1961 rock 'n' roll was here to stay.

My thumb deftly spun the tuning dial away from WIBG and Fabian to 1430 WHAT, a popular black station. Frankie Lymon wanted to know: "Why Do Fools Fall in Love?" That was more like it, more first Wednesday. As I turned the corner to Lawrence Road, a gaggle of giggling girls waited at the school's crosswalk. Dressed identically in their fresh, new uniforms, they looked like a set of blue bowling pins. I boldly entered the flock, the only male, and stepped up to the curb.

I was greeted with more giggling and hushed remarks.

Just last year I would have shied away and hung back till the crowd moved on. Today I stood at the front of the pack, lost in the heady aromas of fruity powders, Aqua Net hair spray, Ivory soap, Bazooka bubble gum, and female giddiness.

The DJ did a smooth segue into "Baby Workout." The giggles segued into squeals. Something touched my shoulder. It was a hand with slender fingers and perfectly filed nails, all but one. The pinky nail was bitten down. I spun around. The hand's owner had startling, clear hazel eyes.

She said, "Don't you just love Jackie Wilson?"

Several girls squealed again, a chorus of broiler drawers opening. They began to hop up and down in time to the music.

"Oh—turn it up!" The hand lightly squeezed my shoulder and lingered. Months of practice paid off. My eyes remained locked on the fascinating hazel orbs while my thumb found the volume wheel and gave it a quarter of a turn.

More hopping and squealing, and something else...

The smile was inviting, playful.

I'm not sure if I returned the smile. An instant later the hand, eyes, and smile retreated, leaving a void in the heavy morning air. The giggling gaggle moved off around me.

"Having second thoughts?" It was Sam the crossing guard, all five foot nothing of him, dressed proudly in his red and white uniform, a human stop sign in the middle of busy Lawrence Road. "School's this way."

I headed across the street in a fog, following the scent of oranges and the sound of high-pitched murmurs. "Hot enough for you this summer?"

Passing Sam a blank stare, I replied with the only thing that came to mind. "Remember last winter when you wished you were warm?"

⨀Chapter Four⨀

The other race, the one for space, continued to heat up as the world population fell into a strange sort of complacency. Space exploration was becoming an everyday occurrence. The U.S. had successfully sent a chimpanzee on an eighteen-minute flight. Then, after Alan Shepard's historic flight in May of 1961, Gus Grissom became the second American in space. His July flight was still being talked about when Russian Gherman Titov orbited the earth seventeen times in his *Vostok 2* capsule. Despite President Kennedy's recent call to action, we were still lagging far behind.

On May 31, Kennedy began his first out-of-country trip with a visit to Paris. At the state dinner, the American president and French president Charles de Gaulle declared a "complete identity of view" regarding readiness to meet with force any Soviet threat to the city. Following World War II, the Soviets had been given control of the eastern sector of Germany, including the eastern portion of Berlin. Many thought the Soviet presence in Eastern Europe a threat to the security of the rest of the continent. Berlin and the rest of the world lived under constant fear of a Russian take-over. At the Kremlin, Soviet premier Nikita Khrushchev continually threatened to close the boarders between East and West. The escalating race for space and its resultant nuclear threat punctuated Khrushchev's ranting

However, it was a different Kennedy who captivated the French people. Jacqueline Kennedy's command of the French language and her regard for French culture made her extremely popular. Acknowledging his wife's popularity in his opening remarks at a Paris press conference, John Kennedy introduced himself as "the man who accompanied Jacqueline Kennedy to Paris."

Getting down to more serious duties, on June 3, 1961, the president met with his communist counterpart, Nikita Khrushchev, at the U.S. Embassy in Vienna. The two discussed trade embargos, the division of East and West Germany, and Communist expansion in politically emerging Southeast Asia. The Russian premier was friendly and gregarious before the world press. Publicly the White House announced the talks as being "frank, courteous, and wide ranging." Behind closed doors, however, Khrushchev stubbornly refused to discuss Castro, Cuba, or nuclear weapons. Both leaders gave open support for an independent government in Laos chosen by the Laotian people. Privately, Khrushchev threatened that he would sign a separate peace treaty with East Germany, effectively cutting off Allied access to East Berlin.

The talks produced no substantial agreements. Little was accomplished at the meetings, and the new American president received his first hard lesson in international diplomacy. What he learned would serve him well in the months to come. Back home, the opposition nodded knowingly, treating the Vienna meeting as proof of the inexperienced president's ineffectiveness on the world stage.

By July the situation in Europe had deteriorated to the point that it could no longer be ignored by Kennedy, America, and the rest of the world. On July 25, Kennedy appeared on television to outline a plan for a balanced military buildup in Germany and elsewhere. It was hoped that the proposal would nullify Khrushchev's continual threats. But instead of calling the Kremlin's bluff, the soviet premier's response was swift and sure. Nineteen days after Kennedy's speech, on August 13, 1961, under Khrushchev's direct orders, construction of the Berlin Wall began. The wall of concrete and barbed wire halted all traffic between East and West Germany and cut the city of Berlin in half. On official recommendations and unwilling to risk a possible nuclear war Kennedy decided not to challenge the construction directly.

Throughout the crisis I remember TV programs like *American Bandstand* and even the evening news being interrupted for updates and hastily assembled press conferences to advise the population of the developing situation. It was during these impromptu press conferences that many say Kennedy showed his true mettle. Remaining calm, at ease, and well informed, the U.S. leader assuaged America's fears, fielded questions confidently, and presented the facts in a clear and understandable manner. Kennedy also disproved his detractors, yielding a firm yet fair hand in dealing decisively with the world's problems. I became intrigued with the young leader who presented world affairs in a way that even I could understand. My father, on the other hand, often played devil's advocate with his overly cautious and protective "we need to be ready" nature. By the turn of another year, I would begin to understand his attitude.

On another world front, nuclear test ban talks reconvened in Geneva, but the Soviet Union resumed atmospheric nuclear testing in Siberia. Kennedy countered by ordering the resumption of underground nuclear testing. In September Kennedy addressed the United Nations General Assembly, endorsing a complete and general disarmament, challenging the Soviet Union to a "peace race." His words, while stirring, fell on deaf ears. Nuclear testing continued unabated on both sides. Amongst minor protests, the president justified the country's position, stating, "In view of the acts of the Soviet Government, we must now take those steps which prudent men find essential."

A deadly game of chess between the two world powers had begun in earnest.

It was nearly impossible to escape the daily headlines and solemn reporters' continual predictions of doom and gloom. In just a few short months, it seemed the country had fallen from unbridled optimism into an abyss of fear and suspicion. Nuns at St. Pius X pointed out the similarities between the global situation just before World War II and the present world mindset. In letters and scathing editorials to newspapers, detractors continued to cite the Bay of Pigs fiasco and his handling of Khrushchev in Vienna as proof positive John Kennedy was unfit to lead the nation. However, in the early years of the new decade, protesters were still reluctant to take to the streets to voice their opinions openly against the government. Marches, sit-ins, and organized rallies were reserved for the still-volatile issue of race relations.

In the cloistered world of the schoolyard, passing mention was made of the news and what was said by parents over the dinner table. A noted change was made in good guy-bad guy chases during play time, with the "dirty red Commie" assuming the role of the villain. But for the most part, my friends and I were content to believe in the president and his stirring words. To an impressionable fifth grader, John F. Kennedy seemed more of a cool older brother off at college somewhere than a world leader. The Berlin Wall and revolutions in Laos were intangible concerns. If the president could spend weekends cruising with Jackie and the kids aboard the *Honey Fitz,* the Kennedy family yacht things couldn't possibly be that bad.

Closer to home for us was a bill signed into law on September 22. The Juvenile Delinquency and Youth Offenses Control Act sought to prevent the spread of juvenile delinquency. It set its ambitious sights on the directionless teens and preteens of America, youths like me who took a less-than-serious view of education. Always a strong proponent of education, Kennedy signed into law a number of bills strengthening and augmenting the country's efforts to rebuild and modernize its aging and failing school system. My friend Chris Murphy joked that it was now a federal offense to ditch class.

During his same address before the General Assembly of the United Nations in New York City, Kennedy expressed the country's support for the faltering world organization. Since before the death of Dag Hammarskjold in an airplane crash earlier in the month, the UN had been under strong criticism as being powerless in the face of increasing world tension and troubles. Many believed the death of the widely popular Secretary-General signaled the demise of the UN itself. Kennedy reassured a shaken world that, "The problem is not the death of one man—the problem is the life of this organization. It will either grow to meet the challenges of our age, or it will be gone with the wind…"

His stirring words spoke not only to the continued existence of an organization dedicated to peace, but also to the continued existence of the U.S. and the rest of the world:

"…in the development of this organization rests the only true alternatives to war—and war appeals no longer as a rational alternative. Unconditional war can no longer lead to unconditional victory. It can no longer serve to settle disputes. It can no longer concern the great powers alone. For a nuclear disaster, spread by wind and water and fear, could well engulf the great and the small, the rich and the poor, the committed and the uncommitted alike. Mankind must put an end to war—or war will put an end to mankind."

Kennedy's words once again found approving but deaf ears. The world situation was heating up faster than mere words, regardless of how strong and sincere, could control. The UN debated and talked and talked and debated and passed resolution after resolution. Urgent communications between world powers increased. Newspapers in the U.S. called for more definitive actions against the communist threat. Meanwhile the Berlin Wall was closed down to traffic from either direction; the situation in both Laos and Vietnam worsened; and secret American spy planes, often flying without presidential consent or knowledge, stepped up their campaigns to make sense out of the disorder.

I could read the increasing anxiety and concern in my father's face and demeanor and I tried my best to comprehend. But I was busy waging campaigns of my own, campaigns of survival in the schoolyard; campaigns of dealing with my new-found popularity—and an arcane campaign to understand my emerging feelings for an enigmatic classmate.

The Philadelphia Phillies were struggling. The Phillies were always struggling. They had been on a downward spiral since the 1950 Whiz Kids took the pennant. After Richie Ashburn left the Phillies, the spiral became a slide. The 1948 Sporting News Rookie of the Year had bought a home in my development, Lawrence Park. His son played in my Little League. Needless to say, our baseball banquets were the envy of the area. Thanks to Ashburn's affable nature and popularity among the other players, the Broomall Little League opening day and end of season dinners were peppered with a who's who of the National League. My short career as a little leaguer netted me autographs of such greats as Robin Roberts, Willie Mayes, Warren Spahn, Maury Wills, Roberto Clemente, and Bill Mazeroski, the Pirates' hero of the 1960 series.

My friend Chris said Cincinnati was the team to beat this year. I told him he was nuts—the Phillies would be unbeatable. That was at the start of the season. We argued all summer. Now the Reds were in first, the damn Yankees were slugging their way to another pennant, and Philadelphia was stuck in the cellar, some thirty games out. I hadn't seen Chris in a week and I knew he would be gloating.

I met Christopher Murphy in Sister Dominica's first grade class. Chris was a goofy-looking kid with ears too big for his head, a mouth too big for his face, and legs too long for his skinny body. He had a natural comedic air about him and moved like a marionette at the mercy of a drunken puppeteer. Eventually he began to grow into his body—except for his sugar-bowl ears. Sister Dominica sat us next to each other in a double row of desks, and a friendship was born.

Chris lived in an old house by the Marple Township Police Station. Because of the distance, Chris got to ride the bus to school. We socialized only in the schoolyard. It wasn't until the summer between fourth and fifth grades, as my trusty old bicycle carried me further from home, that I began to hang out at his home.

My best friend up till that time was Butch Bartley. He lived in the short cul-de-sac behind my street, and our back yards met at an angle. There were nine people in the busy Bartley house: four boys, three girls, plus the two adults. They were crammed into the same three-bedroom, one-and-a-half-bath little box as the rest of the neighborhood.

Butch was a walking contradiction. Big, athletic, and outgoing, he chose me—quiet, small, and shy—for a best friend. An A and B student, always polite and eager to help out, Butch drank coffee like soda and his nails were always bitten down to the point of bleeding. We managed to get into more than our share of mischief. But I always seemed to get caught and into trouble, while Butch came out unscathed. That should have told me something. It didn't. He was the one who dared me to put my toy .38 to my head.

One summer we went off to a four-day camp. A boy was beaten up pretty badly. Everyone knew Butch had taken sadistic pleasure in hurting his victim. Once again he managed to talk and charm his way out of the situation. Years later I would learn that Butch was paying Clark Gilman to beat me up. After I failed the fifth grade, Butch moved on, ignoring me.

"How 'bout them Red Legs?" The squeaky tenor voice echoed across the rapidly filling schoolyard. It was my best friend Chris Murphy. Chris was a hopeless Phillies fan like me. But he seemed to a have a crystal baseball because he could pick teams better than anyone I ever knew. He claimed his picks came to him in dreams.

Baseball wasn't the only thing that came to Chris in dreams. His morning predictions of pop quizzes and surprise tests were usually dead on. He once told me he dreamed he was a condemned prisoner and I flipped the switch to the electric chair. Chris laughed. But the eerie prediction made me shudder.

In proper grade school etiquette, the St. Pius X schoolyard was unofficially divided: the boys' side and the girls' side. A kind of no-man's land ran between the two. Here, girls unafraid of cooties and boys unafraid of their buddies' ribbing sometimes mingled. I turned left at the bottom of the school's long driveway, passing through girls' territory on my way to the boys' side. My radio was back on Wibbage, and Chuck Berry sang about Maybelline. I waded through a sea of blue jumpers and powdered scents, wondering what sort of parents named their kid Maybelline.

"Ya ready to pay up?" Chris met me in no-man's land. He was accompanied by Ben Masters, Ben's kid brother Randy, and David James. If Chris had big ears, chubby David was Dumbo, a painful moniker he was finally starting to shake.

"The season ain't over yet," I replied.

"It is for the Phillies."

David James nodded his agreement.

"More of your dreams?"

"Just common sense."

"We'll see. What's cooking, my brother Hound?"

Chris took my outstretched paw for our secret club handshake. He let out a high-pitched, hair-curling howl befitting a Great Dane with a bad tooth. Nearby several girls stopped jumping in mid-rope and stared. Ben Masters grinned. Ben Masters always grinned.

"Got your tunes with you I see," Chris said, releasing my hand.

"Always."

While the radio became a permanent fixture with me, I hadn't brought it to school much. I carried it for company mostly on the days I planned to ditch. I never saw anyone with a transistor at school and wasn't sure how the nuns would react to the presence of rock 'n' roll in their sacred halls. They thought most music was the work of the devil and Little Richard, Satan himself.

But at that moment my little radio was becoming the center of attention. The jump ropers moved closer, along with some other girls, as did some guys, seventh and eighth graders.

"Oh, I love that song," a girl squealed.

"She was on *Bandstand* last week," another added.

Connie Francis was complaining about lipstick on your collar. Everyone within earshot was hopping in time, like musical pogo sticks. I held the music box out and turned up the volume. I was a pied piper weaving my musical spell on those around me. Guys tapped their feet or snapped their fingers. Girls hopped. Chris slapped my shoulder and Ben Masters grinned. For the first time in my life I was in control, held an audience, and was the center of attention in a good way.

Connie Francis faded. She was replaced by a short station jingle and then the unmistakable voice of Buddy Holly. The hopping changed to a rhythmic sway.

"Who's that?"

"Buddy Holly," I replied to the anonymous question. "'True Love Ways,' it's an old one of his."

"Actually it was released shortly after he died."

The comment came from behind the line of now-swaying jump-ropers. The voice was honey, music itself, and oddly familiar.

"I remember reading about it in the newspaper," the voice said.

Heads nodded solemnly, murmured, and continued to sway. "Buddy Holly's one of my favorites," I found myself saying.

The voice sang its reply. "Mine, too."

I edged up the volume wheel. There was silent reverence as Buddy sang and kids swayed. An eighth-grade boy shook his head, bestowing the ultimate in schoolyard respect: "Cool."

That single, profound utterance, innocently muttered by an upper classman, officially announced to the school population that Billy Neblett, fifth-grade repeater and bad boy, was nevertheless one cool dude. Life was about to get very good.

First Wednesday of fifth grade, part two, went a lot better than I had expected. The school bell rang, and I lined up with a hundred strangers at one end of the yard, while my friends got into line at the other end. They had graduated not only to the sixth grade, but to the second floor.

Sister Philippine, who had flunked me, was long gone. Her replacement, Sister Tres-Martin, wore an expression as if her shoes were too tight. Fortunately, a couple of my new classmates had more serious behavioral problems than I did. Throughout the year they caught the brunt of our nun's sour disposition.

One of these was Jake Cushman. Jake's dad was a famous baseball umpire. At ten years old, Jake already carried the stubborn single-mindedness of a professional baseball ump. His specialty was snide, often off-color remarks muttered into the lapel of his camel sports jacket.

Sister Tres-Martin's specialty was a right-handed slap across the face, followed by a wicked backhand when Jake spit out the corner of his mouth, "That the best you got?" Jake survived to referee professional basketball.

Two other troublemakers who took some of the heat off of me were Vic DeSicca and Stan Dana. Dana was a straight-A student and a grade-A wise guy. Vic DeSicca wore the world's biggest chip on his shoulder. Both were textbook pain-in-the-ass bullies and candidates for reform school. Both decided they would make my life miserable. With taunts and jeers, they tried to turn the school population against me.

Their campaign of terror came to an abrupt end one day when I punched the lights out of one of their friends, right in front of them in the schoolyard. Terry Decker purposely knocked my radio out of my hand and then laughed. I bent down to retrieve it and came up with a fist to his gut. He hunched over just in time for his nose to meet my knee. It sounded like someone stepped on a cricket. He should have stayed down. Instead he stood there in a daze, blood spewing from his broken nose, while I pounded what was left of his face with my fists in time to "Tutti Frutti."

Maybe the nuns were right about Little Richard after all.

If Decker had broken my radio, I'm sure I would have killed him. He went off to the hospital, and I was given a month's detention. I was lucky I wasn't suspended or expelled.

The entire school population was on my side. It was time someone put the bullies in their place. Naturally, parents and teachers didn't see it that way. Me, I was just pissed about the radio.

Still working on my self-confidence, I didn't pay close attention to my new classmates those first couple of weeks. I kept my head down and rarely made eye contact with anyone.

At St. Pius X there were two classes of each grade. Classrooms held about one hundred and twenty students; usually sixty or so were boys. Boys sat up front, filling the first six seats in the ten rows of antiquated desks. I sat in the sixth seat of the ninth row, close to the window.

Two weeks after first Wednesday, the sun returned, along with temperatures in the mid-seventies. It was Friday afternoon, September 22, geography time. A light breeze stirred the stuffy classroom. It smelled of orange blossoms.

Our inane homework assignment was to draw a map of Pennsylvania, filling in important cities and the state capital. The papers were being passed forward. Something familiar touched my shoulder. It was a hand with slender fingers and filed nails, the pinky nail bitten down. I turned in my desk. Bright hazel eyes smiled at me.

I never heard the nun.

"William, is there a problem?"

My whole being was consumed in a pair of sparkly marbles that appeared to speak. "Hi," they seemed to say. "Remember me, from first Wednesday?" Unspoken words touched my heart, ricocheted up to my ears, and rattled around in my brain.

"William Neblett!"

The world existed between breaths, between beats of my heart, in the space from one tick of the plastic wall clock to another.

I became aware of hushed laughter.

The hazel eyes broke the spell, shifting their focus upward and spilling over with panic.

Another hand landed on my shoulder. This one was wrinkled and red with anger. It pulled me from my seat, spinning me around.

"Is there something wrong with your hearing?"

Before I could answer, music flowed from behind me. "It's my fault, Sister. I was passing the homework."

When Tom is chasing Jerry, he sometimes runs into Butch and is stopped dead in his tracks. While Jerry lingers teasingly in the shadow of the hulking bulldog, knowing he is safe, Tom's head slowly explodes. Now it looked like smoke was escaping from around Sister Tres-Martin's ears. I was sure the only thing securing the top of her head was the tightly wrapped headdress of her nun's habit.

The grip on my shoulder loosened. You could hear a rosary bead drop. Finally I was roughly returned to my seat. Sister Tres-Martin marched off to the head of the class.

I accepted the stack of loose-leaf papers, added mine to the pile, and passed them forward. "Thanks. I owe you," I whispered over my shoulder.

"Yes, you do Billy, and I'll collect," was the gentle song that came from behind me.

At three p.m. my hazel-eyed bulldog disappeared in a flurry of blue jumpers. All weekend I was haunted by two sparkling, hazel-colored diamonds. They peered up at me as the yokes of fried eggs; beamed at me as headlights on Dad's Plymouth; laughed at me as the knobs on our television set; smiled at me from a sky of navy blue.

Monday morning I nearly ran over a third grader as I coasted my bike down the school's long drive. My eyes scanned the girl's yard for... what? A pair of anonymous hazel eyes, a gnawed pinky? She called me Billy, not William or even Bill—Billy. I realized I had no idea of her name or what she looked like. But why did I even care?

I parked my big, black two-wheeler in the bike rack. Slinging the green Army school bag over my shoulder, I retrieved my radio from the handlebars, where it hung by its leather strap, and sought out Chris.

A group of sixth-grade boys stood in a circle laughing. I knew I'd find Chris at the center. Sure enough, my friend stood with his black jacket on backwards, arms outstretched, doing a very funny impersonation of Frankenstein's monster. I moved through the circle and Chris spied me.

"Aaruggh, Master..." He hobbled stiff-legged toward me. "Master, more power, Master. Turn up the juice. More power!"

I held out my radio like a cross to a vampire and cranked the volume. Chris stopped and began doing a Frankenstein twist to Chubby Checker. Mercifully, the song ended quickly. Chris returned to his normal, goofy self, and the circle began to break up.

"What is it with you and electricity?" I asked, helping Chris with his jacket.

"I had the dream again last night."

"Oh, no."

"The one where you fry my ass."

"I told you I don't want to hear it!" I switched off the radio in the middle of Fats Domino. "Besides, I need your help."

Chris's dark eyes grew wide. He looked from me to the transistor and back to me. "This must be serious for you to kill your tunes, Daddy-o!" He draped a boney arm around my neck and pulled me over. "Step into my office. What can I do you out of?"

"Well, there's this girl..."

Chris stopped and looked me dead in the eye. I think it was the only time I ever saw my friend serious. Even in class he kept a light, joking demeanor, ready to laugh at the drop of a piece of chalk.

But that day in the schoolyard I saw a different, serious Chris. His open-mouthed expression seemed to say, "From this moment on, nothing will ever be exactly the same."

He was right.

Chris's seriousness vanished almost instantly. "I thought I warned you about those creatures. Nothing good ever comes from mixing cold cream and Clearasil. The fumes do funny things and—"

"Will you just shut up and listen? This girl—I don't even know her name..."

The disarming grin I knew so well crept across the familiar face. Chris threw up his arms in an overt gesture. "Leave it to you to flip out over someone whose name you don't even know." He turned and began staggering around, shaking his head. His unkempt, dirty blonde hair spilled over his forehead. "Kids! Kids these days! What's a mother to do? Oy vey!"

The school bell rang. I left him there in his drama and got in line at my end of the schoolyard.

ᘓᐧᐧᑯᐧChapter Five᙮ᘓᐧᐧ

"**I**t happened in the year eleven-eleven and again in sixteen-ninety one. The last time it happened was eighteen-eighty one. It's happening this year, but it won't happen again until the year sixty-one nineteen." That riddle was on everyone's lips as the new decade entered its second year. Appropriately, 1961 turned out to be an upside-down year in more ways than one.

While Chubby Checker, a former chicken plucker and teen idol from the streets of Philadelphia, was poised to accept a Grammy for his "Let's Twist Again," adults across the country were poised to invade teen territory. In 1960, Checker, aka Ernest Evans, recorded an old Hank Ballard tune called "The Twist." With a peppier, slicker arrangement and the hypnotic, gyrating motions of the portly performer, the twist—both the song and the dance—soon became all the rage. And it wasn't just the teens who were caught up in the new craze. As Sam Cooke would soon put it, "...here you'll find the young and old twistin' the night away..." The first phenomenon of the '60s had arrived.

By 1961 Twist clubs were a worldwide happening, peopled by the rich and famous, the plain and poor, the young and old. Adults had discovered a rhythmic connection to their rebellious rock 'n' rolling sons and daughters. Wives across the country took an afternoon break from housework, twisting with dancers on *American Bandstand*. Dance studio instructors grew fat teaching the new moves to eager, middle-aged students. Celebrities from Grace Kelly to Norman Mailer to Joe DiMaggio to New York Mayor Robert F Wagner, Jr., could be found rubbing elbows and shaking hips with secretaries and truck drivers. Even popular columnist Earl

Wilson headlined the new trend, soon finding himself the butt of another headline: Wilson Does the Twist, But Needs Help Back to His Table.

Riding the dance craze to fame and fortune, Checker would re-release his original 1960 version of "The Twist" in 1962, taking the newest wave of twisters once again to the number one spot on the Billboard Top 40 charts. With an irony befitting rock 'n' roll itself, the music that had alienated generations less than a decade ago now found them sharing a common dance floor.

With music bridging cultural gaps, however tenuously, happenings half way around the world were conspiring to create an ever-widening generation gap. Following the surrender of Japan to Allied forces in 1945, Japan transferred all of its powers to the provisional government of Ho Chi Minh in the Southeast Asian country of Vietnam. With British forces returning power in Saigon to the French, the stage was set for internal conflict. Following months of deteriorating relations, the Democratic Republic of Vietnam launched its first consorted attack in an attempt to evict the French.

In 1950 the U.S. pledged fifteen million dollars in military aid to the French for the war now raging in Indochina. At the same time, China and the Soviet Union were providing weapons to the Vietminh forces of Ho Chi Minh.

By 1954 it was obvious the French had met their match, and the Geneva Convention put an end to the hostilities by dividing the country at the 17th parallel. China and the Soviet Union aligned themselves with Hanoi to the north, but the U.S. rejected the Geneva decision, supporting the interim government in Saigon. With the final withdrawal of the French in 1956, the tiny, divided country became a political pawn in an international game of chess.

In a well-publicized speech, President Eisenhower referred to the situation in Southeast Asia, citing a "domino theory." Whether anyone believed that if Vietnam fell into communist control the rest of Southeast Asia would follow suit, making it "impossible to stem the flow of the red tide," is a moot point. As the Cold War in Europe escalated, the United States found itself in a position of worldwide guardian against the red menace. By 1961 Vietcong guerillas from the north, supplied by the Soviet Union and communist China, and South Vietnamese troops, trained by the U.S. Military Assistance Advisor Group, were locked in a bloody struggle. President Kennedy had inherited another politically volatile situation involving a foreign country.

I found I could easily identify with the new president's problems. I could read the concern and tension and indecision, even the fleeting feelings of helplessness, in his face. They were the same feelings I saw in my father's face as he watched the nightly news or scanned the evening newspaper. They were the same feelings that coursed through my young mind as I was forced to leave my urban roots behind.

My first crack at the fifth grade back in 1960 was a confusing time in my life. Mom's sister, my beloved aunt, had been gone a while. Grandmom D'Nato, Mom's last living relative, had recently passed away. Visits to the old 'hood in south Philly, already growing fewer and fewer, trickled down to the requisite Palm Sunday grave-side vigils. Soon, even these would end.

I felt alone, lost.

Except for Chris, my friends seemed to be changing, finding new interests, just as the world around us was changing. We said a fond goodbye to the fabulous fifties and an uncertain, qualified hello to what began as an optimistic new decade. My daily hike up Cornwall Hill was saddled with unanswered questions about myself and my ever-changing world. I sought answers in the most unlikely places.

School was never much more than an inconvenience to me, broken up by periods of fun and socializing. The boring, repetitive, archaic teaching methods of the nuns didn't help matters. Neither did the fact that I suffered from Obsessive Compulsive Disorder and Attention Deficit Disorder. Neither would be diagnosed in me for decades. All the while I felt confused and increasingly alienated.

Spending time with my aunt only fed the amorphous demons growing in my young brain. Aunt Mary taught me how to count. Riding the trolley or subway, headed downtown on shopping trips or visits to her doctor, she would make a game of counting. I'd count the red cars we passed, or the barbershops we saw, even the squirrels that performed their antics for tossed peanuts in Rittenhouse Square. I counted, knowing how much it pleased my aunt.

The afternoon of her funeral, my sister and I remained at my grandmother's house on Eighth Street with a sitter. I understood what was going on; my mom had given me the talk about death and funerals and burial. A Catholic education assured me Aunt Mary was in heaven looking down, watching me. But I didn't understand why I couldn't go or how adult logic dictated a funeral would be "too hard on the children." I missed my aunt and wanted to be with her. Dad did his best to smooth over the situation. He said the funeral procession would be passing by on the way to the cemetery. I sat by the front window counting. It somehow made me feel close to my aunt. Later that evening my parents couldn't understand the significance when I proudly reported there had been three long limousines, two flower cars, one big black station wagon—the hearse—and twenty-seven cars with their lights on.

My obsessions were beginning to blossom.

Thanks to Mom's non-driving status and my extensive trips with my aunt, I learned to ride the buses around our community and to navigate the elevated subway, which carried us to downtown Philadelphia. I fed my obsessions by counting and memorizing stops and transfers and landmarks. But I kept my obsessions secret. Though she was gone, the private counting game still belonged to my aunt and me.

At the corner of Lawrence Road and Sussex Boulevard, some thirty yards from Sam the crossing guard, sat a SEPTA bus stop. One bright, warm morning in early fall, 1960, my weekly allowance burning in the pocket of my black slacks, I stepped into the gaping mouth of a waiting bus. Depositing my fare, I found a vacant seat and watched as St. Pius X School, my classmates, and a piece of my childhood disappeared over my left shoulder in a plume of grey diesel smoke. As the bus lumbered onto West Chester Pike, a comfortable, excited anticipation washed over me. I had ditched school before, but never like this. I was on a pilgrimage, a personal crusade to discover what secrets lay beyond the next town.

Forty-five minutes and one transfer later, I was deposited in a sleepy hamlet on the outskirts of the Main Line. Before me sprawled Great Valley Auto Salvage, my personal empyrean.

I quickly discovered the yard's vicious old guard dogs loved popcorn and to have their ears scratched, and that the portly old grease-stained caretaker loved to talk. I never inquired as to the needs of his sizeable ears. He let me wander about the yard alone, as long as I first listened to a well-meaning lecture on skipping school, and to one of his protracted yarns of the good old days. I paid admission to my arcane Erewhon with my patience and attentiveness, and an occasional chore for my friendly benefactor.

The eerie, cemetery-like atmosphere of the salvage yard appealed to me. With the background roar of my existence attenuated, I could think about my young life and where it was and wasn't and perhaps should be, and why. Thoughts that normally darted through my mind like distance lightening in the summer sky now paced themselves, allowing me time to savor and analyze every subtle detail and nuance. I'd been pretty much a loner, often preferring my thoughts and private musing over my friends' company.

With the peaceful stillness of a church on Saturday, the junk yard taught me to think—and to listen. In the windswept silence I heard the chromium voices of the forgotten and forlorn vehicles: their cries, their whispers, their hopes and dreams, and their prayers. Each had a unique tale to tell, a vainglorious vision that was slowly fading, like their bright, shiny, Simonized paint in the unforgiving sun. The once noble cars, each as sad and lonely as their genial guardian at the front gate, each with its hood yawning high, a metallic cenotaph to a proud past, spoke to me.

And I listened and understood. Later in my life, their tales, as fresh and alive in my mind and imagination as the new day, would provide inspiration for some of my best short stories.

The sullen old veterans of endless miles became my friends, my confidants and my confessors. Their lessons went beyond part numbers and inner workings and mechanical magic. From them I learned the mechanics of living, and of dying with dignity. That same wisdom can be learned in the stillness of a cemetery; in the clatter of a carnival; among the wild beauty of a field of sunflowers; or in the stark realities of an inner city street. All one needs do is listen.

I thought about my grandmother. The last few years of her life she spent alone and old and nearly forgotten, rusting with time in her own personal junkyard on Eighth Street. She still held much wisdom to impart, stories to tell, dreams to relive. Only no one was listening anymore. I wish I had been listening.

I spent more time at my open-air academy then I did in Sister Philippians' classroom. As I grew older, as the lessons of long division and proper spelling and world capitals faded, the knowledge and insight imparted by my mechanical mentors remained.

Try to explain that to a concerned parent worrying about their truant son who just failed fifth grade.

If I was going to find out her name, or anything else about the owner of the beautiful hazel eyes, I was going to have to do it on my own.

Did I say beautiful?

The word sprang to mind as naturally as the lyrics to a favorite song. As we marched to class in formation, I realized her eyes were beautiful. There was no other word for it.

A pre-teen boy's concept of beautiful is different from an adult's, like chocolate ice cream is different from a Snickers bar. Not better or worse, just different. A thousand images flooded my brain. A thousand endorphins fired with each. My Phil Rizzuto signature baseball glove was beautiful, as was my big, black, Columbia bike with the massive chrome fenders and motorcycle-type seat.

A 1950 Mercury could be beautiful, once it was nosed, decked, shaved, and lowered. The ancient formations in Carlsbad Caverns were beautiful and awesome. Linda Jansen, the lead singer of the Angels, had a beautiful voice—and she was beautiful, too. The picture sleeve of their 45 record "Till" hung on the wall of my bedroom, between my Phillies pennant and a map of the solar system. Yes, she was beautiful.

At St. Pius X Grade school, lay teachers filled in for the nuns, teaching second, fourth, and sixth grades. St. Pius X being the poor school it was, the lay teachers were actually college girls in their final year, teaching as part of their credits toward a teaching certificate. Even to a fourth grader it was obvious they were beautiful too.

I reached my desk. Sister Tres-Martin's fifth-grade classroom was not beautiful.

"Hello, Billy." The melody floated up from behind me. Now that *was* beautiful. I looked around, and more endorphins exploded like sky rockets. The hazel diamonds sparkled. They were set in a slightly rounded face with full, rose-petal cheeks and a lightly freckled button nose. The small, pert lips reminded me of the gracefully curving lines of a Kaiser Darrin sports car.

My tongue ceased to function. What was the old biblical expression? It had cleaved to the roof of my mouth.

Poets and musicians, authors and lovers for centuries have tried to express their exact feelings at moments like this. Words such as *magical* and *timeless* and *destiny* can spring to one's mind.

Not mine.

I think it was Shakespeare who once spoke of being addlebrained by beauty. It was either Shakespeare or Charlie Brown. Either way, they were right. The only word coursing through my mind at that moment was *run*.

And so I did.

Snatching up my school bag, I bolted down the aisle to the security of the coat closet at the rear of the classroom. There I remained for as long as possible, pretending to busy myself with the intricate workings of the bag's three snaps.

"William Neblett! Are you joining us today? Or perhaps you'd prefer to just stand in the closet?"

Nuns don't joke about such things. Nuns don't joke.

I turned, head bowed in embarrassment. Why hadn't I just kept running, out of the classroom, the building, right up the long driveway and into Lawrence Road? There a speeding DeSoto could have saved me, skewering me on the tines of a chrome hood ornament. A poetic end to my misery, befitting any poet or musician, author or lover: "His tongue still cleaved to the roof of his mouth."

Head bowed, I walked the green mile back to my desk. Past Lucy Brighton, giggling her insidious giggle; past Margret Curtis, taking her copious notes of my degradation for the edification of the schoolyard, the community, and the world. Every school, every class, has their Margret Curtis: the skinny, bespectacled, self-appointed conscience of the class. The one who pops up as the dismissal bell chimes and in a whiny, nasally voice declares, "Sister, you forgot to give us homework." The Margret Curtises of the world grow up to head organizations like PETA and run magazines like *Cosmopolitan*.

Finally my desk was within reach. There was just one more demeaning hurdle to overcome. I risked a peek. One hundred and eighteen pairs of eyes dogged my painful progress. But the hazel diamonds weren't among them. Hands folded, facing ahead, eyes averted, their absence offered up a ray of compassion, a life saver in a sea of sharks. Not a lot of help, but a kind gesture.

Sister Tres-Martin rapped on her desk as I sat at mine. Instantly, mercifully, all attention was diverted to the front of the room. It was time for arithmetic.

Those who have never experienced Catholic school in the '50s and '60s need to be made aware of something. Nuns in those days dressed like penguins, but they possessed the memory of an elephant, the cunning of a fox, and the temperament of a sun-stroked rattler. It was possible to get over on one, but they always had their revenge, quietly biding their time till the opportune moment. Sister Tres-Martin's moment came later that same day.

It was three days since the beguiling creature behind me had saved my butt during the paper-passing debacle. I knew I would pay dearly for it one day. It was just a matter of time. This morning's fiasco was also about to come back and bite me.

"Class, put away your history books and take out your readers."

Uh-oh.

My hands frantically searched the compartment beneath my desk top. Geography... Spelling...

Arithmetic...

A copy book...

Car magazines...

Chocolate Tastykake...

Baseball cards...

No reader.

I must have it! Part of the homework assignment I had neglected was to read ten pages. I remembered staring at it while Hy Lit counted down the Wibbage Top Ten. Its weight caused my school bag to tug at my shoulder as I peddled up Cornwall hill.

My school bag.

In the confusion of the morning's events I'd neglected to completely empty my school bag. The reader sat what seemed a mile away, in the classroom coat closet.

I needed a decoy. U.S. History was about the same size. With their hand-fashioned, brown shopping-bag covers, all our school books looked alike anyway.

"Master Neblett?"

Too late. Damn, she must have x-ray vision or something.

"You do have your reader?"

"Yes, Sister, it's in—" No! Not the coat closet!

"Well?"

"It's—it's at home, Sister."

From across the room, Jake Cushman broke out in a coughing fit that sounded very much like, "What a jerk, what a jerk." A look from Sister Tres-Martin worked better than a Luden Wild Cherry cough drop.

She turned her attention back to me, a cruel smile creasing her implacable visage. In the classroom, the only time a nun smiles is when they know they've got you. "I see."

I was dead meat.

"Well then," the smirk grew, "perhaps one of your *friends*"—she spit the word out in a challenge—"wouldn't mind sharing his book with you."

Sure. Any number of them would be glad to. Only problem is they're all upstairs in Miss Keiffer's sixth-grade class while I'm stuck here with you.

To punctuate her point, she waited, surveying the room.

Silence.

"Well it seems—"

"He can share my book, Sister."

There are certain unwritten, universally understood and accepted rules and conventions followed by grammar-school kids the world over. For example: you don't rat out a friend. Cheating off the annoying smart kid next to you is perfectly acceptable, that's why he's there. Asking a girl for help is catamount to saying you like her. Being saved by a girl twice in three days is like being kissed by her in the middle of the schoolyard at lunch time. Nothing could be worse.

For the first and only time in my life I saw a nun beaming. "Excellent!"

Sister Tres-Martin arose, the smirk now a full-fledged, teeth-flashing, fangs-bared leer. She smelled victory and was going in for the kill. She would fell two birds with one stone.

"Thank you, Miss Johns. You may slide over in your seat so Mr. Neblett can join you at your desk."

Okay, there was something worse. I'd take the kiss in the schoolyard any day. This was cruel and unusual. The prospect of sitting next to the beautiful—yes, beautiful—Miss Johns was not an unpleasant one. It was the circumstances that sucked.

I was trapped.

Begrudgingly I rose. One hundred and eighteen pairs of snickering eyes watched. I could feel my macho, bad-boy image crumbling to dust. Donning my best sympathetic face, I turned, feeling as bad for Miss Johns as for myself for what I'd gotten her into.

To my utter amazement and confusion she was smiling, a bewitching, perplexing, and genuinely friendly smile. Her hazel diamonds locked on to my chocolate hollows and smiled as well. A reassuring, "It's okay, I won't bite" smile. It helped. She slid over, cheerfully patting the seat next to her.

There was nothing for me to do. Okay, I could have bolted, this time heading out the door and not stopping till I reached West Chester Pike and a speeding semi. Splat!

I didn't.

Savoring a deep breath, I did my best to smile back, taking my place next to the enigmatic Miss Johns. Looking up, I thought I detected smoke once again escaping from beneath Sister Tres-Martin's headdress. She was no longer smiling, nor was any one laughing.

A bolt of lightning and the world made glorious, perfect sense. I could have kissed my partner right there in the classroom despite the consequences. By not getting upset and by smiling, she had stolen the thunder right out of the nun's planned humiliating victory. My smiling and my acceptance of the situation only sweetened our triumph.

I looked back over at the rosy face. It was a face I wanted to know better, to explore, to learn in detail. Chris was right in his warning me about these creatures. They could be more devious, conniving, and dangerous than any male. It was a lesson I would do well to remember.

Of course, I wouldn't.

Sister Tres-Martin returned to her desk in a huff. I slid into the seat, greeted by the dizzying scent of oranges.

Match point. Set and game to Miss Johns.

Parents have a method of tormenting their children. It's surprising how annoying a few seemingly innocuous questions can be to the adolescent. This need to question is carried and passed down in the genes. The question gene lies dormant until the individual becomes a parent. Then it becomes active and turns cancerous to the unsuspecting offspring. This is why you never hear a single aunt or a favorite bachelor uncle asking, "What did you do today?" or, "Who's your new friend?" or even, "Where have you been?"

These questions, harmless enough on the surface, have the same effect as tugging the ears of a sleeping pit bull. And they carry with them automatic, natural responses that include inarticulate shrugs and groans followed by words sounding like "stuff," and "a guy," and "around."

This parent–child dance has been carried on for centuries and seems to be some sort of rite of passage, necessary to both parent and child. When I arrived home from school, my mother was in the mood for dancing.

"How was your day?"

"All right."

"How was school?"

"Okay."

"What did you learn today?"

To this I could have responded in several different ways. I could have explained that I learned about friendship. How true friendship is selfless and genderless, sacrificing, willing to bear the brunt of embarrassment and scorn, purely in the name of friendship; and how sincere friendship can often be found in the oddest places, among the most unusual circumstances. I could have said that I learned a girl could indeed be a friend, despite what Chris Murphy said.

I didn't.

I could have told how I learned that sometimes battles could be won through the simplest subterfuge, and of the value of a well-planned, well-timed smile.

I didn't.

I could have waxed poetic about the often overlooked color hazel, comparing its brilliance to a noon-day sun, its awe-inspiring beauty to a rainbow, its mystery to that of the pyramids of Egypt.

I chose none of the above.

To my mother's inquiry as to what I had learned today, I responded with the second most popular universal young boy reply:

"Nothing."

However, I *had* learned something today. Something of major importance, something I would remember all my life.

Her name was Amy.

ᏽ Chapter Six ᏽ

W hile the students at St. Pius X Catholic Grade School were adjusting to the routine of classes, nuns, and homework, the rest of the world was adjusting to a new decade of new fears, new threats, and new enemies. With the Berlin Wall now closed to traffic; atomic and hydrogen bomb tests escalating, and the communists winning in South East Asia, the possibility of an all out nuclear war seemed closer than ever. On October 6, 1961, President Kennedy took to the air waves and advised Americans to build shelters from atomic fallout in the event of a nuclear exchange with the Soviet Union. If the threat wasn't real, the fear certainly loomed real in the minds of the U.S. military and the American people. In a move reminiscent of the McCarthy '50s, U.S. members of the Communist Party were required to report themselves to the police. Two days after Kennedy's speech, Rev. Patrick Peyton arrived in San Francisco to hold what he called a "Rosary Rally" at the Polo Field of Golden Gate Park. The prayer for world peace drew an estimated 500,000 people. Then, on October 15, Kennedy called out military reserves in the wake of the Berlin crisis. The Kremlin responded to Kennedy and the American people's prayers by exploding a fifty-megaton hydrogen bomb on October 30. The Tsar Bomba test was the largest explosion ever recorded.

Back at St. Pius X, prayer times were expanded. Priests began making regular visits to the classrooms, speaking frankly about the world situation. Nun's increasingly reminded students to keep our president in our prayers. It was the first time I'd heard anyone directly refer to President Kennedy, the President of the United States and leader of the free world as *my* President. The young leader was already an important presence and influence in my life. Considering the possible meanings of the nun's referral to *my* president, I gradually became aware of a much larger community around me. The schoolyard, Lawrence Park, even sprawling Philadelphia began to shrink with-in my mind. Slowly, the background people of my existence began to take on forms, faces, and names, real, foreign sounding and frightening. I found myself an unwitting member in a worldwide society I could neither understand nor control.

Despite growing signs, increasing threats and mounting fears that October, people went about the day to day business of living their lives. Listening to the news, I began to pay closer attention to the lives of the background people.

A believed extinct volcano on an island in the South Atlantic erupted, forcing the evacuation of the entire population of Tristan da Cunha. In San Francisco a comedian name Lenny Bruce was arrested on charges of something called *lewd and obscene language*. The first Saturn rocket was successfully launched in an un-manned test flight. The United Nations finally were able to come together long enough to elect U Thant acting Secretary General. In New York City, ground was broken for a new Municipal Stadium. The baseball venue would soon be known as Shea Stadium and become the home of the newly formed New York Mets, one of baseball's first expansion teams. And in a decision which would have far reaching consequences, a U.S. Federal Judge ruled that Birmingham, Alabama, laws against integrated playing fields were illegal. With a keen understanding and insight of the rapidly evolving world, Bob Dylan recorded his first album in one day at a total cost of $400. The times were definitely a changing.

With new found fears and anxieties temporarily tucked securely in the hip pocket of our jeans, my friends and I concerned ourselves with a more important and immediate problem: what to be for Halloween. My second favorite holiday was coming up and my mom had already laid in a supply of Food Fair brown paper shopping bags for the orgy of candy and pranks ahead.

Even if dad had purposely planned our house for my near mile hike to school each day, he had unsuspectingly planted us in the middle of Trick or Treat central. 241 North Central Boulevard was ideally situated for Halloween. Regally clad as a pirate, or a hobo, or a gangster or a cowboy, ubiquitous brown bag in hand, I'd start my evening trek down the block, turning up one side of a connecting street and then down the other, finding myself back home. Dropping off the goods and acquiring a fresh sack, my journey took me up and down the next connecting street and back to my home base. And so it continued throughout the night, as nearly every home in the neighborhood was canvassed in a sweeping, zigzag pattern repeatedly terminating back at my point of origin. And, as an added bonus, Catholic tradition observed the day after Halloween, November 1, aka All Saints Day, as a holy day, which meant no school. While public school drones were forced to return to their homes early, the Catholic school crowd continued to terrorize the neighborhood. This year, older and with loosened curfew restrictions, I looked forward to my friends and I enjoying a late night of sugar induced mischief and merriment.

Freckles, hazel eyes, and feminine wiles had other ideas.

It took a while, but eventually the other kids in my class began to warm. Once they decided this crazy kid with the radio and reputation was okay, I started making friends. This was due in no small part to the influence of my newest friend, Amy Johns.

It was October and fall had finally arrived wearing a sweater, amidst leaf piles and football and apple cider in large oak casks. I managed to miss not a single day of school, quite a feat just a year previous. My parents were delighted. Well over a month had passed without a single note or call from school about their son.

In the rarefied realm of blissful expectation in which all parents reside—a realm often bordering on naïveté—Mom and Dad believed I had finally taken an interest in school. Fact being stranger than fiction, I had taken an interest in two bewitching eyes and a beguiling killer smile. No one since my late aunt had spoken to me or treated me or made me feel the way Amy did. Amy Johns was a perplexing mélange of fireworks, candy hearts, and long division. And I never wanted the roller coaster ride to end.

Afternoons were spent beleaguering poor Chris with the inflated and decidedly biased details of my reverie. She spoke soft, looked soft, and smelled soft—like oranges. She was smart, funny, and witty; she laughed at my jokes, and she knew as much about music, and more about baseball, than I did. And she liked me!

Chris of course took it upon himself to school me in the subtleties of dealing with *the enemy*. He had nothing at all against girls. His take on the fairer sex was simple: enjoy at arm's length.

I wanted more.

For many, fifth grade is that surreal time when the opposite sex comes into sharp focus and begins to take on new meaning. Boys start to find the same creatures they once avoided now strangely compelling, even intriguing, if not downright interesting. Girls, always a full step ahead of their male counterparts, begin to initiate the ages-old game of catch me. The rules are simple: once contact is made, the cards are marked and stacked, the dice loaded, and the dance fully choreographed. The hapless male is doomed. In other words, a boy chases a girl until *she* catches him.

Amy and her brood were readily versed in the game. Like all good soldiers they understood the key is to capture the general. As oldest and unofficial leader of Sister Tres-Martin's fifth-grade boys, I walked eagerly, if not willingly, eyes wide open, into Amy's well-placed snare. Once I was captured, the rest would fall like dominoes.

Not that I minded being captured. Amy sat directly behind me and delighted in disturbing what little attention I was paying in class by lightly blowing on the back of my neck. It felt like a swarm of gnats playing tag and, although it was distracting, I enjoyed the tickling sensation—and the attention. I'm sure the nun wondered about the goofy smile that painted my face.

I retaliated with tricks of my own. Sometimes, when it came time to pass our homework forward, I'd accept the stack of papers from behind me, slyly slip Amy's from the pile, and forward the remainders. At first opportunity, usually around morning recess or lunch time, as everyone lined up for the march outside, I'd place the purloined papers back into Amy's desk. Later in the day, as she searched for a pen or history book, she'd discover the errant homework. With a reluctant raise of her hand and a red-faced explanation, Amy would deliver her homework to Sister Tres-Martin. No harm done, except of course later when she connected with a stinging right to my shoulder.

Often we'd pass notes to each other, important things such as whether I'd heard the latest release by the Drifters, previewed on the radio last night by Hy Lit; or if her mom was picking her up after school. Many times the difference between an acceptable D and a failing F on a test lay in a gentle pen tap to my back, telling me the answer to question three was *true*.

In our own fumbling, faltering manner, Amy and I began to form a friendship. Despite Chris's warnings; despite the nun's disparaging, knowing glances; despite parental chidings; despite lunchroom remarks and schoolyard comments, Amy and I became friends. I enjoyed her company and found her to be fun, and as easy to be with and talk to as any of my guy friends.

I parked my bike in the rack and retrieved my school bag and radio. The voice wasn't unexpected.

"Hey, Delinquent."

Through our hushed quips, whispered jokes, and passed notes, Amy and I were growing close. She was certainly a lot more interesting than anyone I knew. And she smelled a lot better, too. It took a while, but Amy hung in there through my stammering tongue, my puzzled and embarrassed gaping, and even one or two more sudden bolts through the door or across the schoolyard to the safety of the boy's side. I had all but gotten over my shyness around her. I was also learning to ignore the taunts and less-than-friendly comments from some of the guys for being friends with a girl.

Somewhat...

The week before, in a fit of gallantry befitting Lancelot himself, I punched out a kid for hollering an obscenity while Amy and I talked in no-man's land. A stern lecture to our class about manners from one of the priests brought about the juvenile delinquent handle. Coming from Amy's sugary pallet, it took on a different significance altogether.

"Hi there, Bulldog," I eagerly replied. Holding the radio forward, I tweaked the volume.

Two hazel jewels rolled back in disbelief. "You gotta be kidding—'Blue Suede Shoes.'"

It was a game we played. It grew out of our mutual love of rock 'n' roll. We constantly challenged one another to identify songs, titles, performers, and more. Along with our hopeless Phillies and ineluctable attraction, it gave us mutual ground on which to build a friendship. The game also provided fodder for what would become my parents' anthem: "You can remember all that music stuff, why can't you remember your school work?"

If Sister Tres-Martin strummed a guitar, looked like Connie Stevens, and sang the state capitals in time to "Rave On," maybe I would.

My lips curled to one side. "And...?"

"Carl Perkins."

"And...?"

She shook her head, giving me a pitiful look. "Nineteen fifty-six."

Damn, she was good. I thought for a second. "On...?"

The smug expression melted into an onerous frown. She stomped her foot like a nervous thoroughbred. "Darn. It's kinda yellow, I think. I have the 45…"

"Times up, sorry!" I taunted. "On Sam Phillip's Sun label. But you are right about the color."

"Okay, Mr. DJ, you win. Now come over here, I have a job for you."

I strutted over to where she stood, savoring my victory. They didn't come often. Aside from myself, when it came to music Amy was about the most knowledgeable person I knew. We were well matched at our private little game.

"Job, as in work?" I switched off the radio. A light autumn breeze filled the air and my young brain with the provocative scent of orange blossoms. To this day I can't drink a glass of orange juice without thinking of Amy.

Amy's best friend was Connie Earnhart. Connie had designs on Tommy Grant. I was the bait. Poor Tommy never had a chance. Considering the extended outcome neither did I.

She pointed to the boys' side of the schoolyard where a group of kids were talking. "You see that kid there, the tall blonde? Do you know him?"

He was in our class, sat in the second row at the front. "I think his name is Tom or something."

"That's the one. Do you know him?"

"Not really. Why?"

"Can you get to know him, find out about him?"

I wasn't sure I liked where this conversation was headed, wherever that was. A sleeping monster awakened in my immature being: I was jealous. Why should I help Amy meet someone who might beat my time? The feelings were strong, real, and confused, if not fully understood. Amy looked at me and smiled and my brain turned to soft noodles.

"I... I suppose... of course, anything," I heard myself reply. At least it was my voice, but damn if I remembered saying something.

"Good. My girlfriend wants to meet him."

My built-in warning system, which tells me that trouble might be up ahead, was frantically sounding the alarm. Not that I ever heeded its council. Even if I wanted to, I couldn't hear it for the loud thumping in my chest.

Amy stood a foot away. Her long, honey-brown hair flittered out to the sides from beneath a cute, pink knit stocking cap topped with a fuzzy, pink pom-pom. Her rosy cheeks were flushed with the crisp autumn air. The infectious smile blossomed, melting the morning chill. Conflicting emotions drew up sides within me. The ensuing battle was called by the school bell.

We wandered toward our assigned line for the march inside. Taking her place with the rest of the girls at the rear of the dyadic formation, Amy called out, "The Poni-Tails."

"'Born Too Late,' 1958," I answered.

Amy shot me a disarming wink. "Delinquent!"

"Bulldog!"

A few days later I switched off my radio, steeled up some nerve, and cornered the boy named Tommy Grant in the schoolyard.

"Hey."

"Hey."

"What's going on?"

"Nothin'."

"Watcha' doing?"

"Nothin'. You?"

"Nothin'."

"You in Sis Tres-Martin's class?'

"Yeah, you too?"

"Yeah."

Well, so much for stimulating conversation. Tommy was quiet, a bit shy, and easy-going. His dad was a big wheel at Chrysler, and we soon found common ground.

"My dad brings home all kinds of neat junk—car brochures and models and stuff."

"Cool. You like to build model cars?"

"Yeah. You?"

"Yeah."

"I got George Barris' *Ala Kart* kit."

"Cool. I got Big Daddy Roth's *Outlaw*."

"Neat. You wanna come over? You can bring your models and stuff. Dad just gave me a bunch of brochures and sales junk on the new '62 Dodges."

"Sure."

And so a friendship was forged, born out of cars and plastic and feminine subterfuge.

The following day, after school and a quick two-step with my mom about where I was headed and who this new kid was, I peddled into new territory. Just beyond the small, sparse woods bordering North Central Boulevard lay South Central Boulevard and the start of the new build-out. Tommy lived on the far side of this new housing section. His updated home backed up to what was earmarked as a future industrial track. The future took its time arriving, and the area sat vacant, a sprawling, heavily wooded expanse crisscrossed with new sewers and a maze of fresh blacktop streets leading nowhere. It didn't take long for me to explore and map this new world aboard my trusty chrome and black Columbia bicycle. Amid new streets and new houses I discovered new friends—and new troubles.

Sporting larger, fancier, and pricier versions of ticky-tacky, the New Lawrence Park effectively doubled our subdivision: the number of families, the population of overcrowded St. Pius X and the size of my turf. On the schoolyard, a silent, subtle rivalry between old and new began to bubble beneath the harmless games of tag and jump rope. It spilled over into the adult realms of community swim clubs, little league bleachers, and back yard barbecues. With all of my positive experiences in hard-core, racially diverse and divided South Philly, I was about to get my first taste of a different kind of prejudice in placid American suburbia.

Despite my friend Chris's insistence, the New York Yankees captured the World Series crown in early October 1961. As Chris predicted, the Cincinnati Reds, skippered by Fred Hutchinson, finished the season four games ahead of the LA Dodgers. But the National League champs were the underdogs from the start, and with good reason. Buoyed on the bats of the "M&M Boys," Maris and Mantle, the Yankees had won 109 regular season games and pounded a Major League record 240 home runs, including twenty-plus round trippers from Yogi Berra, Elston Howard, Bill Skowron, and Johnny Blanchard. The Bronx Bombers' elite pitching staff was led by Cy Young Award winner Whitey Ford with a 25–4 record. To nobody's surprise, the Yankees clinched the title on October 9, taking game number five 13 to 5 at the Reds' home, Crosley Field, and winning the best of seven series 5 to 1.

Despite Jackie Robinson joining the Brooklyn Dodgers in 1947, Major League Baseball, like the rest of the country, was slow to accept integration. Incredibly, the Boston Red Sox refused to sign a black player until 1959, becoming the last Major League club to integrate. It wasn't until the 1954 season that the Cincinnati Reds integrated, signing Nino Escalera. By the time Elston Howard joined the New York Yankee organization in 1955, the United States Supreme Court had struck down Separate but Equal with the

Brown vs. Board of Education decision. That was December 1, the same year Rosa Parks was arrested for not giving up her seat on a bus to a white passenger. Her civil disobedience sparked the boycotting of buses in Montgomery, Alabama, and other southern cities. Parks became an important symbol in the growing Civil Rights Movement. She collaborated with civil rights leaders, including Martin Luther King, Jr., helping to launch him to national prominence in the struggle for black equality.

With the 1960 elections, African Americans found a source of hope. John Kennedy had been a strong supporter of civil rights throughout his political career. Less than two months into his presidency, Kennedy established a Committee on Equal Employment Opportunity, appointing Vice President Lyndon B Johnson as its chairman. That same committee would later become the Equal Employment Opportunity Commission. By May of '61, the Congress on Racial Equality, or CORE, had begun its series of Freedom Rides to the South to defy segregation in interstate bus facilities.

The idea was for an interracial group to board buses headed for the South. The whites would sit in the back of the bus, while blacks occupied the front. At rest stops, the whites would go into black-only areas. Drawing attention to the inequality of the interstate bus system, it wasn't long before the Freedom Riders' buses were attacked and burned by segregationist in Alabama. On May 21 the Freedom Riders along with Martin Luther King Jr. were surrounded by a mob at the First Baptist Church in Montgomery, Alabama. The standoff forced Robert F. Kennedy, the president's brother and attorney general, to send in federal marshals to protect them. But the Freedom Rides brought national attention to the escalating problem. By September the Interstate Commerce Commission, at the insistence of Robert Kennedy, issued new rules ending discrimination in interstate travel. But the conflict between white and black riders continued, stealing headlines and claiming victims.

In August of '61, my dad's employer, Wyeth Labs, sponsored a day at the Philadelphia Phillies. Driving to his work that Saturday afternoon, we boarded buses that would take us to Connie Mack Stadium, located in a depressed area of racially segregated North Philly. I remember my father commenting that the buses were a good idea since it would be "difficult to find good parking in that part of town." As we waited to board, my father was polite and courteous toward three black men who joined the sixty-some men and their families, greeting them by name, yet stopping short of a handshake. On board, my father seemed compelled to explain to me that the men who now occupied the last seats were porters and janitors, adding, "And very nice men."

Again, my young brain tried to process the mixed signals. I was aware of the class struggles, as many whites politely put the desegregation movement. I'd grown up around blacks and other races; ridden buses and the subway with them; been served by them in stores and restaurants; even interacted with blacks my age on the streets of Philadelphia. The Rexall Drug Store in Lawrence Park Shopping Center had a young black dishwasher and busboy. He would often wait on customers at the lunch counter. Yet there were no blacks at St. Pius X Grade School, or in Lawrence Park, or shopping at the Lawrence Park Shopping Center. And my father's stilted actions toward the men accompanying us went against his normally friendly manner. Riding to the stadium, I watched in contemplative silence as the scenery around me slowly changed from open parks and granite buildings to suburban shopping centers and housing developments; then from bustling city business centers and towering skyscrapers to brownstones and white sidewalks; and finally to decaying row homes and dirty streets cluttered with abandoned cars and abandoned buildings. It was a scene I'd witnessed a thousand times as we traveled to and from the city, visiting old friends we'd left behind. But it was as if I was seeing it all for the first time, in a new way, through different eyes.

My father's words came back to me: "and very nice men." What did that mean? Were they *exceptions*, as my father's inflection while describing them seemed to indicate? Did that mean that other blacks—blacks around me, perhaps ones I had encountered—

weren't nice men? Images of the fights and confrontations in Alabama and other places in the South I'd seen on the news flooded my mind. Were they nice men? Did they deserve the beatings and harsh treatment? And what about the white men who were treated with equal contempt for standing up to what they believed? If the leader of our country said segregation wasn't right; if the constitution stated all men were created equal; if the Bible admonished us to love our neighbor; then why were blacks and whites at war with each other?

On the street corner outside of Connie Mack Stadium, a grey-haired black man strummed his guitar in the noon day sun. I stood frozen, captivated by the pictures he painted with his instrument, the images he conjured up with his words. This was pure and raw, real and honest, and better than anything I'd ever heard on the radio or a jukebox. Smiling at me, his eyes seemed full of love and kindness. At the same time they flooded over with pain and sorrow, hurt, and heartfelt emotion.

...and very nice men.

I felt my father's hand tugging at my shoulder. "C'mon," he ordered, completely ignoring the black minstrel, "the game's about to start."

The racial conflicts continued, escalating into the fall of 1961. At St. Pius X we studied the Civil War; learned of southern slavery; read of John Brown and his abolitionists; were taught the fundamentals of the constitution. Our daily routine at school could be interrupted with the live televised launch of a new American rocket into space. For homework we were told to bring in newspaper clippings of our new president, the Berlin Wall, the race for space, even the race to break Babe Ruth's home run record and the World Series. But never a word was spoken about the undeclared war waged in southern cities every day and on my TV screen every night.

I tried to ask my father about the race situation. He was either unable or unwilling to discuss the subject. Giving me the look, he'd shake his head, saying it was complicated and I wouldn't understand; adding it was nothing I should concern myself about.

As I peddled my bike down South Central Boulevard and into the new section of Lawrence Park, I noticed the houses were somewhat bigger and grander. Still identical to one another, differing only in color scheme and roof lines, the new split-levels were a vast improvement over the smaller boxes where I lived. Making my way through the new build-out, I was reminded of the differences between the quaint brownstones and cramped row housing that delineated blue-collar South Philadelphia and poorer West Philly. The New Lawrence Park seemed somehow more affluent and refined. Even the long-promised public swim club had been built in the new section.

Shaking off a feeling of not belonging, I parked my bike and grabbed the box of plastic models from the handlebar basket. Tommy Grant greeted me at the door.

"And who is this?" It was Tommy's mother. She smiled pleasantly, sizing me up, noting the box in my hands. "Are you selling cookies or something?"

"No, Ma," Tommy answered, rolling his eyes. "This is my friend, Billy. He's in my class. We're going to work on our model cars."

"Oh." Her smile widened and she held out a hand. "Well, it's nice to meet you, Billy. Do you live nearby?"

"Yes, Ma'am," I replied uneasily, fumbling with the box. "Over on North Central."

The smile retreated as did the outstretched hand. "Oh... that's—that's over there." She turned, disappearing into the kitchen. "Well, you two have fun, and Thomas—I don't want you and your friend messing up the den."

The feeling of not belonging returned.

⌒✑Chapter Seven✐⌒

The klatch instinct hatches early in young girls. Once a leader steps forward, the hive begins to swarm. Topics such as clothes, hair, and makeup; movie and music idols; boyfriends and marriage become socialistic. No subject, no secret, no gab nor gossip is considered too sacred to share or too embarrassing to expose. At the core of this communal confab are of course boys.

The young male of the species typically compares life experiences and encounters to practical matters such as baseball and brawn: *he'd make a good shortstop; my dad can beat up your dad.* The gentler sex, however, have a more end-specific approach. They equate everything and anything to one single-minded purpose: marriage. A house should be just right, neither too big nor too small for raising a family. Cars need four doors for the kids. And every male is sized up not by athletic ability, brain power, or even appearance, but by that baffling quality understood only by females: What kind of husband and father would he make? Somehow, in the convoluted, complex thought process of all females, the first telling signs of a proper partner have something to do with how well he dances.

"This is your fault!"

"Yeah? What ya gonna do about this?"

"My mom says I gotta go!"

"Mine too."

It was a week before Halloween. I was in the schoolyard surrounded by several classmates; all angry, all waving envelopes at me like switchblade knives.

"This is what happens when you talk to girls!"

"Maybe it won't be so bad." Ah, the voice of reason among the rabble. All eyes turned. Ben Masters grinned sheepishly and shrugged his shoulders. "Maybe…"

The mob turned its attention back to me just as my buddy Chris made his way into the circle. He bravely planted himself between them and me. "Now, now, let's not be crazy about this. Let's hear him out."

Thanks, Chris.

"Then we'll kill him."

Thanks a lot, buddy.

It seemed the local postman's burden had been a bit heavier the previous day. Amid the circulars and electric bills and postcards and letters from Aunt Clara he carried with him invitations—eight of them. Each was pink and white, each prettily hand-written in gay red ink, each smelling sweetly of fresh oranges. Each requested the presence of the named boy or girl at a party the Saturday night before Halloween. And each was signed by Amy Johns, my Amy Johns—my friend.

And so, in their fifth-grade logic, the unwitting male victims of this unwarranted and unprecedented attack turned to me, or rather, *on* me. Meanwhile, across no-man's land, four giggly girls surrounded Amy with squeals and laughter, occasionally stealing a glance our way before returning to more hushed whispers, laughter, and giggles.

"Oh, it will be such fun!"

"What are you going to wear?"

"Look, there he is—he's so cute!"

There was more giggling.

Chris turned to me. Behind him four blue-tied, angry, fifth-grade boys, egged on by other fifth and sixth graders, awaited my reply. I swallowed the urge to turn and run. "So what's the problem?" I asked with feigned aloofness. "You've never been to a party before?"

"Not with girls!"

"My mom says I have to wear a tie…"

"Dummy, it's a costume party!"

"… and dance!"

The discussion escalated along with the volume and the anger. My new classmates, my new friends, had accepted me as one of them; moreover, as their leader. And now they felt they'd been betrayed and for a good reason. Tommy Grant and I had become friends, sharing interests in cars, models, baseball, and a more-than-passing curiosity regarding the opposite sex. As fate would have it, Tommy had had his eye on pretty, blonde Connie Earnhart all along. One afternoon in the schoolyard following lunch, I dragged him over to no-man's land. There Amy waited, accompanied by a nervous, anxious Connie.

"This is my friend Tommy."

"Hi."

"Hi."

"This is my friend, Connie."

"Hi."

"Hi."

The air burned with a roaring silence. Finally Connie found words, sort of. "Watcha doin'?" Well, it was a start.

It didn't take long for Tommy and Connie to become an item. Soon the talk of the schoolyard, the clinging couple was rarely seen outside of each other's company. Connie lived on one of the side streets that ran into North Central Boulevard. Tommy regularly skipped his bus ride home, preferring to walk his new blonde friend to her door. Then he'd hightail it through the shallow woods, across South Central Boulevard, cutting through several back yards, arriving home just minutes before his mother. I wondered how the snooty Mrs. Grant would feel about her only son seeing a girl from the other side.

Fortunately, the new couple's budding relationship drew some of the heat and attention off of Amy and me. And I found it was nice to have a male friend with whom I could share my feelings about liking a girl. But now, as I stood in no-man's land, facing a mob of angry, betrayed fifth graders, I realized Tommy was leading the rebellion. I wondered if his anger was real or simply a product of mob mentality. It didn't matter. We had all been betrayed, victims of feminine cunning.

Just then a cute pink stocking cap and killer smile sauntered over. The small crowd parted like the Red Sea.

"Hey there, Delinquent."

My mind went to mush. "Uh... er... hi, Bull... er... Amy." My cheeks flushed, and the killer smile waned.

"Here." She held out a pink envelope. "I wanted to give this to you myself."

The gathering responded with a collective, pointed, telling, "Ooh..." Ben Masters started giggling. My face flashed like a stoplight. I looked around. Unforgiving, mocking eyes laughed back.

Thanks, friends. Friends?

I looked back at my friend Amy, her arm outstretched, hazel diamonds questioning. With friends like Amy, who needed enemies? She had broken the first unwritten law of the schoolyard. She had embarrassed me, albeit innocently, unknowingly, in front of the guys.

Young male testosterone surged. With a disaffected smirk, I snatched the envelope from her hand. "What's the matter... run out of stamps?" The assemblage erupted in laughter. A flash of hazel fire quickly melted into sadness, disbelief, hurt.

Amy turned and was gone, leaving the air redolent of oranges and disappointment. Breakfast churned in my stomach. Confusion clouded my mind. I felt bad for her and angry with myself. Not fully understanding the reasoning behind my conflicted emotions, I sequestered them behind boyhood bravado.

"Gees, what's her problem?" I blurted out. "It's just a stupid party."

Retreating to the girls' side, Amy glanced over her shoulder. My heart plummeted. She had heard.

Testosterone two, empathy zero.

I surveyed the once again angry mob for help. My only hope was Chris. He stared back at me with a wry, detached simper I'd never seen.

"Don't look at me pal; this is your mess, yours and your new friend's. Saturday night I'll be watching *Have Gun—Will Travel*." With that, he and Ben Masters wandered off.

Thanks, pal.

My narrow, red-striped tie was giving me trouble. Four times I tied the Windsor knot; four times it came out uneven. Pulling the uncooperative piece from my collar, I eyeballed the collection of bow ties lying forlorn in my middle drawer. For some reason I had started wearing blue bow ties in second grade as an alternative to the regulation straight tie. Thankfully that phase had passed by the time I entered the fourth grade. To say my pretty, blonde lay teacher, Miss Jansen, had inspired the switch is an understatement.

An ugly blue school tie caught my attention. It was the clip-on type.

What was I doing?

Mom had told me to dress nicely. She mentioned nothing about ties and jackets. It was Sunday afternoon, and the family was headed into the city. Our destination was one of the large, old-time movie theatres that still populated Spruce and Walnut Streets of busy Center City Philadelphia.

Normally being dragged to a Sunday matinee downtown was an occasion I'd just as soon skip. Sure I relished any chance to spend time in the big city. And the movie palaces of the theatre district, with their gleaming chrome and neon marquees; their towering, gracefully curving screens and thundering sound systems; and their opulent lobbies that smelled of stale popcorn and cigar smoke were a Sunday feast for the senses. But what young boy cared about sitting through three-and-a-half hours of Rossano Brazzi and Mitzi Gaynor singing love songs atop a mountain, or watching a bald Yule Brenner dance? A year ago, Dad and I had come downtown to take in the George Pal, H. G. Wells sci-fi treat *The Time Machine* in its wide-screen, Morloc menacing glory. Dad enjoyed good sci-fi; it was something we had in common. Together we'd sat through screenings of *War of the Worlds, Forbidden Planet,* and more than one Saturday afternoon TV monster mash. But those father–son excursions were exceptions. Normally our visits to the aging film venues were at the request of my mom or sister, and usually to view some corny musical or boring love story. But today promised to be different from anything I had witnessed on the silver screen before. We were going to catch the Hollywood production of *West Side Story.*

I tossed the troublesome tie back into the dresser drawer. Slipping into a new pair of black chinos, I donned a sharp, dark-colored, high-collared shirt. It was the kind that jazzy P.I.s wore on TV—not too square for a cool dude like me, but not too crazy for my square parents. Finishing off my very hip ensemble with black matador boots and a thin black belt stylishly buckled to one side, I slipped my Black Panther locking blade knife into my back pocket. I couldn't have looked sharper if I were on screen alongside Riff and Tony.

Mom called from the living room, "Hurry up, we're going to be late."

"That boy will be late for his own funeral," Dad commented, making no attempt to lower his voice.

Market Street shimmered in the bright October afternoon sun. The city was unusually busy for a Sunday, with people window shopping, catching a late brunch, or enjoying the mild fall day. The large corner windows of Wanamaker's Department Store were festooned in orange and black crepe paper and creepy spider webs. Several mannequins had been lavishly outfitted as ghosts, monsters, and creatures from other worlds. Across the street, Lit Brothers countered with one window sporting an autumn harvest theme, including life-sized scarecrows and bales of hay. Not to be outdone and rushing things just a bit, Gimbels' display showcased rosy-cheeked models in faux fur and continually falling faux snow. It was a Neblett time-honored tradition that everyone seemed to love: whenever we came to town, regardless of our final destination, we would make a circle around the downtown shopping area, enjoying the seasonally decorated store windows.

As Dad searched for an adequate parking spot to fit our old, green, be-finned Plymouth, I took in the concrete and granite grandeur of my city. Thoughts of the endless trips downtown with my mom and my aunt flooded my mind: the rides aboard the cramped trolley cars and swaying subway; the fun lunches at the Horn and Hardart Automat; the afternoons feeding the pigeons in Rittenhouse Square; even the trips to the Rodan and Art museums. An alien feeling of sadness coursed through me. I realized my new life in suburbia had all but eclipsed the city boy I'd left behind. I loved our ticky-tacky house on North Central Boulevard in white bread Lawrence Park. But our move to safe, sane suburbia was softening me. I'd always yearned to return, if just for a time, to the crowded streets, noisy tenements, and gruff, friendly faces that had taught me so much. Now, through the magic of something called Cinemascope, was my chance. I would finally become, if only for a time and only vicariously, the street-wise tough guy I masqueraded as.

West Side Story was a box office smash. The ground-breaking film was nominated for eleven Oscars, bringing home ten, including Best Picture. But it was also an eye-opening slap in the face for those who chose to ignore juvenile delinquency in this country. While many turned blind eyes and deaf ears to the problems of restless youth, others were noting with alarm the increase in urban teen violence. The growing problem, which included escalating gang warfare, mounting truancy, and increasing racial discrimination among youths, garnered national attention through scathing articles in *Time, Look* and *Life* magazines. Now, the updated Romeo and Juliet tale of feuding gang members in modern-day New York City was captivating audiences across the country.

Citing juvenile delinquency as "a matter of national concern" that "requires national action," on September 22, President Kennedy signed into law the Juvenile Delinquency and Youth Offenses Control Act. Kennedy well understood that the "primary responsibility of coping with delinquency resides with families and local communities." He nevertheless appointed a committee on Juvenile Delinquency and Youth Crime, headed by his brother, Attorney General Robert Kennedy. The committee's focus would be to "help local communities in their efforts to stem the tide of juvenile delinquency..." School boards and city councils alike were fed up with directionless teens running and driving wild through their busy streets. In urban areas, gang violence was on the rise, while smaller towns were being menaced by speeding hot rod hoodlums. Most adults placed the blame directly on that old demon rock 'n' roll. In many ways, the federal government seemed to agree. My new idol's aims and my own ambitions were on a direct collision course.

I failed to comprehend the seriousness of my direction or the irony of the situation.

Monday morning in the schoolyard I was once again the center of attention. This time though it wasn't my blaring radio or masterful knowledge of the rock 'n' roll it emitted that put me in control of the gathering circle. Rather it was the attendant coolness of having seen *West Side Story*. With no assistance from the jocks at Wibbage, I regaled the growing crowd in no-man's land with detailed visions of the very hip exploits of the ultra cool Jets. As I spoke I imagined myself as Riff, leader of the dangerous gang, and Amy as my loyal moll at my side.

I looked around. Some girls were skipping rope, their breath steaming in the cool morning air. In the far corner of the girls' side, several fifth and sixth graders chatted and gossiped. Everywhere, blue jumpers bundled in autumn jackets scurried about. But there was no sign of a cute, pink, knit stocking cap topped with a fuzzy pink pom-pom.

My heart sank. Amy hadn't spoken to me since the party invitation fiasco in the schoolyard a week ago, and that hurt.

She was mad at me. That was obvious.

I was mad at myself. That I understood.

What wasn't obvious and continued to confound me was why I was mad at her. True, she had embarrassed me in front of my friends. But hadn't I acted like a horse's ass to her?

And why had I acted that way in the first place?

And why did I care?

The previous Friday night I had sat alone on the steps of the neighborhood Little League baseball dugout, radio in hand, smoking and sipping on a Pepsi bottle half full of my father's whiskey. It wasn't the first time I had sampled my dad's bourbon and it wouldn't be the last. Mom and Dad weren't drinkers. After-work cocktails and weekend beer were strangers in my house. Aside from New Year's Eve, three, maybe four times a year my folks would attend a party, usually in conjunction with one of my mom's plays. The gatherings were always BYOB, and my sober parents would return home with three-quarters of a bottle of Seagram's Seven or

Canadian Club. Then the barely used bottle would sit forgotten until the next outing. By that time I had well sampled the potent liquor and my unsuspecting, unaware parents were never the wiser.

I had been listening to DJ Jerry Blavat doing his popular Lover's Portion program of slow music and romantic musings. He spoke with jaded insight of a Coyote and his Main Fox, of young relationships, of feminine emotions and male pride, and of buses you miss on the corner. With plaintive teenage anthems punctuating his tender chidings, the whole ridiculous situation seemed to make perfect doo-wop sense. In my inexperience with the opposite sex, I had lashed out at Amy simply because of my pride, not wishing to lose face with the gang. It was something I'd learned at a young age: to make light of situations I didn't know how to handle or didn't understand. I had become known among my peers as well as my family as quite the quipster, always ready with a remark, often saying the wrong thing at the wrong moment. My offhanded observations had gotten me into trouble plenty of times. But it was a defense mechanism I'd grown comfortable with and relied upon, the often snide comments coming automatically.

The whiskey burned as it went down, taking with it the chill from the still evening. To my surprise and delight, I found that I liked the way it tasted. And I was learning to enjoy the harsh sensation in my throat. As I sat there drinking, alone with my radio, I listened to the sage advice from the young, hip DJ. I listened and I learned—of the pitfalls of relationships, of pride and feelings and emotions, and of other buses that arrived if you just waited long enough. And I understood.

My tender, eleven-year-old brain and affected heart understood.

Chris had been right. Things were changing—*I* was changing. And nothing seemed to be the same anymore.

I wondered if Amy was listening.

I could picture her in her bedroom, listening to "The Geator with the Heater" speak of young teenage love and as he put it, of being a "yon teen in love." Surely the lamenting lyrics of the Fireflies' song "Because of My Pride" would strike a chord and make her understand.

I missed my friend.

The whiskey tasted good but didn't seem to help. So I took another deep swallow.

I turned back to my audience. Empathy and understanding once again fell victim to stubborn male pride and boyish bravado. The schoolyard crowd had swollen and was hanging on my every word. The feeling was as intoxicating as the whiskey. So I took another deep bite, relating in detail the stirring scene from *West Side Story* of the dance at the gym. Someone laughed and mentioned Amy's forthcoming costume party. A suggestion was made that our childish club the Hounds should be reorganized into a gang and renamed something cool, like the Dudes, or the Rockers, or the Hawks.

Forgetting my radio lessons of just a few nights past and buoyed on a fresh supply of ego and testosterone, I had a better idea.

ꙮChapter Eightꙮ

On Saturday night at 8 p.m., Amy's recreation room resembled the dance at the gym scene from *West Side Story*. The lights were set, the music was playing, and the dance floor was empty. But that was the extent of any comparison of this party to the movie. It wasn't the feuding Jets and Sharks, but rather the angry girls who stood on one side of the room and the stubborn boys who occupied the other. At school dances you could always tell the four toughest guys in the crowd: they commanded the four corners of the hall, their chicks and clique close at hand. Tonight, the not-so-obvious leader of this group was a brown-haired, short version of Riff, standing in front of four sorry excuses for a gang.

Outfitted in my black chinos, yellow dress shirt, skinny tie, brown corduroy jacket, and desert boots, my better idea had been for the boys to come to Amy's party dressed as the Jets. I of course was to be the gang leader, Riff. My mom thought the idea was cute and helped me with my wardrobe; Dad just gave me the look. In a moment of awkward conversation, I had pitched my idea to Amy in the schoolyard's no-man's land during lunch. Still mad at me, her reaction was less than enthusiastic, surprising since Amy was cool and seemed to like my bad boy persona.

Little did I realize she had long-term plans for the two of us that included taming this bad boy.

Rolling her disbelieving hazel eyes, she countered with the offer that our costumes should match. In fact, she had already suggested to the girls that they select an appropriate partner and that all of the outfits should be paired. Amy had proposed something like Raggedy Anne and Andy, or Tweedle Dee and Tweedle Dum. I was lucky to still be alive, let alone the group leader after that one, although the idea of my playing Prince Charming to Amy's Snow White did have a certain fleeting appeal. But if she wanted matching costumes, that was fine with me. I insisted that Amy don a tight red dress and be my street-wise chick Graziella. Connie Earnhart could be Velma to Tommy's Ice. It didn't help matters. She said my idea was dumb; I countered by saying getting involved with girls was stupid. Something was said about calling the whole thing off. The school bell rang and we parted, nothing accomplished, nothing gained; something possibly lost.

It had been easy to convince the guys to attend the coed party once I suggested we come as a gang. My biggest supporter, Tommy, opted to dress as Tony to my Riff. Frankie Lamont made a convincing A-rab, Nick Brown took on the role of Action, and Bob McGuire was a cool Ice. We all met on the corner of Amy's street, purposely stalling until almost 7:45 to make our grand entrance.

Looking this sorry group over, the greeting from Mrs. Johns, Amy's mom, was less than flattering. "Didn't you boys know this is a costume party?"

Amy's hurt look made me feel inside like a Jet that had crashed and burned. On the outside, however, fortified with a couple of long pulls of Dad's bourbon, this Jet was ready to rumble.

Across the room huddled five costumed girls, including a winged fairy princess and a blonde, wigged Cinderella. In a fortuitous nod to their growing relationship, Connie, Tommy's main interest, was dressed as a bride. The girls all talked and gossiped and whispered, pointing and giggling. Perplexed glances ranging from disappointment to embarrassment to amusement to admiration ping-ponged across the paneled den.

From the record player, Wanda Jackson tried her best to enliven the evening, rhythmically shouting, "Let's Have a Party!"

Two girls shyly took to the dance floor, shagging to the infectious tune. Guys tapped their foot in time to the music but talked about monsters, movies, and baseball. Nick Brown, who had also seen *West Side Story*, elbowed me in the ribs, lifting a line from his character. "What are we doin', poopin' around with dumb broads for?"

This party was dying a slow, agonizing death. The fact that Tony and Riff, the characters Tommy and I chose for us, had both been killed in the movie didn't escape me.

Something or someone had to give. Around 8:45, Amy's mom made an appearance, pushing her way through the group of boys, ignoring the girls, and marching up to the blaring phonograph. Deliberately ripping the needle from Danny and the Juniors with a pronounced scratch, she turned, and the room fell silent.

"Okay, boys, line up on my left," she barked like a seasoned drill instructor. "Girls, you're here, on this side."

She didn't wait for a reply, and she wasn't playing a game. Tommy and I looked at each other. Frankie shook his head and shrugged. From the other side of the room, the girls slowly began to line up. It didn't take another command, just a piercing glare from Mrs. Johns, and my gang begrudgingly slinked into formation.

"You all know what to do!" With that, Amy's mom deftly dropped the phonograph needle into the lead-in groove of the next record. "And no one sits till the song is over!"

David Summerville's deep bass vocals filled the room.

"Come let's stroll, stroll across the floor..."

Slowly the two lines clumsily began to snake up and down, nearly in time to the music. In a natural order that was to mark our small circle for the next couple of years, we had unconsciously paired up. Nick chose Marianne Patrick, Bob faced Marlena O'Brien, and Frankie paired with Sherry Roland. As could be expected, Tommy took his place across from Connie, and I found myself heading the line, a smirking Amy directly opposite.

"Come, let's stroll/stroll across the floor/come let's stro-oh–oh-oll/stroll across the floor..."

Positioned at the front, I was obligated to go first. Swallowing hard, tasting Dad's whiskey, and wishing I was back at the baseball dugout, I stepped forward.

"Now turn around, baby/let's stroll once more"

Amy twirled and closed in, arm outstretched. Ignoring the peace offering, I awkwardly spun on my heels and strutted down the line, Amy in tow. One by one or pair by pair, each couple followed in turn, each doing their best to keep some semblance of a beat while struggling to hold on to a last shred of coolness.

"Strollin', strollin' aah-huh-uh/rock and ro-uh-oh-oh-oh-oh-llin'/strollin'..."

Up and down, round and round, in and out it continued; a seemingly endless circle of embarrassment. Tommy and Connie fared better, acting far more amicable as they entered the moving human pathway. By the time the Diamonds had finished musically directing the faltering folly, the two were holding hands.

Mercifully the song ended. Something touched my hand. I turned. A blushing, reticent Amy smiled up at me. "Thank you, Billy."

"Ah, uh, sure… sure."

The killer smile I'd come to know widened. I acknowledged the gesture with an uncertain grin. She squeezed my hand and as if on cue the couples retreated to their respective sides—all but one. Hand in hand, Tommy and Connie found an unoccupied corner. There they stayed throughout the remainder of the party. I had something else in mind.

Slipping unnoticed out the back door, I looked around. Spying a small play fort at the far end of the back yard, I took off. Once safely inside the miniature wooden building and out of view of the house, I retrieved a small bottle from the inside pocket of my sports coat. The shot of Seagram's Seven hit my empty stomach like molten lead. The powerful liquid boiled there for a couple of seconds and then ricocheted up to my brain. My head spun for a moment. My vision clouded. And then everything was fine—better than fine. Everything became right with my world.

Back inside, the Marcells were declaring the romantic benefits of a Blue Moon in perfect five-part, doo-wop harmony. Mrs. Johns had graciously retreated to the living room, leaving two couples to bounce uncertainly around the dance floor. It wasn't perfect, but it was a start. Tommy and Connie continued holding hands and talking in their private corner sanctuary. Amy was chatting with my neighbor Sherry Roland. The two glanced my way, and then quickly returned to their hushed conversation. Summoning bourbon-fueled bravery, I wandered across the room. Sherry saw me headed their way and whispered something to her friend.

Amy turned, her hazel eyes twinkling. "Oh, there you are," she said, flashing her smile.

I met her friendly smile with a toothy one of my own. "Yup, here I be!"

Amy's smile straightened and her pert nose crinkled. She looked at her friend. Sherry held the same puzzled expression.

"And what are you two chicks up to?"

Sherry's nose wrinkled further. She shook her head and moved off. Amy turned her attention back to me, leaning close, sniffing deeply. I was very familiar with the silent interrogation. I just never expected the judgmental action to come from one of my friends.

It wouldn't be the last time.

I just stood there.

Amy was adorable, dressed as a hazel-eyed bulldog, complete with cropped ears, pug nose, and spiked collar. Juvenile Delinquent and Bulldog—our costumes did match after all. They matched our pet names for each other.

The upside-down year of 1961 closed out on a relatively quiet note. Things were certainly quiet between Amy and me. Thursday after Halloween I made what my young brain thought was an honest effort to set things right with Amy. Quickly stowing my coat and army bag in the coat closet, I raced to my desk. Seconds later the anticipated scent of oranges captured my attention. I turned in my desk, smiled, innocently batted my eyelashes, and spoke up.

"Hi, how was your Halloween? Get lots of candy and stuff?" I figured the party was better left unmentioned.

But Amy was having nothing to do with me. She was mad, hurt, and confused, and for good reason.

Noting the liquor on my breath at her party, Amy had shaken her head and stomped off. Naturally I had no clue what was wrong, only that something was amiss and that I was somehow the cause. Still feeling the effects of the whiskey, I in turn threw up my hands, shook my head, and stomped off in the other direction, right into Tommy and Connie's private corner. Tommy looked at me, knowing immediately what was up. "Hey, buddy, what's shakin'?"

"Damn if I know, you tell me!"

The grin on Tommy's face grew. Winking at his girlfriend, he ran an arm around my shoulder. "You look like you need a friend, and I need a drink. I'm sure we can help each other out here."

Without another word, my friend and I made our way out the back door. Once inside the back yard play fort, I reached into my coat pocket and handed over the bottle. Tommy took a long pull, savoring each drop, adding a satisfied "Mm!" as he returned the makeshift flask. Two more rounds each and the liquor was gone.

"So, what's the problem, chief—why the long mug?"

"Hell, I don't know. I mean, you know…"

"Amy likes you—a lot," he confided with a bemused look. "Connie told me. Amy thinks you are one cool dude." Tommy's words danced in my head. I felt nauseous and elated at the same time.

"Well, if she thinks I'm so cool then what the hell is going on? Why the iceberg treatment these last few days?"

Tommy laughed out loud. "Man, you are the ultimate of coolness, except for when it comes to chicks. You just don't get it, do you?"

I eyed him curiously. *Okay, genius, school me.*

"It's all a game, man, just a stupid game, and you my slick friend," he continued, poking me in the chest to punctuate his point, "you have to learn how it's played. Learn the rules."

"Rules?" I didn't like the sound of that.

Tommy brushed back a lock of dirty blonde hair. "Yes, man, rules." The sagacious grin morphed into a smirk. "You gotta know the rules of the game before you can break them!"

His words made some sort of convoluted sense. He was right. Chris had said it, warned me: *girls are different.* Something President Kennedy had said in a press conference came to mind, something about it being "a different time, a different age, a different game with a different set of rules."

"Rule number one, lesson number one." Tommy pulled a roll of mints from his pocket, popped one into his mouth, and then passed them over. "Be cool, Daddy-o!"

I accepted the offering and the lesson. We returned to the party, Tommy to his corner and Connie, me to Frankie and the guys. The rest of the night didn't go any better, but it didn't get any worse, either.

In the classroom, scooting into her desk, Amy gave me a perplexed look. "Halloween was okay," she offered up, and then proceeded about her business. It was obvious we both wanted the same thing: to be friends again. But it was just as obvious neither of us had any clue what should be said or done next. The rest of the day, and month, and year didn't go any better, but it didn't get any worse, either.

The upside-down year the new administration had been having didn't seem to go any better either; but it, too didn't get any worse. Closing out his first year as president, John F. Kennedy sent General Maxwell D. Taylor to South Vietnam to assist its government against attacks by communist Vietcong guerillas. By December, two U.S. Army helicopter units had reached Vietnam, marking the first direct U.S. military support for South Vietnam. In November, Kennedy declared that the U.S. would soon restart atmospheric nuclear testing. This was in response to the Soviet Union's large October nuclear explosion over the Soviet Arctic.

While John Kennedy was leading the American people into a new era, his engaging wife, Jacqueline, took it upon herself to lead a much neglected White House into the 20th century. Rarely seen far from her husband's side while on state visits, back home, Mrs. Kennedy set to work making the official residence a home for herself and her family, and a museum of American history and decorative arts for the rest of the country. Always downplaying her duties as First Lady, in an interview Mrs. Kennedy defined her major role as, "to take care of the President," adding, "If you bungle raising your children, I don't think whatever else you do will matter very much."

But to that role Jackie brought beauty, intelligence, and cultivated taste. Under her careful guidance, the White House took on an air of grace and eloquence its own, becoming a showplace for visiting foreign dignitaries and highly publicized state dinners. Mrs. Kennedy hired Stephane Boudin, along with society decorator Sister Parish and early American furniture expert Henry du Pont, to aid in the revitalization of the White House, personally administering every aspect of the operation. When funds appropriated for the effort became exhausted, she set up a Fine Arts committee to oversee and fund the restoration. She pushed the publication of the first White House Guide Book, the sales of which further funded the undertaking. Next the energetic and imaginative First Lady initiated a Congressional bill establishing the White House furnishings as property of the Smithsonian Institution, and she wrote personal letters to those who owned historical pieces of interest, urging them to donate the items to the White House.

As First Lady, Mrs. Kennedy also devoted much of her time to planning social events. She invited artists, writers, scientists, poets, and musicians to perform and mingle with politicians, diplomats, and statesmen. Then, on February 14, 1962, Jacqueline Kennedy invited America and the world on a personally guided tour of the refurbished White House. Beaming with pride, the beautiful First Lady said, "I just feel that everything in the White House should be the best..."

The filmed tour was a great success, being distributed to over a hundred countries and earning a special Trustees Emmy Award. On a larger and more important scale, the tour and admiration for Mrs. Kennedy took negative attention away from her husband and helped garner allies for the White House as well as international support for the Kennedy administration and its Cold War policies.

Chapter Nine

I never got the reasoning behind half days of school. Like first Wednesday, it was one of those questions no one could answer reasonably well, except with the look. Not that I was complaining. A half day of freedom beat a full day of St. Pius X monotony anytime. It just seemed a waste, getting up early and trudging up Cornwall Hill in the snow and cold only to sit obediently as a large, crudely decorated cardboard box spewed forth its guts of corny, youthful Hallmarks. I may as well have stayed in bed. Guys like me never got Christmas cards or Valentines from the other kids. With the exception of course of the annual stupid prank: a sickly sweet red heart with the forged autograph of the ugliest girl in class, accompanied by snickers and snipes from the usual boneheaded suspects. And I certainly wasn't expecting anything from Amy.

I had toyed with the thought of getting Amy a nice card but nixed the idea one night while lying in bed listening to Hy Lit. Hy's Sunday night Hall of Fame show also featured a Lover's Portion during the final hour, from 11 p.m. until midnight. But unlike Jerry Blavat, Hy did less chattering, letting the romantic music speak for him, occasionally reading a short poem or airing an especially touching letter or dedication from some listener. The music that night spoke to me, stirring up feelings that were alien to my young senses. Aside from some awkward eye contact and a few polite but cold acknowledgements in class when papers were passed forward, Amy and I still weren't talking. I didn't know what I should say to her, if anything. And she made no obvious gestures towards breaking the uncomfortable silence. That picked at me like a chigger under my skin.

At 11:55 a.m. on Friday, December 22—the last school day of 1961—Sister Tres-Martin called out one final name: "Daniel Gibson."

What misguided goose would send that pimply putz a Christmas card? Dutifully, Daniel schlepped up to the front of the classroom. You'd have thought he was headed to the gas chamber.

"Thank you, Sister." Accepting the greeting card, dopey Dan dropped a thin square box on the nun's desk. "This is for you," he droned, and then turned on his heel. The foil-wrapped package, probably white linen handkerchiefs, sat among dozens of brethren.

In Catholic grade school the standard—the only—gift to give a nun was white linen handkerchiefs. Every nun got them, every year, every Christmas, every Valentine's Day, every Easter. Even on last Wednesday, it was a sort of "Thank you for not flunking little Johnny who really should be in reform school."

The nuns had a cottage industry of white linen handkerchiefs. They sold them back to Macy's and Gimbels and Monkey Ward's, who in turn sold them to parents to give to their kids to give to the nuns for Christmas, and Valentine's Day and Easter and last Wednesday. It was like recycling last year's fruitcake from Aunt Clara to bachelor Uncle Bob this season. The nuns used the money from their hanky hustle to replace yardsticks and pointers and other school equipment broken over the heads and butts of the same delinquents who gave them the white linen handkerchiefs.

It was poetic justice refined to its ironic best.

"And now children, before the bell rings, I want to wish you all a very Merry Christmas and a Happy New Year. Be sure to thank your parents for the wonderful cards and thoughtful presents." Nice speech. Sister Tres-Martin was as eager to see us go, as we were to leave. Twelve glorious snow-filled days lay ahead, carefree days of no school, no homework, no killer nuns, no getting up early—and no Amy.

Despite our silent feud I missed my friend. Chris told me girls could be stubborn. He never said anything about addicting. I

105

was a junkie. I had my taste of sugar and spice and everything nice. I was hooked. And I didn't want to wait on the corner for another bus. I wanted Amy.

A rustle of books and papers from behind stirred me out of my rambling thoughts. I wanted to turn around. I wanted to gaze into two forgiving hazel jewels. I sat frozen, staring at the plastic wall clock. I knew how this scene played out. First the countdown: six seconds... five seconds... four... the shapely missile would lift off from her desk... three... two... and be gone... one... forever... at least for twelve days.

Twelve noon, the bell rang. A hundred joyful bodies blasted off from their desks, heading for the coat closet, the hallway, the schoolyard—two by two of course—and freedom. As my paralysis abated something landed on my desktop. I turned in my seat. Honey-brown hair flitting out from under a pink knit stocking cap with a pink pom-pom bounced down the aisle and out the door. Paying no attention to Sister Tres-Martin's urgings for me to vacate her classroom, I peeled open the green envelope. It smelled like oranges. Savoring the aroma, I retrieved the card. A bubbly, buck-toothed bulldog grinned up at me as he spritely danced on his hind legs. A 45 RPM record player was balanced in one paw while he twirled a Christmas wreath with the other.

"Have a rock 'n' roll howl-i-day!"

It was signed, "Amy."

I awoke on Sunday the 24th to a polite snow. A gentle layer of white had silently settled overnight, blanketing the grass but leaving the streets and sidewalks virtually clean and dry. There would be no snow shoveling for me today. I was eleven.

Switching off my radio, I climbed into old jeans and a comfy flannel shirt. I knew what waited down the six carpeted steps. Sure enough, the irresistible perfume of homemade waffles pulled me to the kitchen.

"Good morning and happy birthday!" Dad sat at his post at the corner of the table, manning the antiquated machine that still produced the best waffles in Delaware County. No plastic, fancy, new-fangled gadget here, this iron veteran had belonged to Grandma D'Nato. It weighed a ton and made perfect, golden-brown waffles a half-inch thick and the size of a dinner plate.

Mom passed a fresh batch of batter over to Dad, "Two or three this morning, birthday boy?"

It was a dumb question for a growing, perpetually hungry eleven year old. I gave her the look and took my place at the table.

"Okay, but I have bacon here, too," Mom said.

I nodded my approval and accepted my first waffle. My sister Mary was on her second—not too shabby for a girl.

Mom poured me a tall glass of ice-cold milk. It was the kind that came in glass quart bottles, delivered to your door in the predawn hours. A layer of thick cream floated on top. Shake the bottle well and you got rich whole milk; drain off the cream for coffee and baking, and the remains yielded healthy skim milk.

"So, do you want your presents now, or wait 'til cake and ice cream after dinner tonight?" Mom asked.

It was another dumb question.

Thirty minutes later, with the Log Cabin Syrup-streaked dishes stacked in the sink, we filed into the living room. In suburban America of the '50s and '60s, the term "living room" was a misnomer, for very little living actually went on there. The popular split-level design home consisted of three levels: the main floor containing kitchen, dining room, and the dormant living room; up six or eight steps to the bedrooms and down a half flight to the basement or rec room, short for recreation room. Here lay the trappings of modern suburbia: 19" TV; casual sofa; Pop's recliner; TV trays for dinners in front of the TV; occasionally a pool or ping pong table; and the ubiquitous bar for mixing after-work cocktails and New Year's Eve celebrations.

Except for access to the front door, the living room, with its expensive gaudy furniture, extravagant table lamps, and strange objets d'art, remained off limits. But holidays were a different story. Now was the time to dust off and open the museum to neighbors and forgotten relatives alike. With Grandma's antique china hutch moved just a tad askew, the holiday tree—always fresh cut, never aluminum like the one our childless, jet-set next door neighbors had—was set, trimmed, and lit. That is, if the very cool but aging bubble lights kept bubbling for another season.

The clear plastic, custom made, custom fit, custom tacky covers that entombed the faux French Provincial sofa and chairs creaked and farted under the unaccustomed weight of human bodies. I took my place on the floor beside the sweet-smelling Christmas tree. Herman, our ageless tabby cat, yawned at me from his favorite spot behind Great Grandma D'Nato's handmade nativity set. He was already being crowded by dozens of wrapped and ribbon-bound packages nervously awaiting the orgy of excess on Christmas morning.

Dad handed me what looked like a disguised shoebox. The white and blue paper shouted Happy Birthday. This year they got it right. Being born on Christmas Eve is akin to having no birthday at all. To the adult trying to forget the years, the situation may be ideal. But to a youngster it's pure torture.

And forget all propaganda of "twice as many gifts." Even when grownups remember your birthday, presents are usually wrapped in Christmas colors and prints. And don't let that humongous package from Uncle Joe and Aunt Sally fool you. The painful head scrum and embarrassing, slobbering, lipstick-smeared kiss is always followed by an overtly exuberant, "And this is for your birthday *and* Christmas."

Thanks a lot. The cheery snowman paper and hastily scribed addendum to the tag, "...and Happy Birthday," are a dead giveaway. But this year a significant stack of properly packaged presents waited in their special corner.

From the weight and rattle I knew immediately the box didn't contain shoes. I tore into the neat wrapping like a hungry lion. My reward: a plastic scale model of a 1957 Ford Thunderbird. From the next box came a model of a '32 Roadster. That was sweet! Next appeared a '62 Buick; one of AMT's new yearly three-in-one kits, followed by a Rambler. Well, you couldn't win them all. Other boxes begat more plastic car kits, plus paint and model cement. And Christmas was still yet to come. I was in styrene bliss. It was the dawn of the age of horsepower, and I was a certified car nut.

Three years earlier, as I was recovering from a week-long bout of whooping cough, my father had surprised me with a plastic model kit to help me pass the time. Even then I had a more than passing interest in cars. Glistening chrome; protruding tail fins that would make a whale feel inadequate; monstrous, throaty motors that made your heart pound in your chest as they powered by; hot rods, customs, NASCAR, NHRA; chopped fenders, frenched taillights, louvers and lakes pipes; pleats and pinstripes; spinners, skirts and spotlights all danced in my head to a raucous rock 'n' roll beat. What red-blooded American lad wouldn't be sucked into the seductive hood scoop of big, bad, brash Detroit iron? Cars would soon form another piece of my life's jigsaw puzzle.

The kit Dad bought me that year was a 1930 Ford Model A. It could be built either as a coupe or roadster, stock or hot rodded. I was hooked. I'm sure dad had no idea of the impact that simple, thoughtful gift would have. It opened up new highways that would beget off-ramps in many varied directions, a Pandora's Box in plastic.

Along with space maps and charts, baseball memorabilia, and music-related items, my room was flooded with automobile pictures, posters, and books, plus dozens of the 1:24 scale model cars. My bookshelves creaked under the strain of new car brochures, old repair and shop manuals foraged from trash cans and retiring mechanics, and the latest editions of *Car Craft, Hot Rod* and *Rod and Custom* magazines.

Yearly pilgrimages to the Philadelphia New Car Auto Show and a number of custom and hot rod shows became routine family fare. And each summer Dad found nearby antique auto museums for us to visit. Mom said I had thirty-weight motor oil in my veins. Cars and everything automotive morphed into a jealous rival, competing with music, radio, and even Amy Johns for my attention.

Christmas 1961 had come and gone. New Years Eve and 1962 were just around the corner. The cheery snow that made Christmas more like Christmas was gone, victim to an unseasonal warm spell.

I sat in my bedroom amid new flannel shirts, jeans, socks, and underwear—mothers never forget—a dozen new 45s, a wallet from some relative, a couple of the latest board games, and enough plastic models to stock a hobby shop. I was thinking about Amy and how 1961 had truly been an upside-down year in many ways.

"...now for all you hipsters, tipsters, and home run hitters..." Even my radio and Hy Lit's catchy chaff couldn't pull me out of my funk.

Dad found a way. Passing by, he stuck his head into my room. "Wanna go with me Friday and buy a new car?"

I came up off my bed like a slingshot double "A" top fuel dragster. Mixed feelings made me dizzy. It was time to say goodbye to our beloved, be-finned '57 Plymouth. But it was also time for a new family car. What would it be? Surely Dad needed my automotive wisdom in making the proper choice. That's why he asked me to accompany him. He sought my mechanical counsel.

It was the beginning of the muscle car era, and with a rapidly growing interest in drag racing and NASCAR, I became an avid fan of the Chrysler Corporation. Don Garlits, Richard Petty, and the Ramchargers had replaced Eliot Ness and Superman as my heroes. For hours I extolled the merits of a 426-cubic-inch, wedge-powered Fury, or the class and value of a Polara convertible, or the status-building prestige of a New Yorker.

It did no good.

My dad's obstinate practicality and the family budget dictated a Chevrolet sedan. Well, a new car was a new car, even if it was a Chevy.

The old reliable Plymouth shivered to life, unaware that her days were numbered... or were they? If a family pet can run the moment you go to scoop it up, somehow knowing it's headed for the vet, what must run through the mechanical heart of the family car as it is steered onto the car lot? Does it shrink from the shiny new comers eager to take its place? Or does it step aside gracefully, bowing to the next generation, whispering encouraging remarks and tips on caring for the family? Our stately emerald friend did us proud this mild winter morning as she confidently carried Dad and me through our holiday-enchanted community to the local dealership.

The early '60s were a different time with different attitudes, concerns, and outlooks and a different way of doing things. Today if you want a Ford sedan you buy a Focus. Looking for a Chrysler convertible? Your options are limited. Don't have a family to tote around? Good luck. The coupe is an endangered species, eclipsed by that automotive oxymoron, the sports sedan. There never was, and never will be, anything sporty about four doors.

Buying a new car in the sexy sixties was much more interesting and involved, and a lot more fun. The five U.S. auto makers (remember Rambler and Studebaker?) offered a full line of models, each available in almost every body style, from sedan to hardtop to convertible to station wagon. And a Chrysler didn't look like an Oldsmobile, which didn't resemble a Mercury, which didn't mirror a Cadillac, which never would be mistaken for an Imperial.

In the days before rebates and dealer incentives, an age of window stickers and options lists, you actually got to choose your body style, color, motor size, interior trim, accessories, and more. Next you sat down and haggled out an agreeable price with the salesman. And then you waited. Six to eight weeks you waited while your car was assembled to your personal specifications. No two Galaxies or Bonnevilles or Belvederes in the same neighborhood were ever exactly alike. One could easily pick out their car from across the shopping center parking lot.

The smaller compacts—a new term in the automotive lexicon—were quickly coming into vogue for the young, suburban commuter. Their family friendly size and price made them the hottest thing in the auto industry. Dad had pretty much settled on what we would be getting. In his oh-so-careful and particular way, he eliminated the major competition: Ramblers and Studebakers belonged to another era; the Chevrolet Corvair was too small, too unproven, and mechanically too weird; the Buick Special and Pontiac Tempest twins were a little too expensive; Chrysler's downsized siblings, the Dodge Lancer and Plymouth Valiant, offered excellent value but, to Dad, were too funny-looking; and the popular Ford Falcon was axed because—well—because it was a Ford. That left only the newly introduced Chevy II.

Sadly, today there would be no multiple test drives or comparison shopping, no tire kicking or door slamming, just a quick once around the block in a demonstrator to make sure the new car felt right, and then the negotiations.

A bespectacled, slightly balding gentleman approached us as we passed through the huge glass doors of the showroom. Decked out in a tweed sports coat, yellow shirt, bright green slacks, tan loafers, and red patterned tie that was obviously a Christmas present from someone who didn't like him, our salesman looked more suited for a round of formal golf. He greeted my father like a long-lost rich relative, clasping a bicep with one hand while pumping Dad's arm with the other. I missed the verbal niceties. A stunning, red-and-white Corvette pulled me like a magnet. As Dad explained the situation to the effervescent salesman, I slipped into the bucket seat, manipulating the four-speed shifter and imagining I was Buzz or Todd cruising down Route 66.

Dad's voice brought me back. "Come on, Billy, we're going for a ride."

The all-new 1962 Chevrolet Chevy II was an ingeniously designed, well thought out, not too small, boring upright box. It had a friendly grill and headlight treatment that seemed to say, "Hi! I want to be your best friend!" The interior was bland and deceivingly cavernous for the car's size, the dashboard and controls laid out simply and intuitively.

I wasn't impressed.

The brown demo we climbed into was a top-of-the-line Nova. Demo cars are always top of the line and heavily optioned, providing subliminal cues to the undecided shopper.

"Of course you said you preferred the six-cylinder," the salesman began as we pulled into traffic. "This one has the 283 cubic inch V8. You will find a *slight* difference in power with the six." It was subliminal message number one. He turned to me from the passenger seat. "How do you like it back there, Sport? Pretty neat, huh?"

Sport! Thank God the interior was roomy. He couldn't easily reach back and ruffle my hair. *No, goofy-dressed man, four doors and ugly brown definitely are not neat. Even my dad knows that much!*

I held my tongue.

Our drive down West Chester Pike was uneventful. Dad paid extra attention to the road and the car's handling and less to the salesman's speech about factory warranties and break-in periods and GM quality, *blah, blah, blah.* In the '60s, with a gallon of Sunoco 200 regular gasoline going for twenty-two cents, miles per gallon was only a consideration when figuring the family vacation budget. Yet the light-weight Chevy II that easily swallowed a family of four including Fido and luggage, with its miserly six-cylinder motor, returned 30 MPG without breaking a sweat.

Returning to the dealership, we wandered to the back lot where the real cars were stored, the bread and butter sedans and station wagons. Dealers kept the show room and front lines reserved for convertibles and flashy hard tops, the eye-catching eye candy.

A half dozen Chevy IIs in an abridged rainbow of colors and trim, each wearing the same stupid expression and each with a red "Sold" tag adorning its windshield wipers, sat like puppies in a pound awaiting adoption. Dad obligingly inspected them, allowing the salesman to pop the hood on a six-cylinder job. Then the two adults did what all adult males do when the hood of a new car is opened. They each rested a foot on the front bumper; leaned an elbow on the bent knee, gazed blankly into the exposed engine compartment, and began to talk about sports, the weather, and our new president. After an eternity, the prolix conversation finally deteriorated into guttural grunts and head nods. It was time to get down to business.

The automobile salesman's drab, partitioned cubicle is a sacred place. It is a sanctuary in which one feels free to unburden one's secret needs and desires, as well as his financial situation, with a complete stranger. It is the bedroom where a new vehicle is conceived; the neighborhood bar where testosterone is served and men talk about manly things; the cigar-smoke-filled boardroom where deals are struck. It is the one place where men, unencumbered and unconcerned with the age or sex of their client, still act the chauvinistic mighty protector and leader. You never see curtains or lace in an automobile salesman's cubicle. I watched, fascinated, as large binders were hauled down from metal shelves. Each in turn was opened and placed in front of my father as the salesman flipped the pages and read upside down.

"These are your available exterior colors," he announced with the first book. "Now here we have interior upholstery and color choices. With the model you chose, Mr. Neblett, you can upgrade to this package. It includes…"

And so it went— the salesman dutifully and patiently pointing out the use and value of each option, and Dad politely listening and then nixing each in turn. After about thirty minutes of discussion, the salesman's work-up sheet indicated my father's preferences and the agreed-upon cost of each. The list was a short one: 1962 Chevrolet Chevy II 300 Deluxe, a slightly upgraded model with standard heater and connivance lights. The standard six-cylinder was X'ed, as were the standard three-speed manual transmission and a limited slip rear axle for safety and traction in the snow. Options: basic manual-tune AM radio with a rear seat speaker for the kids—nice touch, Dad. The color: boring Arctic white. Interior: cheap-looking red cloth and plastic. There was no carpet, just a rubber mat; no air conditioning; no power steering or brakes; and, considering the anemic motor, no power. This runt would never make it through my driveway snow wall.

Checking his figures a third time, the shirt-sleeved salesman suddenly and deliberately dropped his pen on the desk. Peering over the top of his glasses, he looked my father dead in the eye. "Mr. Neblett, you seem to be a shrewd man. You know what you can afford and you stick to your decisions. I like that."

What was this? The deal was done, why the flattery?

"And I can tell you want not only what is best, but the best for your family," he added.

"Well, of course. I do have to take everything into consideration, especially my budget," Dad replied. He didn't have any clue where this was leading either.

The salesman slapped his desk. "I'm glad you said that, Mr. Neblett, I couldn't agree more. These days it is important to get your money's worth." He lowered his voice and leaned forward, as if not wishing to be overheard. "You've been very candid about how much you have to spend. Well, I want to see to it you don't leave here disappointed. The Chevy II is a great car. You've made a wise choice. But before we sign any papers—"

Uh-oh, here it comes, Dad. Even I knew about protective coatings and extended warranties and such. But instead of pulling out another book, the salesman rose from his desk. "Please come with me," he said, stepping out of his cubical and gesturing with his arm. Before we could say anything he strode away. Dad looked at me and then stood. We followed the salesman across the showroom floor and down a hallway lined with offices. At its end he pushed open a heavy door and stepped through. We followed.

The salesman located a switch, and powerful overhead lights flickered on. We stood in a small shop used to detail cars. Twenty feet from me stood one of the most beautiful objects I had seen since meeting Amy.

Parked in an open bay sat a gleaming, royal blue 1961 Chevrolet Impala convertible. It had a white top, sharply contrasting, white side-spear moldings, dual chrome mirrors, dual-canted, rear-mounted antennas, white sidewalls and fancy spinner hubcaps. I could tell from the crossed flag badges that a powerful 409 cubic inch V8 lay sleeping beneath the broad hood.

I was off at a run.

Behind me the salesman's voice echoed. "What do you think? I know we don't have to ask the boy."

The door was unlocked, and I climbed into the comfortable bucket seat. Surrounded by rich, two-tone vinyl, plush navy carpeting, and shining chrome, I was in car nirvana. Every option in those thick books must have been lavished on this beauty. There was a center console with an automatic shifter; a sporty steering wheel; a full array of gauges, including a tachometer; and a fancy, push-button AM-FM radio with rear seat speaker.

And that new car smell.

"What—what do you mean?" Dad said, as the salesman took his elbow and steered him over.

"Here, Sonny, step out and let your dad enjoy her."

No way was I getting out. I crawled over to the passenger seat. Poor Dad was almost forcibly ushered into the car.

"Go on, start her up." Before my dad could protest, the salesman twisted the key. The mighty motor came alive. "Just listen to that baby purr."

Dad shook his head. "Yes, but—"

"Of course, let me explain." The salesman leaned into the interior to be sure I heard what he was saying. "You see, Mr. Neblett, I'm in a bit of a predicament. You can help me out. We can help each other."

Oh, this was going to be good.

"This is the last '61 model on the lot. It was left over." He tapped the top of the dash. The speedometer showed less than one thousand miles. "It's brand new, never been titled and already carefully broken in and serviced. And the boss has been on me to get rid of it."

Dad reached over and switched off the ignition. He turned in the seat and pushed his way out. I jumped out and hurried over. "It's very nice," my father said, "very nice, but—"

The salesman held up his hands. "I know, Mr. Neblett, but I can put you in this baby for exactly the same price as the Chevy II. Late last summer a gentleman came in, ordered it, plopped down a nice-sized down payment, but then never returned. We've taken all the proper steps, waited the necessary amount of time. Now the boss wants it out."

I couldn't believe my ears! This was much too good to be true. The way I figured it, in a couple of years Dad planned to buy my sister a used car. He always bought a new car every four or five years. By then I'd have my license. With a little bit of persuasion, he'd probably give me his trade-in, *this* trade in—this car!

Dad stood there looking at the Impala. I summoned my most calm and authoritative voice. After all, this was why he had brought me along. "It's a very good deal, well below sticker. And the Impala is a reliable, proven car."

Dad looked at me and then at the salesman. I was losing him. "And mom will love the air conditioning," I quickly added.

I caught a glimmer of resignation in his eye. Dad examined the window sticker and then leaned into the open car, looking around.

That's it, I thought. *Take your time. Breathe in that new car smell. Picture yourself cruising through the neighborhood, top down, Mom at your side.*

Suddenly images of Amy and me cruising, WIBBAGE on the radio, Amy close by me, my arm draped around her shoulder, honey-brown hair dancing in the wind, shot through my brain.

I looked up at Dad, my eleven-year-old voice cracking. "Blue is Mom's favorite color." I had no idea what Mom's favorite color was, or even if she had one. All women liked blue, didn't they? Sure, I'd read it somewhere, or heard it on TV, on one of those game shows.

"I'm sorry." Dad straightened and turned. He avoided my eyes. "It is a very generous offer. But I'm afraid not."

The salesman looked as if his dog had just been run over by a truck. "You're sure, Mr. Neblett? The resale value alone—"

"No, thank you, no."

My young heart splattered at my feet on the gray concrete floor.

Back inside the cubicle, papers were signed, a check was written, hands shook, and a white Chevy II was conceived.

The old Plymouth motored effortlessly back down West Chester Pike. She had just six weeks left. Then some pipsqueak, underpowered white tin box would take her place in the driveway. I felt bad for her. It wasn't fair. She could proudly step aside for the magnificent Impala. But now the Chevy II's friendly grillwork seemed more a contemptuous sneer.

I couldn't hold it in any longer. "Why, Dad? Why?"

He smiled over at me, and then looked back to the road. In his calm, practical manner he said, "There was nothing wrong with that deal. And the car was very nice. But Billy, I cannot show up at work in a car that's nicer and more expensive than my boss's."

It would take some time, but eventually I understood. My father's words—his reasoning—reflected the structured moods and attitudes of the society, the times, in which we lived: the buttoned-down world of 1962.

I began to see my father in a different light. He wasn't intolerably practical. No, his practicality sprang from wisdom. That same practicality began to trickle down to me slowly, little by little. I applied it to my eleven-year-old logic and rapidly maturing hormones. It was time to take matters into my own hands.

But how? I had missed a perfect opportunity with Amy at Christmas.

ᴄ◢Chapter Ten◣ᴄ

The country awoke Saturday morning, January 13, 1962, to the tragic news that Ernie Kovacs had been killed in an early-morning car accident in Los Angeles.

The 42-year-old actor–comedian had been part of the new generation of television comics. Along with other pioneers such as Steve Allen, Jack Parr, and Johnny Carson, the visionary Kovacs embraced the new medium. Dad and I were avid fans of the talented comedian, tuning in weekly to his popular TV show.

The previous spring, in a speech criticizing televised programming, FCC chairman Newtown N. Minow had called TV a "vast wasteland." However, Kovacs saw the potential in the wildly popular device. His innovative techniques used the versatile television camera to explore new angles and points of view, giving the viewer a different and often distorted perspective on life. Critics weren't quite sure what to make of his weekly, wacky, often surreal comedy show of sketches and blackouts. But the public responded in kind, and the 1962 Emmy for outstanding electronic camera work was presented to his widow, Edie Adams. The inventive Kovacs' work is still being studied and imitated today.

President Kennedy awoke on Saturday morning, January 13, 1962, to business as usual at the White House. The recently excommunicated Fidel Castro was moving closer to communism, still condemning the U.S. for the Bay of Pigs and for not supporting his struggling country. The Berlin Wall was being fortified by the

Soviets, and China and the Soviet Union both continued to support the forces of Ho Chi Minh in Vietnam. The race for space was continuing at a frantic pace, with new achievements on both sides coming almost daily. But NASA and the U.S. space program were just hitting their stride.

Two days earlier, Kennedy had delivered his State of the Union address. The president proposed to Congress and the country sweeping changes, including a new department of urban affairs and housing, a trade expansion act, school aid legislation, tax issues, health insurance programs for the elderly and federal aid for public fallout shelters. Yet in spite of a strong Democratic majority in Congress, within months most of Kennedy's proposals would be defeated.

Just two weeks later, his administration would receive another setback. On January 29 the three-year-long East–West negotiations on nuclear test bans, led by the United Nations, officially failed in Geneva.

Despite Kennedy's troubled presidency, *Time* magazine, in January 1962, named JFK its Man of the Year. But this was just the beginning of what would become a tense and terrifying year for the young leader, the American people, and the world.

I awoke on Saturday morning, January 13, 1962, to James Darren singing "Goodbye Cruel World" through my radio, playing softly beneath my pillow. It wasn't quite the end of the world, but it might as well have been. I was back at St. Pius X Grade School, facing Sister Tres-Martin and my friends—and Amy. The DJ on WIBBAGE back sold the top ten record with some catchy patter, then punched up a Hires Root Beer commercial, followed by a spot for Gimbels department store's annual January White Sale. Next there came a loud, overproduced, obnoxious welcome to the New Year, and then he slid smoothly into Little Anthony and the Imperials' "Shimmy Shimmy Ko-Ko Bop."

I thought of my first encounters with Amy. First Wednesday seemed an eternity ago, and Halloween had faded into an alcohol-induced haze of confused self-pity. Since the ill-fated party, I'd spent a lot of weekend nights alone in the baseball dugout, smoking and drinking and thinking. Not much materialized from those solitary times except an appreciation for breath mints and an ability to consume increasing amounts of bourbon with decreasing after effects.

Sometimes one or two of the guys—Nick or Frankie or Bob—would stop by to shoot the breeze and share my bottle. Tommy made rare appearances, choosing to spend most of his weekends with Connie. He'd update me on the latest news as related to him via Connie from Amy. Mostly it was just the same old adolescent BS: she liked me, she knew I liked her, she didn't know why I was acting that way, I couldn't figure her out, and hey, why even bother. Then the grapevine would reverse itself, and Amy would hear of my drinking and solitary brooding and then greet me in class with a pitiful, disappointed, disparaging look.

Sometimes in the schoolyard the other guys would chime in with comments and advice based on their own budding relationships. A tight friendship was forming, a circle of friends forged of young male bonding and struggling first romances. It was a friendship that would grow and strengthen and last through the troubled months and years to come. But at the moment I was the odd man out. We'd been back at school for almost two weeks. Amy and I were speaking, but barely. I didn't like the situation, and I didn't want to play the role of the disaffected lone wolf any longer.

I rolled out of bed and slipped into my usual jeans and T-shirt. The weather had remained mild and dry, and a high sun in a cloudless sky made attempts to warm the winter day. Mom met me in the kitchen with a cheerful good-morning kiss. Dad grunted his greetings and then inquired as to the state of my homework. I lied, saying the nuns had been kind. In reality I had some easy math problems and a history chapter to read by Monday. The broiler drawer screamed, and I sat down to a breakfast of one-sided toast, scrambled eggs, and milk.

"Your friend's mom called this morning." Mom scraped the last of the eggs onto my plate.

"Who?"

Mom settled down in her usual place, sipping her coffee. "You know, that girl you like, what's her name? Jans... Janston... Johnson?"

Uh oh, this couldn't be good.

Dad looked up from his paper. His puzzled expression read like a neon sign; *Billy likes a girl?* As if deciding the preposterous question wasn't worth mentioning, he flicked an eyebrow, adjusted his glasses, and returned to his reading.

"You mean Amy—Amy's mom?"

"Yes, that's it. What's her last name?"

I nearly choked on a piece of burnt bread. "Amy? You mean Amy Johns?"

"That's it, Johns. Mrs. Johns called this morning."

My mind raced. *Ok—don't panic—there has to be a reasonable explanation for this.* Did Mrs. Johns know about my drinking in her back yard? No, that was months ago, why wait till now to report it? Had Amy told her mom what she learned through the group? No way—despite our current differences, Amy and I were friends, close friends, closer than friends. Well, whatever we were, Amy would never sell me out. I re-ran the laundry list of all the questionable things I'd done in the last month or two. The list was a long one.

Nothing. There was nothing to warrant such a call. Only fathers getting together to talk about their sons trumped the dreaded mother-to-mother conversation. Breakfast churned in my stomach. My buddy Jim Beam waited in the den bar, down just a half-flight of steps. And I had a small bottle hidden in the garage. But there was no way I could sneak away for a quick bracer. My parents were clueless, not blind.

I swallowed hard, trying not to let my voice crack. "What... what did she want?"

Once again, Dad glanced up from his newspaper.

"Oh, nothing much," Mom replied much too casually. "The St. Pius variety show is coming up, and she's the chairman. She knows that I'm an actress and asked if I could help out again this year. I told her I would."

Whew, that was close!

"And since you and Amy are friends, she thought we should get to know each other."

The clock on the wall stopped ticking. My body froze in place. The world came to a sudden, deafening, screeching halt. All movement and activity ceased, with the exception of the growing grin on my father's usually unflappable face. It now spread from ear to ear. I looked at Mom; Mom looked at Dad; Dad looked at me.

Ok—let's not panic—think, remember, a different time, a different game, a different set of rules. Maybe I could use this to my advantage. But I'd have to get to Mrs. Johns before my mom.

And I'd have to get in good with Amy.

And I'd have to do it soon.

As I pedaled my two-wheeler up Cornwall Hill, something kept playing over in my mind, like a stuck record. Or at least tried to.

"...negotiate in fear... out of fear..."

It was Monday morning. The weather was clear, but winter was making a comeback, the temperature in the low forties with a biting breeze out of the north. Normally on cold winter days my bike would remain in the garage, while I'd bundle up like a disgruntled Eskimo and begrudgingly walk to school. I didn't like the cold weather.

"...not negotiate in fear..."

But this chilly Monday morning, I had awakened with a purpose, a goal. And I was not going to be denied.

"...fear to negotiate..."

I had bounced out of bed at 6 a.m., beating my sister into the bathroom. Five minutes later Mom heard me hurrying back to my room.

"Hey, slow down! What's the big rush?" she called.

I didn't answer. Cranking up my radio, I dressed in time to Chuck Berry's "School Days." It seemed appropriate enough for the day ahead. Jerry Stevens must have read my mind. All thumbs and nervous energy, I gave up on the stubborn blue tie and reached for a clip-on as the DJ punched up a short station jingle and then segued into the Edsels. That's it! *I've got a girl named Rama Lama Ding Dong.* At least I think I still have a girl.

I began to sing along. *"She's so fine to me..."*

Having slept but a few hours, adrenalin and anticipation fueled my morning. *"...Rama Lama Lama Lama Ding Dong..."* Again Mom called from her bedroom.

"Hey, Caruso, tone it down! And leave the radio at home!"

The previous night at 10 p.m., after enjoying the antics of comedian Jack Benny on his weekly television program, I had uncharacteristically headed upstairs to bed on my own. There were no gentle reminders from Mom, no stern looks from dad, no negotiating for another thirty minutes. Gardner McKay's narration of his *Adventures in Paradise* filtered up through the heating duct as I settled down, while Hy Lit's *Hall of Fame* radio show filtered up through my pillow. I barely heard the golden oldies Hy was spinning. I had formulated a plan, a plan to get back in good with Amy—a fool-proof, sure-shot, couldn't-fail plan worthy of Tom Lopaka and his Hawaiian Eye cronies. All through Hy Lit's show and on into Frank X Feller, I reran my master plan over in my wily young brain. Finally, sometime during the Allan Dean *All Night Thing,* I nodded off.

So this morning, when I had appeared shortly after 6, Dad glanced up from the kitchen table in surprise. "You're up early."

What? Can't a guy get up on his own without the whole world wondering what he's up to? I realized the folly of my thoughts and sat down. Philly's boring MOR station, 610 WIP, spewed forth news headlines, weather, traffic updates, and the time. Then the deep-voiced Joe McCauley, the self-proclaimed Morning Mayor, cracked a stupid joke and cued in Paul Anka's "Lonely Boy."

Dad had grunted from behind his paper. "Not this guy again."

After a failed attempt at Top 40, the city's oldest radio station was now making a mockery of pop hits, '50s standards, and itself. Showing he had at least some musical taste, it was the only station Dad would listen to, and then only for the news. What a waste of perfectly good air space!

I had finished my bacon, milk, and one-sided toast in silence. I didn't want to disturb my father, nor did I wish to engage in a pointless conversation about why I was up and dressed so early. Instead, I had reviewed my brilliant idea in my mind's eye again.

Now, huffing and puffing my way up the steep hill, I began to have some doubts. What if I couldn't get on Amy's good side? What if she still wouldn't talk? What if her mom didn't like me? The questions came fast and without answers as I turned from Sussex Boulevard, hopping off my bike and coasting it to the crosswalk. Sam the crossing guard gave me the fish eye.

"Did you forget to wind your watch or something?"

"What?"

"You're usually the last one to arrive. Today you're just about the first."

I ignored his observation, smiling politely as I walked my bicycle across busy Lawrence Road. Great, now even the crossing guard is keeping tabs on me. Dad must be paying him or something.

But Sam was right—the schoolyard was nearly deserted. I parked my bike in the rack, retrieved my school bag and radio, and looked for Chris. Having to take the first bus, he'd be here already, somewhere entertaining the guys. Sure enough, the sound of rough boyish laughter and cruel ranking drew me across the yard.

"How goes it my brother, a bit early for a vampire like you, isn't it?"

Damn, him too... "I be good, my main cat... skin me!"

Chris and I crossed palms in a cool dude's version of a handshake we'd seen Kookie Byrns perform on *77 Sunset Strip*.

"Outstanding." Chris added with a broad grin, "Hey, guess what?"

No—not this morning. I wasn't in the mood. "Not the dream again, please?"

"Not last night, Daddy-o, but actually—"

"What, Chris, what is it?"

"I got some good news for you, lover boy. Big time news," he announced. "That is if you are interested in that sort of thing."

I loved Chris to death, but he could be as trying as a bad tooth sometimes. I knew this wasn't going to be easy. "Okay, shoot."

He continued to grin. Ben Masters giggled. Several other guys stood watching, bemused by the situation. Obviously they were already privy to the developing story. Chris held a fist to his mouth as if talking into a microphone. His voice slipped into a perfect Walter Winchell.

"Flash! What couple, the talk of the schoolyard this past year, is currently residing in Splitsville?"

Oh, brother. My friend was in rare form today. I'd have to play along if I was going to get any information out of him. Normally I'd just shake my head and walk away, leaving him to his zaniness. But it was obvious he was talking about Amy and me, so I decided to play along.

"And who might that be?"

"The sweethearts of the swing set, the darlings of the schoolyard, the Romeo and Juliet of the fifth grade—"

"You must mean Tommy and Connie."

"Wrong, Daddy-o."

"Just get on with it, will ya, before I make your dream of being fried come true!"

"Okay, okay." His voice morphed once again, this time aping TV's street-wise Ed Norton. "Geez, what a grouch!"

The schoolyard was beginning to fill up. I looked past Chris, scanning for a pink stocking cap with a pink pom-pom. Nothing. I turned my attention back to Chris.

"So—give already."

He took a deep breath, savoring the moment. "Okay, here's the skinny. Your main man on the inside, Tommy, told me he heard from Connie that Sherry told her that Amy had said she wanted you and her to be him and her once again."

You had to admit, Chris had a way with words. I stood there, stupid, confused expression and all, trying to sort out his speech. "You— you mean—"

Chris nodded, the corners of his grin kissing his droopy earlobes. "She wants to meet you in no-man's land this morning."

"What? When?"

"In about... right now."

Well, this was certainly an unexpected set of circumstances, Amy wanting to talk. "You're sure... You—you wouldn't kid me? I mean about this."

"You know me better than that, Daddy-o. We're brothers."

I held out my hand, unable to contain my excitement. "Birth to earth…"

"… Womb to tomb," Chris replied, affectionately sliding his calloused palm across my own.

"Hey, Delinquent!"

I heard the music before seeing the vision. Amy stood alone in a corner of no-man's land, the smile I'd come to look for in place. As I forced my pace into a casual stroll, something popped to mind. It was a line from President Kennedy's inauguration speech: "Let us never negotiate out of fear. But let us never fear to negotiate."

⊂ℐ∘Chapter Eleven∾⊃

Damn, it's getting colder.

Johnny Mancusso took a deep, hard pull and then passed the bottle over. I rolled down the paper sack containing the bourbon, wiped the spout, and tipped it back. The liquor tasted good, burning all the way down, warming my shivering body. Handing the bottle to Larry Cartelli, I flipped up the collar of my denim jacket. As usual, Larry took two deep swigs.

"C'mon, man!" Timmy, Johnny's brother, blew warm breath into his cupped hands.

It was Saturday night, a bitterly cold Saturday night. For the past hour, Johnny, Timmy, Larry, and I had been singing old doo-wop tunes into the acoustically perfect entryway to Loomis Public School. The ballsy bass of Johnny's *bomp bomp ba bomp* reverberated, echoing sharply off the brick and concrete, blending perfectly with my alto lead.

"When you're with me I'm sure you're always true/when I'm away I wonder what you do"

Despite the cold, or maybe because of it, we were in great voice, the harmonies tight, and the vocals strong. We sailed smoothly into the falsetto finale.

"Don't know why I dooo…"

Just then Johnny broke out the first pint of Four Roses and his brother broke into the Monotones.

"I wonder wonder who, be-dooo who/who wrote the book of love"

We continued to harmonize. Each in turn snatched the lead and segued into his particular favorite golden oldie. Larry finished up "Book of Love."

"You know you make me wanna (Shout!) kick my heels up and (Shout!) throw my hands up and (Shout!)"

Three minutes later, as we were all getting "a little bit softer now," Johnny clapped his hands.

"A! I'll always love you"

Right on cue his brother responded.

"B! Because my heart is true"

On it went, through Frankie Lymon, then the Fiestas and the Cadillacs, and into a couple of liquor-turned ballads. Now, as the second and final pint was drained, we began to look for new ways to keep warm.

It had been a great week, capped off by a night on the corner with my older hanging buddies. The usual inane inquirers were made about my sister. I responded with off-handed remarks about certain individuals' body parts. We all laughed, clowned around, grooved to the songs on my radio, and passed the bottle. It was a good night, the kind that stuck with you through the years. Even the return of Old Man Winter failed to ruin my high.

Monday in the schoolyard, Amy and I had talked. We talked, we discussed, we argued, and we negotiated. As expected, we both had plenty to say; my drinking didn't really bother her, she just didn't want me doing it at her house. I understood and apologized.

I said I'd been upset about the costume thing; she told me she thought my idea for costumes was cool, even though her friends had some reservations.

I told her I'd been feeling the heat from my friends as well. We both decided not to listen to our friends' advice anymore. By the time the school bell rang, Amy and I were closer than ever. Unconsciously, I took her hand as we made our way to line up. It felt good. I didn't even mind the protracted lunchtime ribbing, courtesy of my buddies.

The following Friday afternoon, I had raced back down Cornwall Hill with purpose. Amy had invited me over after school. I rushed into my house, quickly changing into jeans, a warm flannel shirt, and sneakers. It had turned cold again, but mercifully it hadn't snowed and the streets were dry. Bundling up in my heavy denim jacket, I peddled my way out of Lawrence Park. Amy rode the bus to school, her house being located in an older section of Marple Township. I made my way across busy Lawrence Road, and then crossed Old Sproul Road to Amy's development. My excitement was tempered somewhat as the front door opened.

"Hi, you must be Billy." It was Amy's mom. My internal warning signals began firing full bore.

We'd skipped the pleasantries at the Halloween party. I never was very fond of most adults, especially parents, and I'm sure the feeling was mutual. But Amy's mom was younger than my parents and very attractive. That I had noted the night of the party. She held out a delicate hand.

"Nice to see you again."

All of my mother's hard work came to fruition. I swallowed hard and straightened my posture, smiling pleasantly and taking her hand. Hey, this was for Amy. And besides, I needed this woman on my side.

"It's nice to meet you, Mrs. Johns."

Her smile was warm and friendly, helping me feel at ease. She took my coat and I followed her inside, sitting down on the sofa. Ignoring the matched wingback chairs, Mrs. Johns settled next to me. I relaxed even more. At least this wasn't going to be the interrogation I might have expected.

"Amy's told me a lot about you."

Uh oh.

"You know she is very fond of you."

Whew! That was close. Time to put into effect everything I'd learned from hours of watching suave TV detectives. "Well..." I'm sure I was blushing—nice touch. "I like her, too. She's very nice."

To my surprise and confusion, Amy's mom laughed out loud. "Yes, she is. You know, Amy and I are very close. We talk, and she tells me everything."

Everything... I'm sure she read my panic.

She continued to laugh, enjoying her private joke. "Relax, Billy, I'm on your side. I know how boys can be. Besides, Amy hasn't said anything bad..." The smirk was purposeful. "Well, not *too* bad."

What the hell did that mean?

Mercifully the front door opened. I jumped to my feet. Mom would be so proud. "Amy, hi, I guess I beat you here. Your mom and I were just talking."

"Oh! Hi, Billy, hi, Mom."

Mrs. Johns greeted her daughter, helping Amy with her coat and school bag. "Why don't you go get changed, Sweetie. I'll get us all some ice cream."

Amy flashed her killer smile, and my brain once again went to mush. Then she disappeared down the hall.

"Amy tells me you're into music," her mom said, switching on the phonograph. "Did you know I used to sing with a band?"

The record dropped, and the living room filled with a pedal steel and a twanging guitar. I'd heard country and Western music before, while visiting my dad's parents in Joplin. And a couple of times late at night while scanning my transistor's dial, I'd heard the Grand Ole Opry on WSM out of Nashville. I didn't care much for what I heard. But this was different, not quite as Western; mellower, softer, with a pronounced beat.

A pleasant female voice began to sing about walking after midnight. Amy's mom hummed along, signaling for me to sit at the counter that separated the kitchen from the living room. "I was good, too—very good," she said. "I even considered a career as a singer..." She paused, staring off into space, remembering. "But I married Amy's dad." Pulled from her reverie, she began to scoop chocolate ice cream into three plastic bowls. "Anyway..."

I watched and listened, intrigued. Parents weren't singers. Parents were plumbers, and mechanics, and shoe salesmen, and businessmen. And mothers were, well, *mothers* sometimes maybe waitresses or nurses or secretaries. But the father of one of my classmates was a bartender. And our childless next-door neighbors both worked for the railroad. And my mom was an actress. I'd never really thought of parents as being people before.

I studied Amy's mom more closely as she set the bowls on the counter, now singing aloud to the stereo. She was very pretty, an older version of Amy. And she had a very nice voice, something between Connie Francis and Dinah Washington. She caught me staring and smiled.

"You like country music, Billy?"

"Well, I... I don't know. Not really."

Mrs. Johns leaned across the counter, sliding a bowl of ice cream over to me. "That's probably because you've never really listened. I'll bet you like Dion, don't you?"

"Well, sure, Dion and the Belmonts—they're cool." I didn't think any parent knew about Dion and the Belmonts.

She savored the rich Breyer's chocolate ice cream, placing the spoon in her mouth upside down, the way a kid would do. "Yes, they are very cool. But I mean Dion by himself. Have you listened to his solo albums? Do you know who his biggest musical influence was? It was Hank Williams."

I'd heard Hank before. His vocals were high pitched and strained, almost like a yodeler. But the three-chord guitar arrangements were simple yet catchy. Then it hit me—she was right! Dion's latest record, The Wanderer... the guitar work was pure country, pure Hank Williams.

The automatic changer on the record player dropped the next 45. My ears perked up. The sweetest voice I'd ever heard flooded my senses. I became lost in the gentle, tinkling piano and the plaintive lyrics sung softly, yet with heartfelt emotion.

"Crazy, I'm crazy for feeling so lonely..."

It was the voice of an angel.

"That piano, it's just like—"

"Floyd Cramer," Mrs. Johns said, finishing my thought. "Listen to the background harmonies."

I listened. "The Jordanaires—Elvis's backing group."

"Amy was right; you do know your music."

For the next half hour Amy, her mom, and I talked, ate ice cream, and listened to her mom's records. Mrs. Johns was like no parent I'd ever met. She was fun and funny and interesting. And it was obvious she and Amy were close. I envied their relationship. At one point I thought I spied a twinkle in Amy's gorgeous hazel eyes when her mom spoke of Amy's dad. She said I reminded her of him, and that he too had been a bit of a rebel, her parents disapproving of their relationship.

I discovered a lot that afternoon: a lot about myself, as well as about Amy and her mom. I discovered my bad boy image wasn't necessarily all bad and that parents could be cool. I discovered Amy really didn't tell her mom everything.

I discovered that country music could be cool, especially the sweet tender voice of Patsy Cline.

And later that afternoon, huddled together in the backyard play fort, I discovered the sweet, tender sensation of kissing Amy Johns.

It was getting even colder. The whiskey was gone, and a breeze had kicked up out of the north. Joe Capone showed up just as our make-shift quartet finished a smooth version of the classic "In the Still of the Night."

"You guys sound good—and look cold." He laughed, reaching into his jacket. We were hoping for a fifth of bourbon or at least a bottle of wine. Instead he pulled out a can of lighter fluid. "What ya say we get warm?"

We followed Joe to the far side of the school grounds, scrounging some twigs and branches and dried leaves. After several failed attempts and much heated discussion and good-natured ribbing, Joe finally managed to get a small fire going.

"Got any marshmallows?" Joe warmed his hands over the growing flames. We formed a tight circle with him; the fire wavered and struggled to stay lit in the chilling wind.

"Give it another shot," someone suggested.

"Yeah, let's get this baby going."

Joe held the can of lighter fluid at arm's length and squeezed hard. The fire flickered. Then suddenly a flame leaped up, finding the volatile stream of liquid. An instant later the can in Joe's hands exploded.

I was standing directly across and managed to turn away from the blast. As I stumbled to the ground, I felt a burning sensation. The right leg of my jeans was on fire. Fighting the pain, I rolled over, trying to smother the flames.

Looking up I could see my buddies had caught the worst of it.

Joe's hands were blackened, and his coat and shoes were burning.

Larry Cartelli was struggling to wriggle out of what was left of his slacks. The fronts of his legs were already blistering.

Johnny and Timmy, their coat sleeves on fire, were frantically trying to get Joe out of his jacket. All around the grass smoldered and burned.

A neighbor taking out his trash witnessed the whole frightening scene. He called the police and came running to help. By the time the fire department arrived, the flames were out and the Mancusso brothers had run off. Larry Cartelli was taken to the hospital with some first- and second-degree burns to his legs. It took four months for Joe Capone to fully recover. He'd walk with a pronounced limp for the rest of his life.

Hurting and frightened but only slightly burned, I limped home to face my father.

On February 20, 1962, the United States finally got it right. Early that morning astronaut John Glenn became the fifth person, and the third American, in space. Lifting off from Cape Canaveral, riding atop an Atlas missile, Glenn reached a maximum altitude of 162 miles, speeding away from Earth at 17,500 miles per hour. Glenn's Mercury capsule, the *Friendship 7,* reached orbital stage and circled the globe three times during his 4-hour, 55-minute flight. When he passed over Western Australia, residents of the city of Perth lit their house and street lights for Glenn to see.

But the historic flight was not without its tense moments. During the flight there was concern that the capsule's heat shield had come loose. Ground controllers had Glenn keep his retrorocket pack on over the heat shield, instead of deploying it on re-entry. Later it was found that the problem lay in a faulty indicator light. Glenn splashed down safely in the Atlantic Ocean near Bermuda.

In July 1962 John Glenn testified before the House Space Committee saying he favored the exclusion of women from the NASA astronaut program. Within a year the Soviets would place Valentina Tereshkova in orbit, making her the first woman in space. However, from this point on the Russians would be playing catch-up in the ongoing race for space.

Three days after the historic flight, President Kennedy presented Glenn with the NASA service medal in a ceremony at the Manned Spaceflight Center at Canaveral Air Force Station.

The space achievement was a welcome distraction for the president, who was dealing with more pressing problems at home and elsewhere. While the U.S. prepared to put a man in obit, Fidel Castro accelerated preparations to align Cuba with the communists. Negotiating with Khrushchev, Castro continued to verbally attack the U.S. for the Bay of Pigs Invasion and for turning a blind eye to the plight of his people. Old resentments in Congress and big business still burned strongly in Washington, and high-ranking advisors kept pressure on the Kennedy administration to punish Castro. On February 3 the president banned all trade with Cuba except for food and drugs.

The threat of the spread of communism remained the main topic in print and on television. Besides Castro, the Kremlin was threatening to expand the Berlin Wall. China was openly supporting the North Korean government as well as conflicts in Laos and Thailand, while both Russia and China continued to send arms into Vietnam. In response, the U.S. Defense Department created the Military Assistance Command in South Vietnam. In an impassioned speech explaining the government's position, Attorney General Robert F. Kennedy said that U.S. troops would remain in Vietnam until communism was defeated. By February 27 the first U.S. national had been killed in Southeast Asia, as two planes bombed the presidential palace in Saigon. South Vietnamese president Ngo Dinh Diem was unharmed.

Closer to home, in the wake of the Freedom Riders, a bus boycott began in Macon, Georgia on February 12. Ever since Rosa Parks had refused to give up her seat on a Montgomery city bus, the movement for integration had been gaining momentum. Violent confrontations and peaceful demonstrations throughout the South made daily headlines across the country. On the 26th of February, the Supreme Court ruled against race separation on public transportation.

Following the failure of the long-running Geneva talks with the Soviets, JFK announced on March 2 that the U.S. would resume above-ground nuclear testing. On April 25 Operation Dominic began with test explosions on Christmas Island. The operation was a series of 105 nuclear test explosions conducted on the island and in the Nevada desert, continuing through 1963.

By May the U.S. was firing Polaris missiles armed with nuclear warheads from submerged submarines. The warheads detonated above the Pacific Ocean. In retaliation, the Soviets stepped up their own nuclear testing.

The U.S. economy continued to fluctuate in 1962. Ever since his Inaugural Address, Kennedy had been urging Americans and American businesses to exercise restraint in order to strengthen the U.S. economy. For the most part the country complied, placing economic trust in the young presidency.

In the spring of 1962 a strike was averted when the Steel Workers of America agreed to hold off their demands for higher wages. That agreement was contingent upon the steel companies not raising their prices. But before the ink had dried on the new contracts, U.S. Steel Corp. announced a 3.5 percent price increase. Within days other companies followed U.S. Steel's lead with price hikes of their own.

The announced increases incensed the president. On April 11, in an address to the American people, Kennedy called the increases a "wholly unjustifiable and irresponsible defiance of the public interest." He cited the growing crisis in Berlin as well as the escalating troubles in Southeast Asia. The references struck their mark. Four U.S. servicemen had been killed recently in Vietnam. In the days following, Kennedy kept up his pressure until the steel companies retracted their increases.

In news headlines of more interest to my friends and me, Philly's Parkway Records re-released Chubby Checker's monster hit "The Twist" in November of '61. By January the unstoppable dance craze had pushed the record back into Billboard's number one spot for an unprecedented second time. It finished number 9 in the year's top 100. The song and the dance didn't escape the notice of the Catholic Church. On January 26 Bishop Burke of the Buffalo Catholic dioceses declared the Twist impure and banned it from all Catholic schools. A day later San Francisco's Cow Palace hosted Chubby Checker's Twist Party. More than 17,000 fans made it the Bay Area's first big rock concert. In truth, by '62 most teens had abandoned the fad and moved on, leaving an older generation to the hip-gyrating dance.

By Valentine's Day, Joey Dee and the Starliters' Peppermint Twist occupied the number one spot in the nation. While the First Lady was showing the White House to the country, in California the Beach Boys were showing the world a new musical style. Originating on the sun-bleached beaches of Southern California, surf and beach music rode a wave of success across the country. But not everyone was quick to accept the new sound. Radio stations in New York, Philadelphia, Baltimore, Chicago, and LA began featuring battles of the bands. New artists like the Beach Boys and the Four Seasons went up against established rock 'n' rollers, including the Drifters, the Coasters, and even Elvis, with listeners phoning in votes for their favorite. The gimmick caught on and became a regular feature on Top 40 radio throughout the musically evolving '60s.

Meanwhile, the Motown sound out of Detroit was making major inroads into the American music scene with artists like the Miracles, the Marvelettes, Martha and the Vandellas, and Stevie Wonder. At the same time, soul music was fusing the best of R&B and rock 'n' roll, with James Brown, the Isley Brothers, Otis Redding, and Aretha Franklin just hitting their stride. In New York, Bob Dylan gave his first public performance of "Blowin' in the Wind" at Gerdy's Folk City in the West Village.

Even popular music, long the bastion of conservative adults with established artists including Frank Sinatra, Doris Day, and Tony Bennett, began to feel pressure from the younger generation. On April 9 the youth-oriented *West Side Story* took the Academy Award for Best Picture. Then, on May 5, the movie's sound track went to number one. It would remain at the top of Billboard's Album Chart for a record-shattering 54 weeks—20 weeks longer than any other album.

My friends and I listened to the new sounds emanating from the West Coast, enjoyed the smooth, polished sounds of Motown, and accepted the black revolution in soul music. But we stubbornly clung to the past, preferring the four chord structures of rock 'n' roll and the five-part harmonies of doo-wop. Little did we imagine the musical revolutions that were just around the corner.

241 NORTH CENTRAL BLVD, BROOMALL, PA

BILL, ROSE AND BILLY NEBLETT

WILLIAM I NEBLETT

MARY D'NATO (LEFT) AND ROSE NEBLETT

BILLY AND AUNT MARY D'NATO

ROSE NEBLETT – ST. PIUS VARIETY SHOW - 1962

Mary Neblett with mother Rose - 1969

Billy and Princess - 1963

BILLY AND 57 CHEVY - 1964-5

Chapter Twelve

On April 9 President Kennedy threw out the first ball at the Washington Senators' new D.C. Stadium. The Senators had been a hard-luck ball club since before Hall of Fame pitcher Walter Johnson led the team to the 1924 World Series. The new stadium was a ploy to bring back the waning crowds—a ploy that would fail by decade's end.

Closer to home, my Phillies returned to an aging, rundown Connie Mack Stadium for another season full of hopes and anticipation. Talk about a new multi-purpose sports facility had gone about as far as most good ideas seemed to go in Philadelphia politics—to the talking stage and no further. But with talent like Johnny Callison, Wes Covington, Tony Taylor, Bobby Wine, and big Art Mahaffey, the season looked bright.

Amy was more pragmatic in her predictions. Chris and I both laughed when she said it was time for one of the West Coast teams to take the National League Pennant. Amy loved the Phillies as much as Chris and me; she was just a lot smarter than either of us.

Ever since our talk in the schoolyard and my meeting with her mom, Amy and I had spent as much time together as possible. On Valentine's Day I dropped a card I'd purchased at Woolworths Five and Dime on Amy's desk. The guys were riding me regularly by now for my relationship with a girl. It really didn't bother me too much; in fact it boosted my bad boy reputation. But I wasn't about to give them any more ammunition by placing it into the big, tacky red box, to be distributed in front of everyone by Sister Tres-Martin. Instead I discreetly slipped the blushing red envelope under her copy book. Struggling through most of the previous evening and ignoring my math homework, I had finally signed Amy's card, "Your friend, Billy."

Amy must have had the same idea. When I returned from the coat closet, inside my desk there was a pink envelope with tiny white hearts. A paper cut marked my index finger as I nervously slid it open. To my relief, Amy's card was tagged, "Your back yard buddy, Amy." The double meaning gave me pause. And a smile.

The winter remained relatively mild, with a couple of light snow falls in February. Once or twice a week, I'd race home, do a quick Q&A dance with my mom while changing clothes, and then pedal over to Amy's house. We'd spend time listening to records or talking with her mother, or maybe playing a board game. Sometimes I'd be invited to stay for dinner. Mrs. Johns seemed to genuinely like me and encouraged our friendship.

Mr. Johns was a different story. I never was able to figure out Amy's dad. The only time I saw him was across the dining room table. He rarely spoke and never to me except for the cursory hello and occasional "How's things?" That was fine with me, and he seemed content with the situation as well. At least he never grilled me about school or my intentions with his daughter.

When warmer weather arrived we moved outside, walking or riding our bikes around her neighborhood. Even in the cold, Amy's back yard play fort saw its share of action. Slowly learning to cope with initial shyness and awkwardness, by springtime we were making regular visits to our private hide-a-way.

Our circle was growing tighter. Frank and Sherry, Nick and Marianne, and Bob and Marlena were all headed in the same direction as Amy and me. Tommy and Connie remained Tommy and Connie, much to the extended gossip of the fifth grade, the schoolyard, and all of Lawrence Park. The ten of us socialized almost exclusively, sometimes as couples. In March we sat through a Sunday matinee of the St. Pius X talent show. As could be expected, my mom acted her heart out in a funny sketch about newlyweds. Then in April, the Lawrence Park Movie Theatre featured a Friday the Thirteenth Creep-A-Thon. Amy and her friends arranged for a group date. We met at the shopping center about seven, invading the movie house for five hours of giant ants, man-munching locusts, and a killer praying mantis.

The following night Tommy called and said we were meeting in the woods behind his house. The small, secluded clearing tucked among thick growths of trees and wild shrubs had become the guy's favorite gathering spot. The five of us would talk and smoke and pass a bottle of wine or whiskey or beer or whatever else we could sneak out of the house. Most of the abbreviated conversations centered on baseball or cars or music or school or killer nuns. Sometimes we'd shyly discuss our relationships with the girls. Politics would come up, especially when a breaking story or news conference interrupted *American Bandstand*. It seemed I wasn't the only one our new, engaging young president was having an effect upon.

This Saturday night, however, would be different.

As I approached the clearing I could see Nick Brown leaning forward. He was sitting on the ground, his legs draped over a fallen log. I thought at first he was throwing up. Then I noticed Frankie lying sprawled out across the grass. He appeared to be sleeping. Before I could speak, Tommy looked up. He straddled another log, a brown paper sack in his hands. "Hey, there's my ol' buddy Billy. Hey buddy Billy..." He slurred his words and giggled.

It was obvious the guys had been drinking. But they hadn't.

Tommy grinned, motioning with his arm for me to come join him. Then he put the open bag to his face. His deep breathing caused the paper sack to fold in and out, in and out. I watched stupefied. A minute later Tommy began to slowly sway in an uncertain, circular motion. His arms went limp, dropping to his side; his eyes rolled back in his head. Then he too lay on the soft grass, unconscious.

It didn't take long for me to catch on to sniffing glue. I'd smoked some grass before but didn't care for it. I had never felt the high everyone talked about, and the expense and fits of coughing weren't worth the trouble. I wasn't even that fond of cigarettes, lighting up the occasional mild Salem just to fit in and be cool.

149

Glue was different. The potentially dangerous substance produced semi-conscious euphoria and hallucinations I'd never experienced with alcohol. And afterward, aside from some grogginess, there was no discernible hangover or after-effects. Plus the potent odor masked any smoking or drinking I may have been doing.

Glue-sniffing parties became a regular occurrence. Once a week or so we'd meet at our secret spot behind Tommy's house. By summertime I was a glue junkie. And the ruse that my friends and I had been working on our car models was the perfect cover. My parents never caught on.

While I was bonding with my new friends in all the wrong ways, my old buddies were slowly drifting away. It wasn't just Amy or the time I was spending with Tommy and the guys. Having been left behind a grade opened a widening rift in our friendships. A blind man could have foreseen it. Chris and I still talked in the schoolyard. But our afternoons together, playing in his backyard, dwindled as my interest in Amy and glue and alcohol increased.

Chris and I had no secrets. We were closer than brothers. But by May I was beginning to feel his sense of loss and his growing disappointment in me. Monday mornings he'd look into my eyes, shaking his head and forcing a smile.

"Man, you're one mess of flesh; you know that Daddy-o? You been hitting the sauce again, haven't you?" he would say.

No one else knew of my hidden life of drinking, smoking, and sniffing—not my parents, or my sister, or teachers at school. Amy and the girls knew that we drank and smoked and occasionally sniffed glue, but not to the extent that it had grown. With no outward telltale signs of my addictions, I was a typical, normal, healthy, if a bit troublesome young boy. Only Chris, my long-time best friend, could see the seriousness of my path. And I could tell it bothered him.

"Hey, delinquent, come over here a sec."

Amy's smile brightened an already cheery spring day. It was Friday, May 18, and St. Pius X School had plenty to be excited about. Besides being the end of another week, we were being dismissed early today. And Monday was a holiday due to some kind of teacher's in-service day. Everyone looked forward to the long weekend.

I sauntered over to no-man's land. "You beckoned, Miss Johns?"

"Cut the crap and listen," Amy replied. "Mom and I are heading down to Wildwood right after school today. We'll be gone all weekend, just the two of us." She rolled her hazel jewels into a puzzled expression, "Something about her and I not spending enough time together or something, I don't know. Anyway, I want you to do me a big favor—actually two favors."

Amy knew I'd do anything for her, but I wasn't expecting what came next. She moved close to me, pretending to brush some lint from my jacket, and lowered her voice. "I want you to promise me you won't do any drinking this weekend, and that includes sniffing, too." Her pretty face showed concern.

"Oh, ok. Sure. I don't think we had anything planned anyway," I lied. The guys had actually planned a big party in the woods for Saturday night. It was almost certain Amy and her friends knew.

She looked up, her eyes finding mine. "Promise me!"

"Ok, I promise—honest."

Her killer smile returned. "Good. Now there's something else. I want you to spend some time with your friend Chris. The school grapevine says he's been down in the dumps lately. You know he worries about you. And there's talk about him having some bad dreams or something."

I knew right away what that was about. A cold chill caused me to shiver in the warm sunshine.

Amy noticed. "Are you ok?"

"Yeah, yeah, I'm fine. Chris and I will buddy up. And I promise I'll behave. You and your mom have fun."

She winked as the school bell rang. "I'll bring you back a souvenir."

By four p.m. Chris and Ben Masters and I were engaged in a furious game of tag, chasing each other around Chris's spacious back yard. The barbs and antagonisms flew fast and fierce as we teased one another about everything from Chris's inability to hit a fast ball to my liking Amy Johns. At one point Chris cornered me by our old club house, chanting aloud, "Billy and Amy sittin' in a tree."

I ducked past him, making my way to the swing set.

"K-I-S-S-I-N-G," he continued, dancing a little jig for good measure.

"You sorry bastard," I screamed back, trying to conceal my laughter.

Chris took off at a run. I followed, swearing revenge.

At the end of Chris's driveway there stood an ancient oak tree. Its branches reached out and dipped low, spreading shade across the Murphy family's back yard. Running at full speed, Chris leaped, latching onto a low-hanging branch and scurrying up the tree like a monkey. As I awkwardly followed, he climbed higher. Finally, some twenty feet up, we both paused to catch our breath. Clinging to a broad, heavy limb, we faced each other.

"I told you what happens when you get involved with a girl," Chris taunted.

"How would you know?" I countered.

"Hey, I can smell the cooties from here!" He shimmied backwards away from me, holding his nose for good measure. "You need to be—"

Chris never got to finish his words. As he moved back across the limb, his right ankle brushed a power line. His body twitched and then stiffened. The arc of light from the spark blinded me. I regained my sight to see Chris' face contorted in pain, his mouth frozen open in a silenced scream.

The air lay heavy with ozone. It smelled like burnt chocolate.

By the time the police and ambulances left and I was allowed to go home, it was dark. The media circus that had gathered remained, looking for any fresh tidbits of news or forgotten neighbors to interview. Chris's death made headlines across the East Coast. But beyond inarticulate attempts to answer questions about what had happened, I don't think I spoke a word.

I wasn't in shock. I wasn't feeling anything.

I was just numb inside.

Mom held me as we drove home. She was softly crying. In the living room Dad placed a comforting hand on my shoulder.

"I'm sorry, Billy," was all he could manage.

I muttered something and headed up to my room. Most of that weekend remains a blur to me. Later, I was able to piece together events through conversations with Amy and my sister.

I remember drifting off into a troubled, restless sleep. Stark images haunted my dreams. As in his own nightmares, Chris was strapped into an electric chair, my hand on the switch. At times we were back in the tree and I could see his face, twisted in pain, trying to cry out. Sometimes he reached out to me, his outstretched hand always just beyond reach. The images and nightmares dimmed and lessened with time, but would remain with me for a lifetime.

Late Saturday morning I picked at my eggs and toast, mostly just sitting, staring, and thinking. I could hear my parents talking softly in the next room.

"It's not natural, I tell you—he hasn't said a word about it. He needs to cry, grieve for his friend, and get it out."

"Oh, he'll be fine, just give him some time. He'll figure things out."

It made no sense. What was there to figure out? Chris was gone, dead. It was as simple as that. I'd chased him up that tree. He'd been electrocuted, just like in his dreams. No amount of talking or discussing or explaining would bring him back.

Forsaking my breakfast, I told my parents I needed to get out of the house. The rest of the day and night is lost to me.

I did sleep a bit better Saturday night, but mostly just from exhaustion. Rising early the next day, I found myself sitting at Sunday Mass.

Father Dowd began his sermon with, "The loss of our dear brother Christopher Murphy." I could feel every eye in the church following me as I stood up and walked out. My gut burned, and I felt as if my head would explode. I wandered the neighborhood aimlessly, oblivious to where I was or where I was going.

Later that night Amy and her mom arrived at my house. Mr. Johns had read about the tragedy in the newspaper and called his wife. Amy wanted to be with me. Her mom understood. Cutting short their weekend, they had hurried back from the Jersey Shore. Now they sat in the living room with my parents and sister. The adults discussed the events of the last two days with cold detachment. What a terrible thing it was. How could such a thing happen? The township should have done something about the wires.

Finally Amy spoke up. "But what about Billy? How's he doing? Where is he?"

My parents shot each other looks that expressed more confusion than concern. "I don't know," Dad finally confessed. "We haven't seen him all day."

"I've called his friends," Mom added. "They haven't seen him either."

Amy had heard enough. "I think I know where he might be," she said, and rushed out the door.

She found me at the Little League baseball field. Despite the warm spring night, I was shivering. Our eyes met as she entered the dugout. Without a word, Amy sat beside me, taking me into her arms. For the first time I began to cry.

My parents loved me and felt for me and did the best they could. They were just ill equipped to handle the extreme situation. Dr. Spock must have omitted the chapter on dealing with the death of a child's friend.

I guess the rest of the world must have missed that part too. Tuesday at school there was a mention of Chris's death by Sister Tres-Martin, followed by a few Hail Marys for his family and nothing more. Even the other kids seemed reluctant to talk about Chris. Bob Masters and I exchanged curious glances in the schoolyard but never spoke again. On Saturday Chris was buried in a small ceremony with only his family in attendance. Dad promised we'd drive out to the cemetery in a few days. We never did. Once again one of the most important people in my life was gone. And again I was denied the chance to say goodbye.

For the next month I functioned simply by going through the motions: school, home, music, friends, and sleep. Some two weeks after Chris died, I ventured over to Amy's house. Other than school, it was the first time I'd seen her since our night in the dugout. She gave me the space I needed, while at the same time assuring me she was there for me. Each morning in class I could count on well-manicured fingers, the pinky chewed down, to affectionately rub my shoulders. She'd whisper into my ear a sincere, "How's it going today, Delinquent?"

Emerging from the disabling trauma proved a slow and agonizing process. I still ached inside for my friend and blamed myself for his death. Some days I'd find myself looking for his face among the crowd in the schoolyard. And I railed against society for its normalcy in the face of the tragedy.

Within days of Chris's passing, life around me had returned to humdrum suburban routine. I wanted to grab someone, anyone, and scream, "He's dead! Chris is gone! What's the hell's the matter with you people?"

Instead I punched the walls of my bedroom. Otherwise I kept it bottled up inside, as my father had taught me, and watched as life went on. In a little over a year, another tragic event would help teach me and the world that a return to normalcy was actually a big part of the healing process.

When I arrived at Amy's, Mrs. Johns greeted me at the door with a smile and a hug. She looked at me with the same affection I found in her daughter's eyes.

"How's it going today, Delinquent?" she teased. The quip forced a smile and helped me to hold my composure.

"I'm doing good, Ma'am," I replied, sniffing back a tear. "Thanks."

Within a few days, Amy and I were back to normal, and a lot closer for the wear.

My friends were another story.

The day of Chris's funeral I pedaled over to Tommy's house. His mother met me with a look bordering somewhere between contempt and curiosity. Tommy and I rode our bikes up to the shopping center, hanging out and talking about nothing in particular. That night we met the guys in the woods. We smoked, drank, and sniffed some. Tommy and the gang knew Chris only through me, talking with him occasionally in the schoolyard.

Our first encounters after his death produced the cursory awkward, head down, foot shuffling, "Sorry, man. Chris was cool. I liked him." After that, boys became boys again. We passed the bottle of cheap wine. Fond remembrances of Chris were sprinkled with good-natured ribbing, and even direct barbs about my having killed him.

"Well, you know he did warn you," Nick interjected at one point, grinning and slapping my back.

I smiled and laughed and listened, smoking my Salems, sipping the bitter wine. But I didn't respond. It was their way of healing. It would take me a long time to understand that their light-hearted jabs were also helping me to heal inside.

One afternoon, as Amy and I clung together in her back yard play fort, I looked into her sparkly hazel eyes. "Life's a bitch, Daddy-o; you'll never get out of it alive. You might as well enjoy the ride," I heard myself say.

Amy looked up at me. "What? What the heck was that?"

"Something Chris told me a long, long time ago," I replied. "A lifetime ago."

Her smile and tender kiss told me things would be just fine.

ᑕᔆ⍴Chapter Thirteen᠙ᕽᒃ

On May 19, in a widely publicized celebration, Marilyn Monroe sang "Happy Birthday" to President Kennedy at Madison Square Garden. The blonde movie star wore a dress that was described in the media as "skin and beads." In a fortuitous bit of sad irony, when Marilyn finally arrived at the gala, the president's brother-in-law, Peter Lawford, introduced her as "the late Marilyn Monroe." In three months the wildly popular actress would be dead from an apparent accidental overdose of prescription drugs.

The summer was quickly turning into a political and emotional roller coaster for the president and the American people. In May the U.S. sent troops into Thailand to aid the faltering government. Four days later the U.S. found itself involved in the internal politics of yet another Southeast Asian country, as Marines arrived in Laos. Meanwhile the conflict in Vietnam continued to escalate, with more American troops being deployed and more American advisors being killed in action. With the threat of the spread of communism on every American's mind, the country at first fully backed President Kennedy's foreign policy decisions.

In the summer of '62 the Cold War was quickly heating up as well. On July 6 the U.S. exploded a 104-kiloton nuclear device in Nevada under the guise of testing "atomic detonations for large-scale peaceful purposes." The following day, Operation Sunbeam began a series of four nuclear bomb tests. Undeterred, the USSR continued its own nuclear testing with the explosion of a 40-megaton bomb. All the while the Kremlin was petitioning the United Nations for the Geneva talks to be re-opened.

The Soviets were busy in space as well, keeping cosmonaut Micolaev in orbit for four days. By August two Soviets had circled the Earth at the same time in separate capsules. But unconfirmed reports of tragic failures began to leak from behind the Iron Curtain. Several rumors told of cosmonauts perishing when their spacecraft plummeted to Earth, crashing violently upon re-entry.

Our own space program moved forward with several major successes. On May 24 astronaut Scott Carpenter became the second American to orbit the earth, aboard the *Aurora 7*. In June, Bell Laboratories' Telstar satellite was launched from Cape Carnival, beaming the first live television pictures from Europe to America. The feat inspired a rock song titled "Telstar." The instrumental became the first song by a British group to hit the number one spot in the U.S. And then on August 27 the *Mariner 2* space probe was launched atop an Atlas D booster rocket. By year's end it was passing within 20,000 miles of Venus, sending back detailed information about the planet's surface.

On August 5 my family and I had just left a small motel west of Indianapolis on the second day of our vacation to Missouri. We were listening to a Top 10 countdown on WSMJ when the news of Marilyn Monroe's death came across the car's radio. Dad's parents lived on a twenty-acre farm just outside of Joplin. Grandma and Grandpa had chickens, some pigs, a couple of cows, and plenty of places for an inquisitive young boy to explore. Aunt Millicent, Dad's sister, lived on the farm as well with her husband Pete and their kids. Plus, Uncle Jimmy and the rest of my cousins lived nearby in the city.

Normally I looked forward to our bi-annual visits, but not this year.

By school's end I was handling Chris's death pretty well. Amy was the comfort and understanding, the companion and confidant I'd looked for since losing my aunt. As much as my young heart could comprehend, I was sure I was falling in love. And I was sure Amy felt the same. We didn't speak aloud of such things. There was no need.

Wednesday, June 6, was the last half-day of school. By 12:15 p.m. it was all over. I was officially a sixth grader and free of Sister Tres-Martin. The next evening I sat across from Amy at the dinner table. Her mom had called my mom and asked if I would like to join them for supper. I knew something was up; Mom had spoken with Mrs. Johns for quite a while. It didn't take twenty minutes to extend a dinner invitation, even for mothers.

Conversation at the table was pleasant but strained. Mrs. Johns made small talk about the struggling Phillies and Patsy Cline's latest release, which was making Top 40 air play. Mr. Johns asked if I wanted to be an astronaut. Rolling my eyes at Amy, I ignored her dad's question, telling her mom that Patsy's 45 "She's Got You" was already in my collection. By the time we finished the chocolate cake dessert, I was ready for the other shoe to drop. Chocolate cake was my favorite.

Amy's mom smiled pleasantly, glanced at her husband, and then turned to her daughter. "Why don't you and Billy go for a walk? It's a beautiful night out; you can walk off some of that cake."

Minutes later the romantic "Stranger on the Shore" flowed from my transistor while Amy and I strolled hand in hand in silence. It wasn't like Amy to be so quiet. We never seemed to run out of things to talk about.

Tonight was different.

"Mom was right, it is a nice night tonight," Amy said, sighing deeply.

"What is it?"

"What do you mean?"

"What's on your mind, Bulldog?" Inside I was certain I didn't want to know.

Up the street from Amy's house there stood an old barn that dated back to Revolutionary times. Like her back yard play fort, it was one of our places. We sat on a log at the property's edge, the tension as thick as the night air.

"Remember last May, when Mom and I went to Wildwood?"

That was the day Chris was killed. "Of course I do." I forced a smile. "How can I forget?"

The silence that followed lasted an eternity. Finally Amy spoke. "We were looking at houses there."

My young heart splattered on the ground at my feet. My anguish must have been obvious. Amy gave me a perplexed look. Then she started to laugh, touching me tenderly.

"Oh, no—no, silly, we were looking for a house to rent." Her laughter faded. Now she wore the same look of anguish. "For—for the—the summer, we were looking for a place to rent for the summer."

My young heart remained on the ground at my feet. Okay, it wasn't as bad as I thought... just bad. "So, you mean you..."

Amy nodded. It was easy to see she was trying not to cry. "Actually, it's just for a couple of months. We'll be back in August."

Fate had never been very kind to me. I'd come to accept the irony that seemed to permeate my life. "When?" I asked.

"We'll be back on the fifth. But we'll still have all of August together."

"I leave for Missouri on the fourth of August."

Most of that summer remains a blur to me—a drunken, glue-fogged blur. Amy left for the shore. My constant companion, my radio, offered up little comfort. During the summer of 1962 you couldn't kick a cat without hearing Bryan Hyland's monster hit "Sealed with a Kiss." I fell into a routine of sleeping late, moping around the house, singing and drinking with my hanging buddies, and getting high with the guys. Sometimes it was just a couple of us, as Nick and Bob and Frankie continued to develop their own relationships. Tommy and Connie were already deeply into theirs.

Often I sat alone in the Little League dugout, drinking and missing Amy and thinking about Chris.

Amy and I wrote a few times. We exchanged post cards and souvenirs. While visiting Meramec Caverns, I dropped twenty-five cents into a souvenir coin machine. One side of the aluminum disc read "Meramec Caverns, The Ozarks Stanton, Missouri." On the other side I had engraved "Amy & Billy." In a bit of romantic irony, two days after mailing it to Amy I received an identical coin in the mail. This one read, "Wildwood by the Sea, Wildwood, NJ/Billy & Amy."

Usually our two-week excursions to Joplin never seemed long enough to me. I enjoyed the time I got to spend on the farm, and my cousins and I had lots of fun together. But this year, away from Amy, without alcohol or glue to numb the loneliness, time stood still.

One afternoon, while the adults were away, I snuck off behind the barn with some apple jack wine I'd found stashed deep in Grandmom's cupboard. It was gone in a couple of gulps, tasted awful, and had little effect. It was just as well. Before we left for Missouri I'd been hitting the whiskey and the glue tubes pretty heavily.

Uncle Pete, Millicent's husband, suspected something was up with me. Early one morning the two of us walked deep into the woods behind the farm. He'd told the others he was going to teach me to shoot a pistol. But instead we talked about drinking and getting high, and girls and life. He didn't lecture me or pass judgment, allowing me to talk about Chris and vent and reason things out for myself. And he never told my parents. The two-week respite and my uncle's concern should have done me a lot of good. But I was too stubborn to stop.

We returned home late on Saturday, August 18. Sleep was almost impossible. By noon the next day, Amy and I were back sitting on the log at the barn by her house. We hugged and talked; kissed and talked, and hugged some more. She was even more beautiful than I remembered. Amy was deeply tanned, her light brown hair lightened even more from the sun. She wore the souvenir coin on a chain around her neck. I'd attached mine to my key chain.

The following week the annual Lawrence Park Back to School Carnival arrived in town. Amy and I met every night at the fair, spending time alone and with the rest of the gang. Dad was unexpectedly generous, slipping me money for the rides and games, the side shows and the fair food. In an unprecedented move, both families permitted us to remain until closing time, Amy's mom picking us up each night around midnight.

I don't believe I touched glue or alcohol once during those last two weeks of August. By the first Wednesday of sixth grade, our relationship had progressed well beyond friendship or infatuation. Amy and I were in love.

While school kids across the country enjoyed the last, fleeting days of summer vacation, the U.S. was secretly sending spy planes over Cuba. The government had officially ended covert reconnaissance missions after pilot Francis Gary Powers was shot down over the Soviet Union in 1960. But now, with Castro openly embracing communism, President Kennedy authorized the CIA's limited use of the U2 spy plane. On August 29 the dangerous gamble paid off: SAM missile launch pads were identified in Cuba. At the time, even the White House wasn't fully aware of the implications the discovery would have on the U.S. and the world.

In the South, the new school year began with violence. In June the Supreme Court had ruled compulsory school prayer unconstitutional. It was a decision that came as a surprise to many, further defining the separation between church and state. But it would be the issue of desegregation that would ignite the summer of '62 and, for a time, divert attention from the Cold War and developments in Cuba.

On July 10 the Reverend Martin Luther King, Jr., was arrested during a demonstration in Georgia. Two weeks later, in Albany, Georgia, 160 civil rights activists were jailed after a demonstration. Although King repeatedly called for peaceful demonstrations and sit-ins, determined segregationists were making violence an almost daily part of the struggle. In August, Shady Grove Baptist Church in Leesburg, Georgia, was burned. The following month a second black church was torched in Macon, Georgia. By September 17, the first federal suit to end public school segregation was filed by the U.S. Justice Department. Three days later it all came to a head.

On September 20, black student James Meredith was blocked from enrolling at the University of Mississippi by Gov. Ross B. Barnett. A *Life* magazine photograph showed seven sheriffs gathered together to keep Meredith out of the building. The picture, combined with the nightly TV news reports and images, polarized the country. The U.S. Supreme Court had already ruled that Meredith had the right to be admitted to the state school. But Gov. Barnett stood his ground, forcing Attorney General Robert F. Kennedy to send U.S. Marshals to protect and escort Meredith.

The ensuing riots and violence on the school campus resulted in President Kennedy's ordering police from the 503rd Military Police Battalion and troops from the Mississippi Army National Guard onto the scene. The violence continued, culminating in two deaths and over 150 Marshals and Guardsmen injured.

Finally, on September 24 the U.S. Circuit Court of Appeals ordered James Meredith to be admitted to the university. On September 30, on his fourth try, Meredith was permitted to register for classes. The protests and violence continued; Meredith himself was harassed by many of the other students during his two semesters on campus.

On a more positive note in the fight for integration, on July 3 Jackie Robinson became the first African American to be inducted into the National Baseball Hall of Fame.

For my friends and me, the new school year started off well. The gang was fully defined now: Tommy and Connie, Nick and Marianne, Bob and Marlena, Frankie and Sherry, and Amy and I were inseparable. As sixth graders we moved up to the second floor. Fate landed us together in the same classroom. And our new lay teacher, Miss Conway, proved to be an attractive distraction and a giant step up from fifth grade as well. I even managed to talk her into letting me take the seat directly in front of Amy. For the next couple of years the group's friendship would see us through the worrisome times ahead.

But at the moment, things couldn't be better. It didn't take long for us to fall into a comfortable routine. Tommy continued to walk Connie home from school. His parents remained clueless to the serious young romance. Once a week I'd high-tail it over to Amy's house, often arriving before her school bus dropped her off. Mrs. Johns would have cookies and milk for me. We'd talk about music, school, the Phillies, or my mom's latest acting role on stage or TV, or in some movie that was being shot locally. Then Amy and I would spend time together, walking or riding our bikes around her neighborhood, listening to records, or just hanging out.

Friday nights were usually spent with the guys. We continued to meet in the woods behind Tommy's house. Our glue sniffing was becoming a weekly occurrence. We'd smoke, pass a bottle of bourbon, and talk. Topics included anything from cars to our girlfriends to school to the race issue or the Cold War. Then the bags and tubes of glue would appear. I'd return home around midnight to parents who'd already gone to bed, or who were out with friends or at one of Mom's acting functions. About once or twice a month, on a Saturday night the bunch of us would meet at the Lawrence Park Movie Theatre. Afterward we'd wander over to the drug store for sodas and milkshakes. The lunch counter was manned by a hip young black man who always had WDAS playing on his portable radio. Curtis was cool and funny, always singing along with Jackie Wilson and James Brown and Sam Cooke, using his broom or mop handle as a microphone. We liked Curtis, the lone black man in our colorless world, never realizing the extended subway and bus ride he took each day from his home in West Philly, or the abuse he endured for his job in white-bread suburbia.

When I didn't have a movie date with Amy, I still hung out at nearby Loomis Public Grade School with my older friends. We still sang and drank and joked around. The others had all graduated from St. Pius X, moving on to recently opened Cardinal O'Hara

High School. But our nights of hanging out would continue, and their influences would continue to shape and change me. As the years progressed, Amy would be the first to notice the subtle differences, as my personality began to sullen somewhat. Yet she refused to give up on me.

For the moment, though, life was good and we all clung to the fading innocence of our youth.

One Saturday night, after watching King Kong and Godzilla tangle in the movies, the ten of us sat at the drug store lunch counter. Curtis was dancing his mop around the floor and lip-syncing Bobby Lewis' "Tossin' and Turnin'." Amy laughed aloud at the antics of the rubber-legged soda jerk, bouncing on her stool in time to the catchy tune.

Dropping my straw back into my chocolate milkshake, I leaned toward her. "Hey, why don't we have a party?"

Amy's look wasn't encouraging. "We tried that already, remember?"

Memories of that night returned. It had been a disaster. Then images of Amy and me strolling down the line of swaying couples flooded my brain. The mental pictures made me smile. I watched as she continued to dance in her seat. "We'll have it at my house," I said. "C'mon, it'll be fun."

Her smile matched my own. "Okay, but this time you'd better behave!"

"I promise," I replied, crossing my heart and holding up my right hand for good measure.

"And this time I expect you to dance with me."

I looked at Curtis, who was now slow-grinding with his mop-headed partner to the Danleers' "One Summer Night." My mouth was suddenly dry. Draining my shake, I swallowed hard. "Oh… Okay."

166

As Sam Cooke put it, the Cokes were in the icebox and the popcorn was on the table. It was a cool Saturday night in October, and me and my baby were out on the floor. It hadn't taken a lot of convincing for my parents to let me have a party. Mom was a pushover, and Dad readily gave in when she mentioned to him that they would finally get to meet some of my friends. It didn't take any convincing the guys either, although I did make them promise to be on their best behavior. That included no smoking or drinking. Tommy pointed out that the rules applied to me as well. What took a lot more doing was getting them to agree to some dance lessons.

While pitching the idea of a party to my mother, she inquired about our last get-together at Amy's house. I simply said that it had been all right, although no one had danced much. That was all she needed to hear.

Fresh out of high school, Mom had worked at the Philadelphia USO during World War II. Later she became a dance instructor at Author Murray Studios. Now the gypsy in her took over. After a few mother-to-mother phone calls, for the next three Saturday mornings, my sister and father went bowling while the ten of us gathered at my house. With patience and glee, mom taught us the box step, the fox trot, the waltz, the Lindy, the jitterbug, the shag, the cha-cha, the mashed potato, and even the pony and the twist.

Now I was in the middle of our den, the rug rolled back, confidently twirling my partner to the Silhouettes' "Get a Job." The song ended and Amy hugged me, sneaking a quick kiss to my ear. It was already 10:30 and we'd danced and talked and laughed and shared some orange soda and danced some more. I knew what lay ahead, and I began to sweat nervously. I glanced across the room. Tommy held Connie by one hand, slipping a 45 onto the record player with the other. I knew what that meant.

I grabbed Amy's hand. "C'mon, it's hot in here. Let's get some air." Before she could protest I dragged her out the back door.

"Hey, what's the matter? It's cold out here."

Making sure we hadn't been followed, I pulled her close. "Nothing, I just wanted some air is all. You're wearing me out in there."

"Right. I know what you want."

"No, honest, just air, there's no booze anywhere. I don't even have my smokes."

Amy shook her head, giving me her *you sorry idiot* look. "No, silly—this…"

She pulled me to her, and we kissed. As I had thought, from inside came the Platters' "Smoke Gets in Your Eyes." All I needed was for my dad to wander downstairs and catch Tommy and Connie grinding away in a dark corner of his den. I prayed Mom could keep her promise and keep him upstairs.

The kiss ended. Amy looked up at me. I wondered if it was the night air or what I saw in her eyes that made me shiver. Taking me by the hand she led me back inside. Little Anthony and the Imperials began to sing:

"You don't remember me, but I remember you/was not so long ago, you broke my heart in two"

We found our way to the dance floor. Amy folded herself into my arms, pulling me close. After few faltering, nervous steps I began to relax. It was our first slow dance. Half-way through, Amy looked up at me. The same look was in her eyes. But there was something else, a tear.

"Tears on my pillow, pain in my heart, caused by you"

"What's—what's wrong?" I asked.

The tear ran down her cheek, followed by another. Holding me tightly, she buried her face in my shoulder. I could barely hear her soft words. "Oh, shut up."

⋘Chapter Fourteen⋙

The innocence of that night would soon be overshadowed. While Amy and I shared our first slow dance; while Tommy and Connie discussed their future together, and the gang discussed the possibility of making our parties a monthly occurrence; forces here and overseas were conspiring to put an end to everything for everyone. Permanently.

The results of the covert reconnaissance flights over Cuba during the month of August had been purposely kept from President Kennedy. The Joint Chiefs, who had urged the overthrow of Fidel Castro, wanted more evidence to present to the president. Most were convinced that nothing short of an all-out attack on the island country would end Castro's rule and the threat of communism in the Western Hemisphere. After the Bay of Pigs, Kennedy had reluctantly agreed to explore new options for the overthrow of Castro's regime. After months of discussions, plans, and heated debates on ways to disrupt the Cuban government—including the displacement and possible assassination of Fidel Castro—the highly classified Operation Mongoose had proven totally ineffective. Now the CIA, backed by the Joint Chiefs, saw its chance to convince Kennedy to attack Cuba.

On August 31, 1962, Senator Kenneth Keating told the Senate that there was evidence of Soviet missile installations in Cuba. He personally urged Kennedy to take action. Two weeks later, in a speech before the United Nations, Soviet foreign minister Andrei Gromyko seemed to confirm the evidence, warning that an American attack on Cuba could mean war with the Soviet Union. While Gromyko spoke to the UN, the Soviet freighters *Omsk* and

Poltava were arriving in Cuba with the first shipments of MRBMs—medium-range ballistic missiles.

By the end of September, Kennedy had ordered regular secret U2 spy plane missions over Cuba. On October 14, Air Force Major Richard S. Heyser returned from his reconnaissance mission with photos of missiles being transported in Cuba. The next day the National Photographic Intelligence Center positively identified the missiles as Soviet surface-to-surface MRBMs. On October 16, after being showed the photographic evidence, President Kennedy called together a team of advisors to discuss possible diplomatic and military courses of action. Activities on both sides of the world had begun that would bring mankind to the very edge of total destruction.

With the exception of a few dozen high-ranking officials in the U.S. and the Soviet Union, the world remained oblivious to the dangerous situation developing just ninety miles off the coast of Florida. Along with my friends, my biggest concern was what to be for Halloween. Amy's mom was bringing her over, and the gang had plans to meet up at my house on Halloween night and attack the neighborhood.

Amy and I paired up as a couple of cool beatniks. But inside I had begun to grow restless, unsure of the reasons for my feelings. Life was good. School was its usual boring routine but bearable; at least I didn't have to contend with the nuns on a daily basis. And having Amy and my friends close by made the daily grind tolerable. But I began to feel the old wanderlust return. I was spending more time listening to the DJs on my radio, dreaming of how it might feel to be like Hy Lit or Joe Niagara.

One day in the middle of October, Amy was absent from school. Sherry Roland told me Amy had a bad cold and probably wouldn't be back for at least a couple of days. On Wednesday morning, with nothing but a spelling test and the empty desk behind me to look forward to, I hopped aboard a SEPTA bus.

I'd done some research and planning, and some thirty minutes and one transfer later I was deposited at what could only have been the gates of heaven. As I crossed the busy street, before me lay an expanse of lush, green lawn. Nestled in the center of the well-manicured acreage there stood a large, ultra-modern, split-level-style building. Just beyond, five magnificent towers of Babel reached their way to the heavens, each topped with a gleaming, revolving red beacon. These were the same towers that I could actually see from my bedroom window; the same towers that beamed endless hours of rock 'n' roll directly to my transistor radio. I was at the home of radio station WIBG.

During the summer of '62 my dad and I had reached a sort of compromise. If I agreed to cut back on my trouble making, do my best in class, and stop skipping school, he would allow me to attend public high school starting with the ninth grade. My practical father understood I'd never be able to completely keep out of trouble. He would content himself with no more suspensions or detentions and my graduating from St. Pius X.

It was an offer too good to refuse. I was well aware of the deal I'd made with my father. I certainly didn't want to do anything to jeopardize it. But the song of the radio siren was just too strong to resist. I had to see for myself the source of all the magic that emanated from my tiny transistor.

Unable to get past the friendly and very pretty but stern receptionist, I spent my day sitting on the steps of WIBBAG, listening on my radio to the patter of the DJ's and the rock 'n' roll they spun. I continued to ditch school a couple more times during the next month until it grew too cold.

My parents were never aware of my truancy. Their minds, along with the minds of the rest of the world, were occupied with the terrifying developments that threatened to destroy the world. While Kennedy sought alternative means to defuse the growing situation in Cuba, the Joint Chiefs and especially the Air Force continued to strongly argue for an air strike.

Following another U2 flight on the night of October 17, the military discovered the presence of intermediate-range SS-5 nuclear missiles—IRBMs—in Cuba. UN ambassador Adlai Stevenson wrote to Kennedy urging restraint in his actions, saying, "The judgments of history seldom coincide with the tempers of the moment." On the 18th, President Kennedy met with Andrei Gromyko at the White House. Kennedy did not reveal to the Soviet foreign minister that he was aware of the missile build-up in Cuba. Gromyko did his best to assure the U.S. president that any Soviet aid was only for "the defense capabilities of Cuba." By now the count of missiles believed to be stationed on the island stood at forty IRBMs.

On October 20, after some twenty to thirty Soviet ships were spotted en route to Cuba, Kennedy and his advisors began discussing the possibilities of a defensive quarantine. The next day General Walter Sweeney, commander-in-chief of the Tactical Air Command, informed the president that no air strike would destroy all the missiles in Cuba. The same day another U2 flight revealed Soviet bombers, as well as Mig fighter jets being assembled and cruise missile sites being built along Cuba's northern shore. The possibility of a Soviet-Cuban retaliation strike, likely involving the use of nuclear missiles, had become a reality.

The president advised former presidents Hoover, Truman, and Eisenhower of the situation and sent the first of several letters to Soviet Premier Khrushchev. On Monday, October 22, in a televised speech, President Kennedy spoke to the country:

"This government, as promised, has maintained the closest surveillance of the Soviet military buildup on the island of Cuba. Within the past week, unmistakable evidence has established the fact that a series of offensive missile sites is now in preparation on that imprisoned island.

The purpose of these bases can be none other than to provide a nuclear strike capability against the Western Hemisphere."

Along with my dad and the rest of the family, I watched and listened to the frightening speech. Our young president was informing the nation of the very real possibilities of a third—maybe nuclear—world war. I don't think I had ever before seen my father frightened. But that evening, as he discussed the president's speech with my mom, my sister, and me, his face grew pale and grim with concern.

The next day St. Pius X buzzed with the news. Father Dowd made visits to each classroom, explaining the president's words as he understood them. He deliberately avoided the word "crisis," and he held prayer sessions for divine guidance.

My friends and I discussed as best we could our limited understanding of the situation. To the young mind it was simple: Cuban communists were threatening our country. Filled with John Wayne Saturday-matinee bravado, we fully expected the U.S. to attack and sink the tiny country. Amy tightly held on to my hand in no-man's land, telling me of her father's comments and concerns and of her own fears. I did my best to assuage them, repeating the stirring resolve of the schoolyard.

But the truth was inescapable; the world was poised for war. Even WIBG continually broke into regular programming for updates on the escalating troubles. For the next six days, as the U.S. military forces went to the DEFCON 3 stage of readiness and the entire world watched, waited and prayed.

On Tuesday, October 23, in response to the president's first letter, Khrushchev replied that there was a "serious threat to the peace and security of peoples." The same day President Kennedy signed Proclamation 3504 authorizing the naval quarantine of Cuba. By the end of the day, U.S. ships were taking up positions along the quarantine line, some 800 miles from Cuba.

Twenty-six Soviet ships had been confirmed heading towards Cuba from the USSR, but Kennedy ordered his Chiefs, "No shooting without my explicit orders."

Later, while his brother, Attorney General Robert Kennedy, met with Ambassador Dobrynin at the Soviet Embassy, the president decided to give Khrushchev more time, pulling the quarantine line back to 500 miles. The gamble paid off. The next day all but one of the Soviet ships en route to Cuba were observed slowing down or reversing their course. After a tense standoff, the Lebanese ship *Marucla*, chartered to the USSR, was stopped and boarded by crew members from the USS *Joseph P Kennedy Jr.* No signs of nuclear weapons or components were found, and the *Marucla* was cleared through the quarantine. Still, the military decided to go to DEFCON 2, indicating a readiness for war.

For the next several days, Kennedy and Khrushchev exchanged letters, each pointing the finger of blame, and each offering proposals to end the crisis. All the while Castro continued the development of the missile sites, attempting to camouflage the build-up from CIA reconnaissance flights. In a public statement, the Cuban leader authorized his country's air-defense forces to fire upon all American aircraft within range.

Finally, on Friday the 26th, a possible solution to the standoff was offered. In a meeting with ABC News correspondent John Scali, Aleksandr Fomin, the KGB station head in Washington, proposed the dismantling of the Soviet missile sites under UN supervision in exchange for a public pledge from the U.S. not to invade Cuba. A letter from the Soviet premier to the president confirmed the offer. Meanwhile, Kennedy and Khrushchev were privately discussing the removal of U.S. built Jupiter IRBMs deployed in Turkey and Italy.

Despite the promise of a possible settlement, on Saturday the situation worsened. An American Air Force pilot, Major Rudolf Anderson, Jr., was killed when his plane was shot down during a recon mission over Cuba. Kennedy, in a calculated move, and suspecting that the Soviet forces in Cuba had acted without the approval of Khrushchev, ordered the attack on Cuba to begin on Monday morning. On TV and radio, U.S. citizens were advised of precautions to take in case of an attack and reminded of the stop, drop, and cover routine. It was the closest the U.S. had ever come to all-out war with the USSR.

But Kennedy's dangerous bluff paid off. On Sunday, October 28, the president received a letter from Khrushchev sharing his concerns that the crisis was spiraling out of control. The Soviet leader agreed to accept the proposal. As Kennedy responded to the Kremlin, Khrushchev informed Castro of his decision. By the end of the day, Khrushchev announced over Radio Moscow that he had agreed to remove the missiles from Cuba. Kennedy then announced to the country and to the world that the crisis was over, publicly stating that Moscow would remove all nuclear weapons and bases in Cuba and that the U.S. had promised not to invade Cuba or take steps against Castro. In private, the U.S. also agreed that it would dismantle all of its IRBMs in Turkey and Italy.

Only two weeks after the agreement, the Soviets had removed the missile systems and their support equipment. By December, the Soviet MiGs and bombers had been loaded onto three Soviet ships headed back to the USSR. On November 20, President Kennedy lifted the naval quarantine of Cuba. It would be months, even years, before all of the facts of those thirteen days in October would be fully detailed and understood. Many Americans never realized just how close the world had come to nuclear disaster.

November 1962—the country had much for which to be thankful. President Kennedy's handling of what would come to be known as the Cuban Missile Crisis had established the leader and the U.S. as the dominant players in the game of world politics. Although some continued to criticize the administration, immediately following the crisis Kennedy's approval rating reached one of the highest points of any president. But beyond establishing the young president's influential presence, the defused situation became the first step in the cooling of the Cold War. On June 20, 1963, a hotline known as the Red Phone was established between the White House and the Kremlin. In the event of another crisis the two world leaders could communicate directly and privately at a moment's notice.

On a larger scale, talks on nuclear testing and arms limitations would soon gain momentum, prospering a greater hope for the future. The world was slowly returning to a tenuous normalcy. But not everyone shared in the promise of peace. As the year ended, North Vietnamese leader Ho Chi Minh pledged to wage guerilla war for ten years if necessary.

With a nuclear crisis averted, Kennedy finally turned his attention back to domestic issues. On November 20, the president issued an executive order banning racial discrimination. Although the order only covered housing owned, operated, or leased by the federal government, it was another important step on the long, rocky road to equality. Then in February, JFK sent the first of several messages to Congress concerning civil rights. The president urged legislation that would strengthen the enforcement of the Civil Rights Acts of 1957 and 1960 dealing with voter registration.

On the East Coast winter arrived early. Hiking up Cornwall Hill in the cold, sleet, and snow was bad enough. With my trusty old bike parked in the garage, after-school visits to Amy's house came to an end. Still, my buddies and I stubbornly continued our Friday night visits to the woods, drinking and sniffing glue, usually huddled around a small, hastily constructed fire. But we had somehow managed to talk our parents into allowing us to hold parties once a month, at a different person's home.

The Saturday before Thanksgiving, the gang gathered at my neighbor's house. Sherry Roland's father was a large, hulking, no-nonsense individual who didn't care much for teenagers, rock 'n' roll, or smooth-talking juvenile delinquents with an eye for his daughter. We kept the music low, refrained from smoking and swearing, and said, "Yes, Sir," and, "No, Sir." But Mr. Roland's repeated trips to the den portended disaster.

By about 10:30 the music had slowed, the lights had dimmed, and conversation had dwindled to whispers and giggles. Sherry's dad had had enough. Exiting the front door, Mr. Roland stealthy circled the house. He reached the darkened back yard just as Tommy was sliding into second base. Catching the passionate young couple by surprise, the enraged parent grabbed Tommy by the arm, flinging him handily halfway across the grass. He then turned his attention to Connie, launching into a torrent of name calling and accusations. His raging reached the rest of us in the den.

I looked at Amy. Both of us knew immediately what was going on. "Tommy," we said in unison. By the time we reached the back yard, Connie was in tears and Tommy was screaming obscenities at Mr. Roland that would make a sailor blush.

There's a lot to be said for gallantry; still more to be said for sagacity. Tommy was never the brightest one among us, although perhaps the most passionate. I can't say much for the judgment behind my actions either.

I spied the lunging figure out of the corner of my eye. Without thinking I leaped forward. Tommy crashed into me full force. We both then landed atop Sherry's father. The three of us tumbled to the hard, frozen ground. Amy grabbed Connie, attempting to pull her to safety. But an angry Mr. Roland came up swinging blindly. Glancing off of Tommy's shoulder, the back of his hand caught Amy's chin, knocking her to the ground next to me. That was all I needed. Rising to my knees I connected with an ineffectual left to his jaw, busting two knuckles in the process. The enraged parent may have been as strong as an ox, but he had a glass stomach. Instinctively, my right fist found his mid-section. He folded over like a greeting card.

By now a comedy of errors worthy of the Three Stooges was enfolding. You couldn't say the group didn't stick up for each other, both the guys and the girls. The rest of the gang had made their way to the back yard, each trying to put a halt to the fracas. Nick was attempting to pull Tommy from Mr. Roland. A hard elbow to his right eye was his reward. Sherry, seeing her father tussling on the ground, flew into the pile. Afraid that she might get hurt, Sherry's boyfriend, Frankie, grabbed her around the waist. The pair tumbled backward, landing in the middle of Mrs. Roland's dead rose bushes. Meanwhile, poor, hysterical Connie was lashing out violently at Marianne, who was only trying to help and comfort her.

It's unsure who called the authorities. A nosey, eavesdropping neighbor is my guess. Regardless of who sounded the alarm, three police units and an ambulance responded to the riot in progress, lights flashing and sirens wailing. By the time they arrived, the Roland back yard resembled the aftermath of a full-scale battle. Luckily they were met at the street by Sherry's level-headed mother. She managed to stall them, averting what could have been an ugly confrontation and some very serious trouble for all of us.

Surveying the carnage around him, Mr. Roland's outrage simmered somewhat, turning to concern. Helping his daughter out of the dormant rose bushes and finding her not seriously harmed, he joined his wife in the driveway. Together they convinced the police that everything was under control. After about fifteen minutes, with the authorities gone and the neighbors dispersing, Sherry's dad revealed his true make-up.

The ten of us had moved back into the den, licking our wounds, comforting one another, laughing and trying to figure it all out. Scratched and bruised, Frankie and Sherry sat together on the sofa. Marianne tended to Nick's black eye while Bob and Marlena tended to each other's bruises. Connie had calmed down and was back in Tommy's arms. She unabashedly proclaimed him her hero, tenderly kissing his swollen cheek and placing a towel to his bleeding nose.

Ignoring her own cut and swelling lip, Amy gently held ice to my aching, distended, discolored left hand. "Think I'll ever play the guitar again?" I joked, kissing the top of her head.

"Damn, I need a drink," Tommy called out.

"Hell, I think we all can use one," Marianne replied.

Our laughter was cut short.

"I'll pretend I didn't hear that!" Mr. Roland strode into the den and we all froze. Savoring the moment, his condemning stare lingered on each of us in turn. And then he smiled.

"The police are gone, and none the wiser," he proudly announced, adding a bit sheepishly, "thanks to Sherry's mom. And the neighbors can think what they want for all I care." His smile widened as he again surveyed the room. "No one the worse for wear I take it? No broken bones?"

A series of negative grunts and groans answered his inquiry.

Sherry's dad began to shuffle nervously, his gaze now finding the floor. "I'm—I'm sorry about all of this. I guess I didn't handle things very well." Head still bowed, he glanced up at his daughter. "Your mom always said I have a quick temper." Shifting his gaze to Tommy, he held forward a meaty hand. "What do you want to do about this, son?"

Surprised, Tommy looked at me. I nodded toward Connie, who stood at his side. Connie whispered something and Tommy smiled. "About what, Sir?"

Mr. Roland sighed heavily, "Okay then." Looking over to the sofa, he wagged a finger at Frankie. "And you—you let this be a lesson to you. You take good care of my daughter!" The stern but friendly smile returned. "Now, let's get you kids cleaned up before your parents arrive."

Sherry's parents kept their promise. When a couple of concerned parents phoned, they simply replied that some new crazy party game the kids were playing had gotten out of hand. There was nothing for them to be concerned about. Mom iced and bandaged my hand but never asked. Dad gave me some curious looks but held his peace. Incredibly, Amy confided everything to her mom. She told me later that the two had a long talk and then a good laugh about the incident and promised one another never to tell her father. The rest of the gang survived as well, and our clique remained intact.

In December we held an informal Christmas party at Connie's house. We bought each other gifts, the guys swapping model cars, pen knives, and baseball cards, the girls exchanging bath powders and LP records. Amy slipped a cool, gold-filled ID bracelet onto my wrist, whispering into my ear that she wished it read "Delinquent" instead of "Billy." With her mom's help and funds borrowed from my dad, I presented Amy with a sweater. It was soft and pretty and highlighted her eyes, and she loved it. But it wasn't what I wanted to give her. The more personal gift I had in mind would have to wait. The gathering was fun and uneventful, with couples making regular stops beneath the mistletoe.

The real party came a week later.

On Saturday night, December 29, the gang met at Tommy's. With his parents out for the night, and none of our parents the wiser, the house was ours. But we had something else in mind. Earlier in the day the guys had cleared out our secret meeting spot and dug a pit for a fire. Now, armed with blankets and marshmallows and flashlights and a couple of purloined fifths of bourbon, the ten of us made our way deep into the woods. With the fire providing warmth and the new moon providing intimacy, we laughed and joked and told stories, passing the bottle, while clinging to the moment. Later, huddled together under our blankets, eagerly sacrificing innocence for memories, everyone reached second base.

ᶜᵛᴼChapter Fifteenᶜᵛᴼ

We returned to Miss Conway's sixth grade on January 2, 1963. The new year started off the way 1962 had ended, with more snow and bitter cold. Christmas and my birthday had begat more model cars and some record albums. But turning twelve signaled a slight shift toward more adult gifts: more clothes, more books, more stuff deemed near useless to a boy turning twelve. Because of the weather, most of my afternoons were spent listening to my radio and assembling AMT's new 1963 model collection. My prized possession was a 1963 Lincoln Continental Convertible. The detailed model kit could be built as an exact replica of President Kennedy's very cool, navy blue, executive limo.

I also had plenty of time to practice my guitar. I was getting pretty good and could strum and sing along with most of the WIBG hit record survey. Amy and I stole as much time as possible, shivering together before school in no-man's land. But January's monthly party ended up being canceled, and even my weekends of sniffing, drinking, and singing finally fell victim to the weather. It didn't take long before I was climbing the walls.

Surprisingly, it was my father who came up with the solution.

The local bowling alley was forming a youth league. Thanks to Mom's organizational skills and her tact with handling parents, the gang became a team—actually three teams. Tommy, Connie, Amy, and I were the Rockin' Bowlers; Nick, Marianne, Frankie and Sherry became the Boppin' Bowlers; and Bob and Marlena formed the Stompin' Bowlers along with another sixth-grade couple. The names may not have been very original, but they were definitely cool.

Dad sidestepped my request for team shirts with his practicality: "Let's just see how long this lasts first."

On Saturday mornings for the next few months, we all met up at the Lawrence Park Shopping Center. Attempting to be cool, the bowling alley piped in some lame rock 'n' roll music. We bowled and even danced for a couple of hours. What we lacked in skill we more than made up in fun and friendship, Tommy's ubiquitous flask notwithstanding.

Afterward the bunch of us hung around the shopping center, window shopping, looking at clothes, and rummaging through the new releases in Woolworth's record department. Often the girls wandered off together doing girl stuff while Tommy, Nick, Bob, Frankie, and I read the latest hot rod magazines and checked out the model cars at Hobbyland. Then we would meet at the Rexall Drugs lunch counter for cherry Cokes and chocolate milkshakes and to talk rock 'n' roll with our black friend Curtis.

Around 12:30 we'd head over to the movie theatre for an afternoon of cartoons and comedies, space ships, monsters, and classic horror. Our Saturday outings saw us well beyond an otherwise bleak winter and became some of the most memorable times of my youth.

On Thursday, February 14, I managed to sneak aboard Amy's bus after school. Our Saturday outings with the gang were exciting and fun. But this was Valentine's Day, and I wasn't going to be denied. I had saved my allowance, even asking if there was anything I could do for extra money. Dad wasn't sure what to make of that but took full advantage. After a month of garage cleaning, whole-house vacuuming, and snow shoveling nearly every house on the block, I was rich. My $12.99 was hard earned and well spent. My purchases, however, were wrought with confusion, embarrassment, and uncertainty.

Amy's mom was surprised to see me. After a quick phone call to my mother, she invited me to stay for dinner. By now Mrs. Johns and I were buddies. She was someone I could talk openly with about most any subject, usually over a bowl of ice cream. While Amy changed out of her school uniform, I confided in her mom, explaining about the card and gift tucked into my school bag. She smiled politely, assuring me that Amy would love it, adding in one of her famous "When Amy's dad and I were dating" stories for good measure.

Following a feast of my second favorite meal, spaghetti and meatballs, and a quick reminder from her mom that she needed to get me home soon, Amy and I sat alone in her den. Sensing my nervousness, Amy took my hands. The envelope she placed in them carried her trademark pink with white hearts and smelled of oranges; the card inside was an adult one, with a poem about love and friendship. It was signed at the bottom with a delicately scrolled *L---* and her name in red.

I read the words over a second and then a third time, not sure what to say. But inside I knew I'd made the right choices. The card I selected for her also contained a poem as well as daisies, her favorite flower. Amy's expression as she opened it told me her mom was right—she loved it.

So far, so good...

My hands trembled and I began to sweat. The hastily wrapped package seemed no worse for wear after a night and a day bouncing around in my Army surplus school bag. Hiding the small box from my parents had been easy; wrapping it was another story. While my mom and dad enjoyed *The Many Loves of Dobie Gillis*, I managed to smuggle some paper and ribbon up to my room. Tomorrow I would face my mother's puzzled look when she discovered the red and pink paper scraps in my trashcan. But at the moment I faced a more pressing and important situation. I began to have serious doubts about my purchase.

"Oh, thank you." Amy smiled as she accepted the gift. My brain once again turned to mush.

"It's—it's for you." Smooth move there, Einstein.

Fortunately she didn't notice the shoddy job I'd done packaging my offering. She didn't have the time. In seconds the paper and ribbon lay strewn on the floor. She held the square purple box in her hands, curiously studying the delicate lace figures silhouetted on the top. I gritted my teeth and hoped for the best. Cautiously Amy lifted the lid. Right on cue the tacky red plastic heart began to beat, its windup mechanism pulsing rhythmically up and down, up and down.

"Oh, my—that's so—so—that's so cool!"

I started to breathe again.

Amy read the inscription on the heart aloud as it continued to beat in her hands. "My heart beats for you!"

"Oh, Billy…" She sighed, her smile lighting up her pretty face.

"I know, kinda silly isn't it?"

"No… oh, no, not at all. It's—I love it!

My own heart began to beat again. "Really?"

"Really, I do." The kiss was sweet; lingering.

On the ride home, Amy's mom gave me a wink in the rear-view mirror.

On Wednesday, March 6, I awoke to an eerie feeling of déjà vu. Answering the call of Dad's frying bacon, I wandered downstairs. Out of the plastic table radio I heard the plaintive "Why Can't He Be You." A cold shiver darted through me.

Dad looked up from his paper with a puzzled expression. "Are you all right?"

Before I could answer, the music faded, replaced by WIP's DJ. "Country singing sensation Patsy Cline died last night in a plane crash near Camden, Tennessee. The private aircraft went down in inclement weather just 90 miles from its Nashville destination. Along with Cline, killed in the crash were Cline's manager, Randy Hughes, and country musicians Hawkshaw Hawkins and Cowboy Copas. The popular singer had managed to cross over from country into pop music with hits such as 'Walkin' after Midnight' and 'I Fall to Pieces.' Patsy Cline was thirty."

I felt queasiness in the pit of my stomach. Another popular singer was dead; another artist I admired was gone; another plane had fallen from the sky. I thought about a cold day in February and the three rock 'n' roll stars who had perished doing what they loved. It wasn't fair. R&B singers Jessie Belvin and Chuck Willis were gone, both killed in car accidents. Eddie Cochran had also died in a car accident while on tour in England. Bluesman extraordinaire Guitar Slim succumbed to pneumonia after a battle with alcoholism. Johnny Ace had died of a gunshot wound backstage in Houston. These were more than just background people. I didn't know them personally, and yet they had deeply impacted my young life. The all-too-familiar empty feeling inside of me returned.

Ignoring Dad's offer of breakfast, my mind reeling with unanswerable questions, I returned to my room and dressed for school. I hardly noticed that the cold weather had finally broken. It was a clear, sunny morning with temperatures promising nearly 50 degrees.

As I rounded Hastings Boulevard, DJ Jerry Stevens reported the tragic news. Then, breaking station format, the morning jock played "Crazy" and "She's Got You," two of Patsy's biggest hits, back to back. I edged up the volume on my transistor.

The SEPTA bus driver seemed to share my pain and sense of loss. He smiled, nodding knowingly as I paid my fare and found a seat. Like a moth drawn to a flame, I followed the music emanating from my radio. I spent the remainder of the day sitting on the front steps of WIBG, thinking about death and about life. I wanted to touch people the way my Aunt Mary and Chris had touched me. I wanted to leave my mark the way Patsy Cline and Buddy Holly and Ritchie Valens and the rest had done. Realizing I probably didn't have the talent or the discipline to be a musician, my choice was clear.

Just then the front door of the radio station opened, and a familiar face poked out. He looked around, his firm gaze landing on me, the ever-present cigar planted confidently in the corner of his mouth.

"Hey, kid, run across the street and get me a cheese Danish and coffee, two sugars." The unlit cigar rolled from one side to the other as he smiled, flipped me a five-dollar bill, and disappeared back inside. It was Joe Niagara, WIBG's famous afternoon DJ.

Ignoring the busy traffic on Ridge Pike, I flew across the street to the small deli, made my purchase, and returned in what I am sure was record time. Boldly entering the station, I marched straight up to the pretty but stern receptionist. Before she could protest, I held up my keys to the kingdom: the brown paper sack with a cheese Danish and coffee, two sugars.

"I have a delivery for Joe Niagara!"

Eyeing me just long enough for the sweat to begin to bead on my forehead, she finally spoke. "Do you know where Studio B is located, Billy?"

Who did she think I was some amateur or something? "Of course I do," I replied with counterfeit confidence, and started across the lobby.

I had no idea where Studio B was located.

Guided by the exhilarating aroma of vinyl records and Phillies Cheroots, I crossed the expanse of thick, green carpet, scaled an open flight of steps, turned down a paneled hall lined with posters, photos, gold records, and other radio memorabilia, and headed straight to Studio B.

Hey, I was no amateur.

I paused, waiting patiently.

Finally the flashing red *On Air* light blinked off.

Summoning a deep, calming breath, I knocked lightly, pushing the heavy oak door open. Nearly every square inch of the small, soundproof studio was cluttered with equipment, audio tapes, record albums, and stacks of 45s. From overhead dangled two large, impressive-looking microphones. Joe Niagara sat behind a broad, U-shaped counter. At either end lay massive turntables. Perched next to one was a gleaming, chrome, open-reel tape deck; to the other side rested a stack of tape cartridge machines. Directly in front of Joe sat the immense master control panel housing a myriad of knobs, leavers, controls, meters, and flashing lights. I remember thinking this is what the inside of the Mercury space capsule must look like.

Joe turned, signaling me to the stool opposite him. Holding up one finger, he slipped into a pair of headphones. With the flick of a switch, the husky Altec monitor speakers clicked off, and Joe Niagara clicked on.

"You can't get any higher on the WIBBAGE survey—its way, way up there where the air is rare. The number one song in Philly land for another big week—it's Paul—and Paula—on WIBG!"

He snapped off the mike, and the studio filled with music.

"Hey, hey Paula/I wanna marry you"

Removing his headphones, Joe re-fired the half-smoked cigar. "What do you think, kid?" he asked, accepting the coffee and Danish.

I sat there, mute, trying to take it all in. As if reading my thoughts, Joe sipped his coffee, cued up another 45, and grinned. "Yeah, I know…"

For the rest of the country, 1963 started off with events that would foreshadow the uncertain times ahead. On January 2, the Viet Cong shot down five U.S. military helicopters in the Mekong Delta, reportedly killing 30 American soldiers. With the increased presence of U.S. advisors as well as military personnel, Ho Chi Minh's North Vietnamese army had begun purposely targeting American troops. The action would directly affect the country's future involvement in the escalating war in Southeast Asia.

On the other side of the globe, Premier Nikita Khrushchev was on a tour of East Germany that included the Berlin Wall. In a speech, the Soviet leader stated that the USSR now had a 100-megaton nuclear bomb. It would be the first of several mixed messages to come out of the Kremlin over the next few years. The following month, in a rare gesture of detente, Moscow offered to open nuclear testing to onsite inspections, while at the same time warning the U.S. that an attack on Cuba would mean war.

On February 6 Washington reported that all Soviet offensive arms were out of Cuba. Two weeks later, the Soviet leader told President Kennedy that it would remove several thousand of its estimated 17,000 troops in Cuba. Then, on February 27, it announced that some 10,000 armed soldiers would remain stationed in the island country.

By March, Kennedy was in Costa Rica meeting with the presidents of six Latin American countries. The leadership cartel pledged mutual support in the fight against communism. In June, before the graduating class at American University, President Kennedy announced a "strategy of peace" to end the Cold War. In his commencement address he called on the Soviet Union to work with the United States to achieve a nuclear test ban treaty, declaring that the U.S. would not conduct nuclear tests in the atmosphere as long as other countries followed suit.

After intensive talks, on July 25, the U.S., the Soviet Union, and Great Britain signed a treaty in Moscow prohibiting the testing of nuclear weapons in the atmosphere, in space, or under water.

With the threat of nuclear war on the back burner at least for the moment, JFK could concentrate on civil rights. In January, George C. Wallace was sworn in as the governor of Alabama. During his speech, Wallace made a pledge of "segregation forever," repeating over and over the now-famous saying, "segregation now."

It wasn't long before the new governor made good his promise. By April, police were using dogs and cattle prods on peaceful demonstrators in Birmingham, Alabama. In May, Birmingham police commissioner Bull Connor turned high-powered fire hoses on protesting high school students.

With vivid, disturbing images of the violent clashes between police and protestors appearing in *Life* and *Time* magazines, as well as in local newspapers across the country, the focus of the civil rights movement landed on Birmingham. Proving the point, on June 11, Gov. Wallace stood in the doorway of Foster Auditorium at the University of Alabama. The governor personally blocked two black students, Vivian Malone and James Hood, from enrolling at the school.

That evening, in a radio and television address, President Kennedy told the American people that the civil rights issue represented "a moral crisis in our nation." Issuing an executive order, the president placed the Alabama National Guard into federal service. As the troops arrived on campus, Wallace finally stepped aside.

A week later, Kennedy sent the most comprehensive civil rights bill proposal to date to Congress, calling its passage "imperative." The bill provided provisions for equal access for all to facilities that were open to the public. It would also allow the federal government to initiate public school desegregation lawsuits.

Despite all efforts, the civil rights issue would burn through the summer and fall of '63.

School remained boring and uneventful, broken up only by lunches with Amy and the gang, and our young, pretty teacher's antics as she struggled with her first teaching job and a class of borderline juvenile delinquents.

As more cooperative weather approached, I once again began to ride my bike over to Amy's a couple of days a week after school. When we weren't eating ice cream and talking music with her mom, we were snuggled together in the back yard play fort, learning more about life and about each other.

Then, on the one-year anniversary of Chris's death, Mrs. Johns drove Amy and me to visit his grave. Afterward, at the local Dairy Queen, the three of us talked frankly about life and about death over chocolate sundaes. It was a talk I'd longed to have with my own parents since the death of my Aunt Mary. Instead, that night I got drunk.

One afternoon in May, with her mom off shopping, Amy and I were amorously making out on the den sofa. Then she pushed away and looked at me.

"What do you want to be?"

Her question took me by surprise. Holding Amy at arm's length, I studied her pretty face. It was determined and serious. "When—what—what do you mean?"

"You know, when we grow up. What do you want to do? Do you ever think about the future?"

My internal warning system was at full alert. This was a dangerous topic. Once again Amy smiled her killer smile. Once again my brain turned to mush, and all I could hear was her soft voice.

"Gee, I… I don't know. I like cars… music… and radio." I replied.

Amy was aware of my encounter with DJ Joe Niagara. I had no choice but to tell her. I had ditched school a couple more times, and she was the only one who seemed to notice or even care. During my subsequent visits to the station, I had met other on-air jocks, including my idol, Hy Lit. Figuring lectures about school and delinquency would do no good and that I would be hanging around the station anyway, the DJs asked me if I would like to work as an intern.

That was a no-brainer. But I knew I would have to clear it with my parents.

Once again, Amy's mom proved to be helpful and supportive. Talking it over with me, she reminded me of the promise I had made to my dad. The last thing I wanted to do was blow this opportunity because of ditching school. Mrs. Johns offered to talk with my mom.

After that conversation, my mom spoke with my dad, laying the groundwork for my big confession. It wasn't easy, telling him that I had cut school despite my promise. He listened, giving me the chance to reason it out and explain the situation. Then he did something totally unexpected, something I'd never seen before. He didn't yell or get upset. He didn't even ground me for missing school. Rather, he and I reached another agreement: I could work at the station on weekends and then two or three days or nights a week during summer vacation. Once again, my school work had to be maintained and there would be no more skipping. This time I was determined to up hold my side of the bargain.

The gang's monthly traveling parties continued on schedule. In March we gathered at Nick's house. April brought warm temperatures and a fun patio party at Marianne's. And then it was Tommy's turn. Tommy and Frankie lived across the street from each other in the new section of Lawrence Park. Taking a cue from our first uncomfortable encounter, I had done my best to stay clear of Tommy's parents, especially his mother.

The night of the party I was first to show up. I wanted to be there when Amy arrived. If Mrs. Grant's look was suspicious, her husband's glare was downright unfriendly. I did my best to shrug it off. Who cared what Tommy's stupid parents thought, anyway? But as more guests arrived, the couple's prejudices became apparent. With the exception of Amy, my friends and I lived in the old section of the development. Tommy along with Frankie lived in the new build-out. Amy's house was located in an older section of Broomall. To the snobbish Grants, old Lawrence Park was the other side of the tracks. And Amy's house was located in the ghetto.

I watched intently as each of my closest friends arrived, each running the embarrassing living room gauntlet, each rudely interrogated under the guise of polite small talk, each the recipient of a disdainful leer. Nothing seemed good enough for the haughty couple. Mrs. Grant looked as if she'd swallowed a sour pickle when Nick disclosed his dad worked as a bartender. By the time Amy arrived, I'd heard enough. Images of Bull Connor and the Birmingham high school students filled my mind. Only it wasn't the bigoted police commissioner, but rather Tommy's dad directing the high-powered fire hoses, his wife beside him, releasing vicious attack dogs. When Amy unwittingly entered this strained atmosphere, I grabbed her by the wrist, quickly ushering her past the irritating couple.

As we reached the steps to the den, I called back over my shoulder, "This is Amy, my girlfriend. Her dad's a Jew and her mom's black." Struggling to contain our laughter, the two of us disappeared downstairs.

We didn't see or hear from the prejudiced parents for the remainder of the night.

My summer of '63 officially began with another Sunday trip to downtown Philadelphia. This time it was just my dad and me. We were headed to the once-glamorous Goldman Theatre to see the American premier of *Dr. No*. In a recent press conference, President Kennedy had admitted that he was a fan of the Ian Fleming spy novels. Previously the English author had achieved only moderate commercial success. Now, not only did the presidential disclosure spark ticket sales at the box office, copies of Fleming's novels began to fly off book shelves across the country. I had no prior knowledge of Ian Fleming or James Bond or Double-O-Seven, but I left the movie house that sunny afternoon a fan. In the car, on the way home, Dad told me about JFK's revelation. By September I had devoured *Live and Let Die, Moonraker,* and *Diamonds Are Forever* and was looking forward to next year's theatrical release of *From Russia with Love.*

Reading and radio made up the bulk of my summer, along with, of course, singing on the corner and more drinking and more sniffing glue. I didn't have much choice. Amy and her family were once again headed for an extended vacation.

∾Chapter Sixteen∾

S chool ended the same way school always ended, which was the same way school always began—on a Wednesday. Only this was just a half day. It was another thing I never figured out. My friend Chris once said the half day in June was St. Pius' way of making up for the half day in December before Christmas vacation. I pointed out that it still made no sense, why school started and ended on a Wednesday. Chris just grinned and said that I thought too much.

Whatever the reason, sixth grade ended with another half day on Wednesday, June 12. Miss Conway looked prettier than ever, probably from the relief of being done with her first year of teaching and being done with the junior JDs in her class. I knew many of the guys who were coming up from fifth grade. She'd better get plenty of rest over the summer.

Unlike the nuns, gifts to lay teachers were more varied and practical. But only a bit more varied. Just as the nuns had their hanky hustle, lay teachers seem to collect scented writing paper. Somewhere, somehow, someone decided that Catholic school lay teachers spent their summer vacations frantically writing to friends and family about their experiences during the school year. And so, as the last of a few dozen nattily wrapped five-by-seven-inch boxes found their way to her desk, Miss Conway looked up with weary eyes.

"Thank you, Daniel. Be sure to thank Mrs. Gibson for the thoughtful gift."

Dopey Dan schlepped back to his desk. I made a mental note to bring a stop watch with me to seventh grade. I was curious how much class time was wasted waiting for Dan when he was called to the blackboard.

The thought passed quickly. I had better things to concentrate on.

Images of a bikini-clad Miss Conway muddled my brain. I pictured her frolicking in the sand, maybe lunging for a volleyball, like the women in the nudist magazines. I could see her slowly layering on sun-tan lotion and gracefully emerging from the ocean, the sun glistening off of her dripping-wet body as she returned to her lounger and the half-written, peppermint-scented letter.

A sharp jab to my right shoulder returned me to reality. "Hey, Delinquent, stop ogling Miss Big Boobs up there and talk to me. Are you coming over after school today?"

I turned in my seat, rubbing my shoulder. She should talk. For a seventh grader, Amy was filling out very nicely.

"I have plans with the guys," I replied. "How about tomorrow? We can spend the day together."

Amy always seemed to know when I was up to something. Of course, according to her, my teachers, my parents, and even my friends, I was *always* up to something. I guess they weren't all that wrong. But I always knew when Amy knew. Her eyes would narrow just a bit and she'd smile with a cute, cat-like, "I know you're up to something" half-smile. She was smiling her cat smile now. And she wasn't wrong.

"Okay, but be careful," she cautioned. "And remember, I leave on Sunday. You've got two months to *play* with your buddies. Try not to overdo."

It was intoxicating the way Amy cared about me. Unfortunately, intoxicating can often turn to smothering, at least in the eyes of the recipient. But for the present I was enjoying her caring nature. "Don't worry, I won't have that much time to *play*. Remember, I'm a working man now."

Amy tried her best to stifle a laugh. She succeeded only in snorting loudly and nearly falling out of her desk. "Some job, you fetch coffee and donuts, and clean and file records three days a week for no pay."

"It's called an internship and its good experience for when I become a big-time disc jockey. And besides, Hy Lit said I could work with him at the record hops."

The fetching feline smile returned. "Yeah, I know what that means—you and all of those girls…"

"Hey, look who's talking. You're not exactly gonna be Miss Lonely Hearts on the beach with that bikini of yours."

This time she connected with a jab to my left shoulder. "It's not a bikini, it's a two piece." But her smile grew, and she blushed. "You like it, huh?"

Now I smiled, too.

"Remind me to wear it for you when I return," she said with a wink.

My after-school plans with the guys included a long night of partying. It probably wasn't our proudest moment. We met in the woods behind Tommy's house just after dinner. I had talked one of my older friends into getting me a fifth of Seagram's Seven. Frankie brought along another bottle of bourbon, and there was plenty of glue to go around. Sometime during the evening, Tommy produced a bottle of his father's gin. It was the first time I'd ever tasted the compelling clear liquor. I puked hard before returning home. Yet by the time I was old enough to drink legally, gin had become my poison of preference.

Amy and I made the most of our last days together. Thursday Mrs. Johns packed us a picnic lunch. We pedaled our bikes over to Springton Reservoir. Sitting by the water's edge, we talked and laughed and kissed. On Friday Amy and I spent the day riding our bikes around Broomall. We stopped at Betsy Parker's on West Chester Pike for chocolate milkshakes and candy. The old-fashioned soda and candy shop had been a favorite hang-out for local kids and teens since the twenties. Cuddled together in the wooden booth, I used my knife to carve our initials alongside countless other hearts and arrows. I wondered how many of the love-struck couples who had shared our booth, were still together.

Meanwhile, Amy slipped a couple of quarters into the be-chromed Rockola. We listened to Connie Francis and Elvis and the Duprees and the Elegants and the Crests. When Smokey Robinson and the Miracles' "You Can Depend on Me" played, Amy buried her face in my shoulder and cried. That night the gang gathered at the Lawrence Park Movie Theatre for one last outing before summer pulled us apart.

Despite my new job at WIBG, I would have plenty of time on my hands to discover the world of secret agent 007, James Bond. Bob's parents were packing him off to some cousin's house out west for the summer. Of course Tommy and Connie would be off in their own private world. But worst of all, Amy and her parents were returning to Wildwood and the Jersey Shore. The night before she left, Amy came over to my house. Hand in hand we wandered up North Central Boulevard to the Little League baseball field. We sat in the bleachers pretending to watch the game. Later, with the game over and the crowd gone, we cuddled together in the gentle darkness of the home team dugout.

"I hate this," Amy said without looking up.

"Same here."

"I'll miss you."

"Me, too."

"It is only for a couple of months."

"So we'll have August together."

"And of course there's the back-to-school carnival…" Amy's hazel eyes glistened in the waning moonlight as she turned and looked at me. She was so beautiful, I wanted the night to never end. I wanted to spend the rest of the summer right there, sitting on the dugout bench, staring into those gorgeous, mystical eyes.

Sensing my feelings, she placed a hand to my cheek. "I love you, Billy."

"I love you, too." The words were out before I realized. I waited.

The sky didn't fall.

The moon didn't explode.

The world didn't come to an end.

My heart did skip an uneasy beat. And I felt my face flush and once again heard my own voice. "I love you, Amy."

On Sunday she was gone.

My first day of working in a radio station turned out to be memorable in many ways. I was officially a member of the WIBG radio staff, albeit an unpaid one. I didn't care; I was living the dream life of every American rock 'n' roller. Tuesday morning I proudly boarded the SEPTA bus, taking my place alongside the other commuters. Arriving at the station, I was greeted by the very pretty but stern receptionist. She cast me a friendly welcome. Ken, the overly serious promotions director, introduced himself and showed me around the facilities. Within thirty minutes I was sitting by myself in a cramped office, stuffing envelopes. It wasn't exactly as I had pictured things.

Around noon, my new buddy Joe Niagara rescued me. We walked down the long hallway to one of the smaller production studios. Joe introduced me to DJ Bob Gale and to WIBG's program director, morning man Jerry Stevens.

"Hey, Billy," Jerry said, warmly shaking my hand. "We need your opinion on something."

What? Me, an unpaid kid intern on his first day, giving my opinion to the jocks that I admired, maybe even worshiped? I swallowed hard. "Oh—oh, okay... yeah." I'm sure my voice cracked. This wasn't exactly as I had pictured things either.

"I think you guys are crazy," Joe declared, setting a stylus into the lead-in groove of a shiny new 45.

Seconds later the ballsy JBL monitor speakers boomed out something new, something strange, something weird but oddly pleasing. Joining them in evaluating the music now filling the room, I watched the others. The three men sat motionless, staring at nothing, listening intently. Joe chewed at the cigar in the corner of his mouth, a barely perceptible smile shadowing his rugged face. It was a smile I'd grow to know and love over the next two decades.

Some two-and-a-half minutes later the music faded. There was a long, uncomfortable silence. Finally Jerry Stevens spoke up.

"I'm sorry, Joe, I just don't see it, not at all."

Bob Gale was more direct. "It's garbage, just garbage. The Brits have never known anything about rock 'n' roll. They're still worshiping Eddie Cochran! Sure he had a couple of decent singles, but—"

Joe puffed deeply on his Cheroot and interrupted. "Rock 'n' roll is evolving, changing, growing. It always has, always will. Look at Motown, the Beach Boys... Phil Spector."

"Phil Spector is a genius; these guys are a bunch of weird-looking nobodies."

I sat there in awe. Regardless of the strange sounds we'd just heard, these highly respected men were debating the very fate and future of rock 'n' roll. The decisions made within this room determined what was heard by millions in the Philadelphia area and, possibly, the entire country. That was the kind of awesome power wielded by the Philly music scene and WIBG radio in the early '60s.

Joe Niagara was determined. He replaced the 45 with another. "This—this—it may not be the next big thing in rock 'n' roll, but we *do* have to take it seriously. We owe it to our listeners." He set the needle in place and looked at me. "You understand, don't you kid?"

I stared blankly and nodded, overcome by the whole situation. The second record started, just as different and strange as the previous one. Yet, there was something...

The trio didn't wait for the song to finish. "You, kid—what do you think?" It was Jerry Stevens.

Nervously I looked from man to man. "Well... I..."

"C'mon, c'mon." Bob Gale was growing impatient with the others. "You know what you like. Would you buy this crap?"

"Hey, take it easy on the kid." Joe leaned toward me. "Don't let these guys scare you, Billy. Go on, tell us what you think."

I picked up the first 45, examining it closely. It was a record label I recognized. Vee-Jay, this was the label that recorded the Four Seasons, Jerry Butler. The group's name made me laugh.

"The Beatles," I said softly. Not catching the word play, I wondered if it might have been a misprint. "I—I don't know. I kinda like it, maybe..." Recalling *American Bandstand,* I looked about the room, shrugging my shoulders. "It has a beat, kinda, but I don't know if you could dance to it. I'll give it a 75."

The comment brought about laughter. I wasn't sure if I had spoken out of turn or not. Joe assuaged my fears. "See, there you go. The voice of America's record-buying teens."

Program director Jerry Stevens wrinkled his face. "But would you buy it, Billy? If it came on your radio would you listen, or turn it off?"

The question frightened me. What if they took my thoughts to heart? What if I was wrong? I thought about Amy. She was a diehard greaser like me. So were all my friends. I could feel the stares of the three men. I bit my bottom lip and shook my head. "No—no, I'd probably turn it off. It's okay—I mean it's not bad, really, but... it's just not what I'm... what we're—used to listening to." I felt bad. "I'm... I'm sorry, Joe."

Joe smiled his cigar smile. "Don't be, kid. Who knows, maybe you're right. Maybe it's just not the right time yet." A stream of blue cherry smoke filled the studio as he spoke. "The Beatles' 'Please Please Me' and 'From Me to You'—someday... someday, I'm sure."

Jerry Stevens rose and stretched. "So it's decided, we shelve them, for now anyway." The others nodded their agreement. Making me a part of their inner circle, Jerry looked at me. "Billy?"

Nervously I nodded.

"Okay, so, I'm deciding, for better or worse it's on me—for now the Beatles are a no-go." Pausing in the doorway, Jerry Stevens turned. "It's a business, kid—a fun, exciting business, but just a business. Only in this business there are no absolutes, no definitive answers. No rights, no wrongs. At best it's a guessing game, and sometimes we out-guess ourselves. Who knows, this may be the biggest thing in rock 'n' roll history. Or..." His smile was reassuring. "Or we may never hear of the Beatles again."

"Segue the next couple of records with a jingle then go into a stop set. I'm gonna go get some air." Hy Lit flashed his agreeable smile, adjusted his trademark tinted glasses, and winked. "You're a natural, kid." Then he disappeared out the studio door.

The lights from the control console cast a soft, yellow glow across the room. I sat at the U-shaped counter, surrounded by a confection of the latest and best broadcast equipment. At my left elbow a stack of 45s teetered like the Tower of Pisa. LP albums, open-reel tapes, spent Pepsi bottles, and the remains of an extra-large, double cheese and pepperoni pizza lay strewn about the studio floor. Overhead the Cleftones' classic "Heart and Soul" spilled from the Altec air monitors.

My internship at WIBG radio found me pulling records, handling the phones, and running errands for two of the country's top DJs. When the engineer wasn't around to see, I even got to man the control board, mixing records, running commercials, and honing a trade that would carry me though adulthood. Mom and Dad weren't happy but tolerated the situation. Then again, what parent wanted their kid to grow up to be a slick-talking rock 'n' roll disc jockey? Their take was the usual over-simplified parental thinking: *Let him be, he'll grow out of it.*

Little did they know.

Philadelphia was ground zero for the burgeoning rock 'n' roll boom. Teens from Philly and across the Delaware Valley, from South Jersey down to the seashore, delighted in the rock 'n' roll, soul, and doo-wop emanating from a station they could call their own. Adults took a different view. Most parents and civic leaders thought rock 'n' roll was just so much noise, with earthy rhythms and a jungle beat that drove young people to perdition. But rock 'n' roll was here to stay. By the early '60s hundreds of stations across the country were rockin' to the new beat, and WIBG was the number one rocker, with Joe Niagara and Hy Lit the top jocks in the nation.

Working with Hy Lit at places like Little Flower and St. Anne's high schools was fun and prepared me well for the disco years to come. And the attention from the opposite sex was exhilarating. But there was something about being on the air that captivated me. From the moment I first set foot in a studio, I knew where my future lay. Joe and Hy were understanding, patient mentors. I took to radio like a needle in a record groove. I discovered there was something mystical, almost spiritual, about an on-air studio at night. When it's just you, the music, the listeners, and the sympathetic glow of the meters, dials, and indicators, you can feel the energy, taste the alchemy. It is the perfect setting for weird and magical things to happen.

Hy Lit returned just as the last commercial was ending. All great DJs have an impeccable inner sense of time and timing. It's part of what makes them great. I punched up a short, personal DJ jingle, potted up microphone A, and gave Hy a nod.

"WIBBAGE, the big 99, and you're rockin' with Hy Lit... 8:22 in the nighttime, in the City of Brotherly Love, with one of Philly's favorite sons. He'll be joining us Saturday night out at Holy

Cross High School, Mr. Lee Andrews along with his Hearts, for Sam and Sherry in Germantown..."

I hit the remote start of the massive QRK turntable. The opening chords of "Teardrops" filled my headphones just as Hy concluded his patter. "... on the Big 99—WIBG!" He smiled, gave me thumbs-up, and I cut the mike. "Nice job, any calls?" Hy fired up a Kool.

"Just the usual—oh, and a Lisa from Chester called. She sounded kinda upset." I read the note in my hand. "She said that you just have to play Tommy Edwards' 'It's all in the Game.' I told her you played it already but she insisted that it was *desperately important* that you get it on."

Hy accepted the paper with the request and grinned. "It always is, Billy, it always is. Pull the record."

"You're going to play it again?"

He snubbed out his half-smoked cigarette, downed a slug of cold coffee, and took my place at the controls. Ten minutes later Hy read the heartfelt dedication over the air, added some poetic words of advice and encouragement to the distressed young couple, and punched up the touching ballad. "That's what we do, kid... that's what it's all about."

Life was good the summer of '63, very good.

You'd think that I would know better.

Naturally I didn't... or didn't care. The life I was living *felt* good, *seemed* perfect. But with Amy gone and most of the gang off doing their own thing, I often found myself alone with my thoughts and my addictions. I continued to drink and to sniff glue. When not working at the station or with Hy at a record hop, I was either high or drunk or both. It seemed to fill in the empty places and dilute the loneliness. I hadn't bothered to notice the marked increase in the emptiness and the loneliness.

Nor was I aware that my addictions weren't with glue or alcohol, but rather lay in the solitude of my self-imposed empty and lonely life. Like it or not, realize it or not, I was a loner. On the outside, I lived a seemingly fun, crazy, idyllic life, openly vying for the attention of anyone who would bother to notice. But I was afraid of letting anyone get too near. Deep inside of me I knew that if I allowed myself to get too close to a person, they would eventually leave me, just as my friend Butch had, just as my grandmother and aunt had, just as Buddy Holly and Patsy Cline and Ritchie Valens had; just as Chris had.

I loved and cared for Amy as well as my young years permitted. But even with her, my girlfriend and friend, I kept a safe, comfortable distance, permitting myself to give just so much and allowing her to get only so close. I didn't understand. And yet, at times it seemed as if Amy understood—understood that one day I would push her away, hurt her.

My demons of confusion and insecurity haunted my nights and clouded my days... except when I was high.

And so I continued to live the life that gave me pleasure, made me feel alive, and made others like me. I continued to smoke and drink and get high and play the part.

Somehow I was able to hide my drinking and glue sniffing from my parents and teachers and most of the guys at the station. I even managed to conceal the loneliness behind jokes and music and my radio and feigned aloofness and a counterfeit cool. On Saturday nights I'd stay sober just long enough to schlep records and equipment to some high school hop with Hy Lit. Frequent trips to the men's room, or outside for some *fresh air,* helped keep my spirits and my confidence up. Girls would gather around, and I'd play the role of the cool dude with the boss job who knew the DJ and spun the best records, and who, if you treated him *just right,* would play your favorite song *just one more time.*

I took my lead from my mentors, but found the fame and popularity as overwhelmingly intoxicating as any liquor or drug. No one bothered to explain that part of the job. Nor did they explain that I should *do as they say, not as they do.* So I followed their lead. It wasn't unusual for Hy to find me, having abandoned my duties, in some dark corner or empty closet, making out with one of the local girls whose name I didn't even know or care to know.

His chidings on the ride home would be to enjoy it while I could, but not to let it go to my head. "It's a great business, Billy; it's whatever you want to do with it. But if you're not careful, it will do you!"

His advice fell on deaf ears; I was already hooked. A new piece of my afflicted personality was being cultivated—that of an obnoxious star. By the time of my first on-air job, it would be in full bloom.

Friday nights were usually spent at the corner school with my older friends. Often I'd already be half drunk by the time we gathered. Procuring my evening's entertainment, usually a pint of gin or bourbon, I'd sit in the bleachers, obvious brown paper bag securely in hand, and watch the Little League baseball game. Then I'd make my way up the grassy hill to the public school playground, where we'd spend the night carousing, rough housing, joking, singing, and passing the bottle.

This Friday night would be different.

She had been sitting in front of me since the second inning. Her hair, straight and blacker than a raven, caught my eye. It was thick and long, reaching down to the small of her back.

Taking a long pull of courage from my paper bag, I reached out, delicately running the back of my hand across several locks of her silken hair. It was soft and shimmered in the late afternoon sun.

She turned, looking me in the eye. "Like what you feel?"

"Oh. I, er, I was… just…"

"Well if I'm gonna let you play with my hair, the least you can do is share your bottle."

Her ebony eyes were blacker than her hair. I felt as if I were staring into a dark, mysterious abyss. "Sure, ah, sure… here."

She accepted the package, placing the bottle to her lips. Her silky hair gently brushed my bare legs as she tilted her head and drank. "Mmm, Seagram's Seven, nice." Stealing another long sip, she returned her gaze, studying my face. "You're sure aren't much of a talker, are you?"

"What—what do you mean?"

"I mean for a DJ, you don't talk much. It's okay, I like that." She smiled, brilliant white teeth contrasting sharply with her deeply tanned, smooth skin. "I saw you last week at the Holy Cross dance."

"Oh... oh, I..." Retrieving my bottle I swallowed deeply. The bourbon burned my throat and steadied my nerves. "I'm not a real DJ, not yet anyway... someday. I work with Hy Lit over at WIBG."

"I know."

"Oh—well, my name is Billy."

She continued to stare at me, as if trying to decide something. "I know that, too. I'm Ronnie."

By now the alcohol had recharged my coolness. "It's nice to meet you, Ronnie. I'm surprised I didn't notice you at the dance."

"If I'd wanted you to, you would have. Dances really aren't my thing. I was bored so I went with some friends." Ronnie took another long drink, finishing off the bourbon. Studying the empty bottle in the bag, she seemed to make up her mind. Taking me by the hand, she stood. It was then I noticed she was dressed all in black: black shorts, black T-shirt, and black Keds. "C'mon, my parents are away. We can get some more."

Ronnie was everything Amy wasn't. She was tall, easily an inch or two taller than me. Her legs were long and slender, accenting her thin waist. Even her breasts were small, firm and pointy. Unlike Amy, Ronnie smoked and could drink as much as me. Kissing her was different, too; not better or worse, but different. Her slim body melted into mine, giving herself up to me with each lingering kiss. I knew she could feel me as our bodies pressed together. I couldn't help myself.

I learned she lived on South Central Boulevard and always dressed in black. Ronnie attended Paxon Hollow Junior High School, and like me she was going into the seventh grade. Her father was some sort of doctor, and both her parents were away on vacation. And she was an only child, left on her own for a couple of weeks. "It's no big deal. They go away a lot. I can take care of myself. And my next-door neighbor comes by to look in on me, at least when she remembers. Besides, I like it, being by myself."

That was all I ever learned about her.

Ronnie and I spent a lot of time together. We didn't talk much, which seemed somehow comfortable and natural. When I wasn't working, we'd meet up at the Little League field and watch the game. After, we'd walk a bit, always in silence, always ending up at her house. Kissing always led to touching, which led to heavy petting. Ronnie would rub me through my jeans, allowing me to lift her shirt and bra and fondle her breasts.

Yet as much as she gave herself to me, there always seemed to be a distance. Ronnie possessed some invisible barrier that she held firmly between herself and me. She kissed and touched with passion and aloofness that was at once both exciting and confusing.

I wondered if Amy felt the same vibe coming from me.

ᒐᔑᗯChapter Seventeenᗒᔑᗒ

In his June 11 speech explaining his position on sending troops to Alabama, President Kennedy had assured the country that "now is the time to act." Southern segregationists took the president's words to heart. Just hours after federalized National Guardsmen arrived in racially besieged Birmingham, Alabama, civil rights leader Medgar Evers was shot and killed by members of the Ku Klux Klan in front of his home in Jackson, Mississippi. Evers was the field director for the NAACP in Mississippi and a key figure in the desegregation of the University of Mississippi, mentoring James Meredith through his attempts to enroll. Although Klan member Byron De La Beckwith was tried twice in 1964, both of his trials ended in a hung jury. Thirty years later, he was finally convicted for Medgar Evers' murder.

The murder polarized the black community, not just in the South, but across the country. Desegregationist's all over the U.S. began to find their voices. On June 18, 3,000 blacks staged a boycott of Boston public schools. The following day, JFK sent his strongly worded civil rights bill to Congress. In August, a youth council from the NAACP began sit-ins at lunch counters in Oklahoma City. That same month, James Meredith became the first black to graduate from the University of Mississippi, amid antagonizing protestors. The ceremonies remained peaceful.

While lawmakers debated the president's far-reaching legislation, across the U.S., civil rights activists—black and white— stepped up their sit-ins, protests, and marches. Clashes between the two factions, often ending in violence, became commonplace on the evening news throughout the summer of 1963.

The unrest culminated in a massive march on Washington, DC.

A coalition of several civil rights organizations, known as the Big Six, was busy organizing a peaceful march on the nation's capital. Although each favored a different approach to the civil rights problem, and each held different agendas, leaders from the Congress of Racial Equality (CORE), the Southern Christian Leadership Conference (SCLC), the Student Nonviolent Coordinating Committee (SNCC), the Brotherhood of Sleeping Car Porters, the National Association for the Advancement of Colored People (NAACP), and the National Urban League all worked together.

The march, to be held in August, was billed as the March on Washington for Jobs and Freedom, or simply, the Great March on Washington. Designed to draw national and international attention to the plight of blacks in the U.S., it also marked the 100th anniversary of the signing of the Emancipation Proclamation by Abraham Lincoln.

But not everyone supported the march or its objectives.

White supremacist groups throughout the South, including the Ku Klux Klan, voiced their opposition. For a time the Klan discussed plans to disrupt the march. Even President Kennedy originally discouraged the march, fearing it might make the legislature vote against civil rights laws that were currently bogged down in Congress. But once it became clear the march would proceed, the president voiced his full support, inviting its leaders to visit him at the White House.

However, some civil rights activists were concerned the planned events might turn violent, damaging the international image of the movement. The march was condemned by Malcolm X, the spokesperson for the Nation of Islam. He felt it presented an inaccurate picture of racial harmony, calling it a "picnic" and a "circus," ultimately labeling the march "the Farce on Washington." In his "Message to the Grass Roots," he accused the leaders of diluting the original purpose of the march, which had been to show the strength and anger of blacks, by allowing white people and white organizations to help plan and participate in the march. Members of the Nation of Islam who attended the march were warned that they faced a possible temporary suspension from the organization.

While march organizers continued to disagree over the purpose of the event, on August 28, 1963, more than 2,000 buses, 21 special trains, 10 chartered airlines, and thousands of private cars—along with regularly scheduled planes, trains, and buses—converged on Washington. Beginning at the Washington Monument, the march proceeded orderly and peacefully, ending at the Lincoln Memorial with a program of speeches and music. Advocates, both black and white, from all over the country and from all walks of life and society, added their names and support to the estimated quarter of a million participants. Charlton Heston, representing a contingent of actors that included Harry Belafonte, Marlon Brando, Diahann Carroll, Ossie Davis, Sammy Davis, Jr., Lena Horne, Paul Newman, and Sidney Poitier, read a stirring speech written by novelist James Baldwin. Music included performances by Marian Anderson and Josh White. Gospel great Mahalia Jackson sang "How I Got Over." Peter, Paul and Mary performed "If I Had a Hammer" and Bob Dylan's "Blowin' in the Wind," while Dylan sang several songs, including "Only a Pawn in Their Game," a gritty ballad about the Medgar Evers murder. Together with Joan Baez, the two folk singers led the crowd in choruses of "We Shall Overcome."

Media coverage of the march was extensive. Speeches and performances were broadcast live by over five hundred cameramen, technicians, and reporters from the major networks as well as by numerous foreign correspondents. While the speeches in general urged the American people to action and called upon the government to pass legislation to aid the cause of civil rights, John Lewis' planned words brought about controversy.

Lewis, a representative of the Student Nonviolent Coordinating Committee, was the youngest of the speakers. His speech, which had been written by a number of SNCC activists, slammed the administration for its inability to protect southern blacks and civil rights workers. Cut from the original dialogue were inflammatory statements calling Kennedy's civil rights bill "too little too late" and asking "which side is the federal government on?"

Another section clipped from Lewis's address claimed that, "We will march through the South, through the heart of Dixie, the way Sherman did. We shall pursue our own scorched earth policy and burn Jim Crow to the ground nonviolently." Even the revised version of John Lewis's speech was controversial and inflamed many in attendance, stating that, "the revolution is at hand... we will take matters into our own hands... we want freedom and we want it now."

Other speakers, including A. Philip Randolph of the Brotherhood of Sleeping Car Porters, called for a decisive yet nonviolent solution to the race problem. Most notable among those addressing the massive crowd was the Reverend Martin Luther King, Jr.

King had come to national prominence in the 1950s. As newly elected president of the Montgomery Improvement Association, King was instrumental in leading the community-wide bus boycott, which followed the arrest of Rosa Parks for her refusal to give up her seat to a white passenger. In 1957, Martin Luther King, Jr., along with Charles K. Steele and Fred L. Shuttlesworth, establish the Southern Christian Leadership Conference. King became its first president, and the SCLC became a major force in organizing the civil rights movement.

Stating, "We must forever conduct our struggle on the high plane of dignity and discipline," King urged nonviolence in civil disobedience and for the movement not to sink to the level of the racists. As the number of racial clashes throughout the South grew and the violence escalated, King became more personally involved in the demonstrations, often finding himself arrested and jailed for his participation and leadership. In April of 1962 he wrote his influential "Letter from Birmingham Jail," stating that individuals have the moral duty to disobey unjust laws.

As key speaker at the March on Washington, Martin Luther King, Jr., delivered his famous "I Have a Dream" speech. Starting off from a prepared text, King said that he was there to "cash a check for Life, Liberty and the Pursuit of Happiness." He also urged his fellow protesters not to "allow our creative protest to degenerate into physical violence. Again and again, we must rise to the majestic heights of meeting physical force with soul force."

Soon, however, King began to depart from his planned script. Citing the American Dream and drawing from religious themes, he spoke of an America where his children "will not be judged by the color of their skin but by the content of their character," calling on everyone to "let freedom ring."

He concluded, "And when this happens, when we allow freedom to ring, when we let it ring from every village and every hamlet, from every state and every city, we will be able to speed up that day when all of God's children, black men and white men, Jews and Gentiles, Protestants and Catholics, will be able to join hands and sing in the words of the old Negro spiritual, 'Free at last, free at last. Thank God Almighty, we are free at last'."

His speech and the March on Washington made a lasting and far-reaching impression on the American people and on the struggle for racial equality, which continues to be felt today. On January 23, 1964, the 24th Amendment abolished the poll tax, which had been installed after the Civil War in eleven southern states to make it difficult for poor blacks to vote. That summer, the Council of Federated Organizations, a network of civil rights groups that included CORE and SNCC, launched a massive effort to register black voters. The council also sent delegates to the Democratic National Convention to protest and attempt to unseat the official all-white Mississippi delegation.

On July 2 President Johnson signed the Civil Rights Acts of 1964, the far-reaching legislation that had been initiated by President Kennedy the previous year. With the push throughout the South for racial equality, the summer of 1964 would become known as the Freedom Summer.

But despite the advancements brought about by the March on Washington, the road to racial equality would remain a long, troubled, and violent one. Less than one month after the march, four young girls attending Sunday school were killed when a bomb exploded at the Sixteenth Street Baptist Church, a popular meeting spot for Birmingham civil rights workers. Following the bombing, peaceful demonstrations turned to riots in several southern cities including Birmingham, leaving two more dead.

Martin Luther King, Jr., would fall victim to the continuing violence when he was assassinated as he stood on his hotel balcony in Memphis, Tennessee, on April 4, 1968.

With Amy away I began spending more and more of my free time with Ronnie. Often she'd accompany me when I met with my older friends. As always we'd gather at the public grade school up the street from my house. Aside from harmonizing old doo-wop tunes, there was the ever-present fifth of bourbon to pass around and the occasional dime bag to sample. Ronnie was cool and didn't lecture me about my drinking and smoking, often joining us. The guys seemed to like her and accepted her into our group. They knew about Amy but were true to the unwritten street code and never mentioned her around Ronnie. I thought this older bunch of guys was the epitome of cool, and I longed to be like them. I would do anything to get their acceptance and approval. But their negative influences were beginning to manifest themselves in some seriously bad behavior—behavior well beyond what my father and other adults of the time termed simple rambunctious boyhood antics.

Dad refused to subsidize the bus rides to my internship at WIBG. And I was requiring increasing amounts of money to satisfy my growing addictions to alcohol and glue. Other guys my age were busy mowing lawns or running paper routes. That seemed like too much work. One evening, while sharing a fat rolled joint, Johnny Mancuso gave me an idea. Sunday mornings, if I wasn't too hung over, I'd rise early and thumb my way down to West Chester Pike. Finding a suitable paper box, I'd deposit my fifty cents and liberate about a dozen copies of the Philadelphia Sunday Bulletin. Then I would hightail it over to the busy intersection of City Line Avenue, where I'd sell my misappropriated newspapers to passing motorists.

Parents being parents, my folks chose to believe I was attending church. I bragged about my new enterprise to my doo-wop buddies. It wasn't long before they presented me with a few handy pocket tools for breaking into newspaper boxes as well as cigarette machines and pin ball games. No one in my home ever questioned why I always seemed to have an unlimited supply of quarters.

I had also recently begun to steal the tubes of glue I was sniffing. The friendly, inattentive, grandmotherly ladies who ran Hobbyland made it easy. This soon led to the filching of other young boy necessities, such as candy, baseball cards, pocket knives, sunglasses, and even small presents for Amy. But, incredibly, just like my beloved transistor radio, my most serious and dangerous transgressions stemmed directly from my father's desire to bond with his maturing son.

One bored afternoon Tommy, Frankie, and I were hanging around the shopping center, doing our best to stay out of trouble. Taking a roundabout route back to Tommy's house, we crossed Reed Road and began to explore. Behind Lawrence Park Shopping Center lay a sprawling expanse of open fields that at one point in the past were part of a large working farm. The main house had long since burned down, leaving only a couple of dilapidated, abandoned out-buildings. Rumors about the property and the barn had been circulating around our town for decades. While the property dated back to Civil War times, the most popular and persistent of these rumors involved runaway slaves and lynchings and ghosts. Naturally we had to investigate.

I handily popped the rusted lock from the rotting wood with my knife. The three of us peeled back the ancient door and cautiously slipped into a musty, rundown barn. To our dismay there were no ghosts or rotting corpses. There was something better.

The dusky sunlight filtering through the hundreds of cracks in the weather-worn wood slats revealed a very cool surprise. Preserved under an inch of dust lay a nearly rust-free Model A body sitting atop a lowered '32 Ford frame. The fenderless roadster sported a chopped windshield, chrome teardrop spotlights, and frenched-in taillights. Showing its vintage, it was powered by a hopped-up, late model Ford flathead V8 engine, complete with open headers and three Stromberg carburetors.

We were in car Nirvana.

It was obvious the vehicle had been setting forlorn for many years: the tires had begun to dry rot, the pleated leather interior was cracked and torn, there were large, dried piles of chicken crap everywhere, and squirrels and rats had claimed the open engine compartment as home. But to three wide-eyed, impressionable young boys, it could have been Ed Big Daddy Roth's famous Outlaw roadster.

After hours of examining the forgotten hot rod, I returned home filled with fanciful dreams of resurrecting the discarded custom. Dad had other ideas. Glossing over the obvious breaking and entering charges, his practical thinking in sorting out the difficulty of locating the owner, securing a proper title if one existed, and then rebuilding and refitting the vehicle won out.

However, I was not about to be so easily dismissed. An interest in cars was one of the few things my dad and I shared. And he was well aware of my over-the-top fascination with anything automotive, especially hot rods. We watched NASCAR races on TV and attended hot rod and custom car shows together. Compared to my preoccupation with radio, a career as an auto mechanic delighted my parents. To that end, Dad and I had talked over the possibility of picking up an old junker. We'd park it in the garage, where I could tinker and learn. My infatuation with the homeless hot rod my friends and I had found seemed to push the idea over the top. But what turned out to be my first car was anything but a junker.

My sister Mary had a girlfriend whose boyfriend was sixteen. His first car was a gorgeous, low-mileage 1954 Dodge Coronet that he shared with his mom. Unfortunately, the car was broadsided at a busy intersection. His mom was uninjured, but the vehicle suffered extensive damage. Three months of rehabilitation in the high school's auto shop left the once proud Dodge battered and broken but still street worthy. In June we purchased the ungainly, black-primered car for $40. Since it was still legally titled and licensed, one of my father's few restrictions was not to do anything to impede the car's running condition. I was free to practice and hone my mechanic's skills, even allowed to try my hand at some simple customizing.

Overnight I became the envy of our clique.

My dad entrusted the keys to the Dodge, which I had dubbed "Princess" for unknown reasons, to me. But I quickly discovered our small, single-car garage too confining to accomplish many mechanical repairs. With Dad at work and Mom off to some photo shoot or play rehearsal, I would carefully back my car out of the garage, then spend the day tinkering and fixing and learning, slipping Princess back inside before my father's return. But one day I managed to flood the engine and was caught red-handed. Dad gave me his sternest, most disappointed look and appropriated my car keys. I could tell he wasn't very upset, perhaps maybe even a bit bemused by his son's irresistible disobedience.

Undaunted, I studied my Chilton's repair manuals the way my folks wished I studied my school books. In an age before steering wheel locks, keyless ignitions, and burglar alarms, I taught myself how to hot wire a car, bypass an ignition system, and jimmy door locks. By mid-July I had memorized every vulnerable point on every popular make and model automobile. Who needed car keys?

It wasn't long before I put my new-found skills to use.

It was a warm August night, and my street corner buddies and I had been hitting the Old Harper and the harmonies pretty heavily. Around eleven, Allan Sarafino, Louie's older brother, showed up in his cool '60 Impala. We'd long since finished the bourbon, and he and Matt Thomas took off in Matt's Mercury in search of more liquor.

"Hey, I got a cool idea." It was Joe Capone.

"You, an idea? That's scary."

"Yeah—the last idea you had sent us all up in flames."

We all laughed.

"No, listen, man, wouldn't it be funny if we stole Allan's new car?"

Larry Cartelli shook his head, spitting a wad of Bazooka gum onto the pavement. "Are you crazy, man? Allan loves that car, he'd kill you!"

"Yeah, right—says you—"

"No man, he's right. We could move it, hide it."

The idea of stashing Allan's beloved convert brought about more laughter and discussion.

Finally someone spoke up. "Forget it, man; he took his keys with him."

"I can start it." The words were out before I realized. All eyes landed on me. I met their incredulous looks. "No, really." I had made up a set of wires with alligator clips and a small push-button switch for starting my Dodge. Carrying them in the back pocket of my jeans made me feel cool, like a true JD. I eagerly held them up to the disbelieving group.

"What the hell?"

"Hey, wait up. Let's see what the little dude can do."

I froze, trying my best not to let my nervousness show. Okay, now was the time to put up or shut up. This was my big chance to prove myself to my older buddies, to show myself a true juvenile delinquent. Taking a deep breath, I headed to the school's parking lot, the others in close tow. Luckily, Allan had left the top down. Not having to deal with the door lock would make things simpler.

By now I had managed to calm my nerves, and I carried the confidence of a seasoned pro. Giving the guys a reassuring nod, I popped the hood of the Chevy. This would be a piece of cake. In seconds I had hotwired the coil and bypassed the ignition switch. I gave the throttle a short pump and pressed my remote starter button;

the muscular 348 motor came to life. The roar of the throaty exhaust was matched by a chorus of whoops and hollers and cheers.

"Cool, man, cool!"

"I told ya he could do it."

"That's boss."

"Okay, let's ditch this short and get back and watch the fun." Larry Cartelli opened the driver's door. "C'mon, man let's go." He was looking at me.

The nervousness returned. The furthest I had driven any car was pulling Princess in and out of my garage. Again all eyes found me, challenging me, daring me. I dropped the hood, smashing my index finger in the process. Ignoring the pain and maintaining my shroud of cool, I slipped behind the steering wheel. Thank God the car was an automatic. Timmy and Johnny Mancuso piled into the back seat while Larry Cartelli claimed shotgun.

It was decided we'd leave the Chevy a block away, over on South Central Boulevard. The ride lasted maybe three minutes. They were the longest three minutes of my young life. I don't think I breathed the entire time. I had to sit forward on the seat in order to reach the pedals. The hood stretched at least a mile before me. Fortunately there were no stop signs or cross streets or traffic to distract me. We pulled up in front of Paul Christopher's house, retrieved my "tools" and were back at the schoolyard. I received a hero's welcome. At the moment, all I wanted was a drink.

Figuring it wouldn't be a good idea to hang around when Matt and Allan returned, we decided to call it a night. I'd had my first taste of driving and was primed for more. But the adrenalin rush of doing something so bold, so crazy like hot-wiring a car—actually stealing a car—hit me like my first shot of alcohol, my first sniff of glue. I was hooked.

By the end of the year I was sneaking Princess out of the garage for joy rides with Amy and the gang. And my skill at snatching cars became a developing talent I would put to good use in the near future.

✒Chapter Eighteen✑

I can remember reading about the March on Washington in the newspapers. And of course radio and TV coverage was extensive. I remember being impressed with the sheer numbers and the focused effort. And I remember my father worrying and mumbling something about "the true nature of the peaceful demonstration." But I really don't remember many of the details. I had more important things to think about.

Amy would return from Wildwood the second week of August. I was still meeting Ronnie at the Little League field, but her parents had returned from vacation. Our time together was limited to walks in the woods, hanging around the public grade school, or making out after the Little League game. None of this deterred us from sharing a bottle of Seagram's Seven and some heavy petting. Oddly, the first time, Ronnie led me over to the visitor's dugout. The third base side became our spot, while the home team dugout remained exclusively for Amy and me. Sometimes fate has strange ways of conveying its message.

Ronnie fascinated me. I wasn't in love. But her quiet nature and free spirit appealed to me. Like me, she was a loner. Yet she was totally comfortable with herself in every way. I envied her.

During Amy's first weekend back, Hy Lit had two big record hops scheduled—one at Cardinal O'Hara High School and one across town at St. Anne's. I had promised to work both. Amy seemed put out by my decision to work instead of be with her.

On her second day back, we sat on the log at the barn by her house. I could sense her disappointment. But there was something else, something I couldn't quite put my finger on.

"You've had lots of time while I was gone. Why do you have to work both nights?"

"It's what I do, you know that. I just... just..." I struggled for words. I was sure she wouldn't understand. How could she, when I couldn't even explain?

"I know it's *what you do*. I just thought we'd spend our time together before school starts, that's all." Frustration showed in her pretty face. I didn't know what to say, how to answer her. The thrill and excitement of working with Joe and Hy was all-consuming. If I could have quit school and worked full-time I would have.

"We've got the rest of August to be together. And don't forget about the Back to School Carnival."

Amy smiled. That seemed to appease her, at least for the moment. But truth be known, I was looking forward to the weekend. It wasn't that I didn't want to be with Amy. I loved being with her. But the mistress of fame and popularity sang a sweet, irresistible siren song. I was drawn like a moth to a flame, fully knowing I would only get burnt. This wouldn't be the first time confusion and conflict between my personal and public life would rear its ugly head. In a few short years I'd be faced with the difficult choice between career, friends, and family. At times I'm not always sure I made the correct one.

The rest of the month was no less challenging. I divided my time between interning, hanging with the gang, seeing Amy, and singing with my older buddies. Most of the time, I managed to remain just shy of totally drunk or high. I even continued to see Ronnie, stealing a couple of nights a week with her at the ball field and an occasional afternoon at my house. But Amy was slowly becoming more difficult and needy, demanding more of my time. I reasoned that things would return to normal when we returned to school in a couple of weeks. At the same time I began to wonder if she suspected something.

The Lawrence Park Shopping Center Back to School Carnival returned with more rides, more games, and more food booths. I even got to show off a bit in front of my hometown. On opening night, Joe Niagara held a record hop on the front steps of the Lit Brothers Department Store. I stood on stage proudly spinning records before friends and neighbors alike, while Joe entertained the sizeable crowd with his patented patter and engaging personality. Claiming that he needed to pick something up at the drug store, my father led my mom through the gathering, and I thought I spied a glimmer of pride in his eyes.

The entire gang had returned from vacation and reformed. They danced and sang along to the rock 'n' roll I played, which blared from two large, portable speakers. Amy smiled up at me curiously, but what I thought I saw in her eyes confused me. I did my best to ignore the uneasy feeling turning in my stomach. The cheerful, encouraging crowd made it easy.

By 11 p.m. the equipment was packed in the back of the radio station's truck. Pointing toward Amy with his cigar, Joe patted my shoulder. "Nice job, Billy. I see you've got more than one fan out there; is she someone special?"

Amy stood in the parking lot, chatting with Tommy and Connie and the others. Despite everything, I had missed her the last two months. "Yes, sir," I said. "I guess maybe she is at that."

"It's important that you know that," Joe replied. "Always be sure of what's important in your life." He sighed, taking a long, contemplative draw from his Cheroot. "It's not always so obvious, kid; sometimes not obvious at all." Joe smiled and slipped me a $10 bill. "Go on, have fun with your girlfriend. Win her something special. I can take care of this stuff back at the station."

Accepting the folded bill, I wondered why all parents couldn't be like Joe and Hy—cool and hip and understanding of what it's like to be young. Thoughts of Amy's mom and Mr. Roland and Tommy's parents flashed through my mind. I wondered what President Kennedy thought of rock 'n' roll and what kind of a parent he'd be when his two small children became teens. Then my dad's expression as he looked up at the stage returned to me. Life was confusing, confounding. And it didn't seem to be getting any easier.

I put the thoughts out of my mind as I slipped the sawbuck into my jeans. I had something to do, something I'd been planning for a while. Little did I realize I was about to make my young life even more confusing.

"Thanks, Joe. See you at the station tomorrow." Hopping down from the make-shift stage, I joined Amy, Tommy, Connie, and the rest of the gang.

By midnight, the ten of us had covered the fair, playing the games, sampling the rides, joking with the carnies, and washing down the fair food with the contents of Tommy's flask. After several tries, Tommy managed to win a big, stuffed dog. Connie squealed and hugged the dog and then Tommy and then the dog again and then both of them. Her over-the-top exuberance wasn't lost on the fact that the nine bucks Tommy burnt trying to win the cheap toy would have bought a half dozen stuffed dogs at W.T. Grant's.

Amy and I shared a large, soft pretzel and a cherry snow-cone followed by pink cotton candy. I spent a few bucks on the ring toss, going after some trinket, but my mind was elsewhere. A couple of times I thought I saw Ronnie in the crowd. Shrugging it off, I steered Amy over to the Ferris wheel. Dominick had taught me well. I slipped the operator a couple of dollars with our tickets.

"I thought you didn't like Ferris wheels?" Amy said.

I glanced up at the towering ride. "I never said I don't like Ferris wheels. Its heights I'm not too fond of."

Knowing Amy well, and wanting everything to be perfect, I waited until a pink seat came around. The operator gave me a knowing wink as he secured the bar across our laps. As we began our slow climb to the top, I spied Ronnie walking alone across the parking lot. Conflicted feelings of guilt and excitement shook me. I was with Amy, and yet seeing Ronnie stirred something inside of me, something different.

As usual, Amy read the confusion on my face. "Hey, you okay? You look a little green."

"Yeah, yeah, I'm okay, it's just—just the height. I'll be okay."

Amy moved closer and placed a hand on my leg. "You're thinking about Chris, aren't you?"

Memories of that day in May returned. I had laid there, some fifteen or twenty feet up, my arms and legs desperately clutching the tree branch, unable to move, unable to pull my eyes from Chris's lifeless body. It had taken the fire department's hydraulic bucket and two fire fighters to bring me down. "Yeah, but I'm fine…"

I slipped my arm around Amy, drawing her near, and watched as Ronnie disappeared down Warren Boulevard.

The operator had gotten my message. After a few minutes of circling up and down, up and down, our seat came to a halt at the top of the wheel. I held Amy close as we both took in the view. All of Lawrence Park lay at our feet. I could make out my street in the distance and Loomis Public Grade School. I wondered if any of the guys were there singing. Off to the left, the peak of St. Pius X Church could be seen, cast in the stark, white glow of car headlights snaking their way up busy Lawrence Road. It was a beautiful, warm night, with a sharp Carolina moon cradled high in the sky. All confusion and doubt seemed to disappear, taken up into the cloudless, star-filled sky. Amy was in my arms. She was beautiful. I wanted the moment to never end.

With unsure hands, I reached into my jeans pocket.

The ring was silver—plated silver over some cheap metal. It had an open design with delicate filigree swirls and flowers that resembled daisies, and it had cost me five bucks at Woolworth's jewelry counter. In the mellow mantle of the crescent moon, its polished surface shone with a gentle glow. My hands trembled as I held it before Amy.

"Oh…"

It wasn't exactly the response I was expecting.

"Oh," she repeated softly.

I tried to speak. I found my tongue had cleaved to the roof of my mouth once again. Amy looked at me, a mixture of uncertainty and fear clouding her hazel eyes. "Are—are you asking me to—to go steady?"

Good question.

Well, was I? Wasn't that what we had been doing all along? Nothing had ever been spoken, but it seemed like we did have some sort of unspoken understanding. Or did we? What about the girls I picked up at the record hops, and what about Ronnie? And why exactly *was* I giving her this ring? It occurred to me I might have figured all this out beforehand.

I glanced down at the ring and then looked at Amy. Right on cue my brain went to mush. "Uh, yeah—yeah, sure..." That had to be the lamest proposal in the history of teenage romance.

Amy continued to stare at the ring. "Gee, I... I don't..."

Again, not exactly the response I wanted. "If you don't want to, I mean, we can—"

"No... it's just that I wasn't—"

The Ferris wheel started up with a jerk. We both lurched in the seat before regaining our balance. Clinging tightly to Amy as the ride began to move, I realized I no longer held the ring. This definitely wasn't how things were suppose to go. Panic set in—had Amy noticed? I anxiously scanned the floor of our seat. Nothing. The ring was gone.

Nearing the bottom, the Ferris wheel slowed. I figured our ride, along with our relationship, had reached its end. We were barely moving now. A big, wide, tobacco-stained grin with two missing front teeth greeted us. "Looking for this?"

Amy snatched the ring from the operator's greasy palm, and the wheel once again sped up. Giving me her "Honestly, Billy, sometimes I just don't know about you" look, she unfastened the silver chain that hung around her neck. It held the souvenir coin I had sent her from Missouri. Slipping the ring into place, she began to refasten the necklace. I reached out. "Here, let me do that."

Amy jumped in her seat, nearly upsetting us. "No! No, that's all right, I've got it."

September 4, 1963, marked the first Wednesday of seventh grade. The Hot Line between Washington, DC, and Moscow was in full operation; the CBS Evening News was now operating each night for a full thirty minutes; Charlie Finley's lawyers were working on moving the Kansas City A's baseball team to Oakland; and unknown singer Allan Sherman had moved into the number two spot on Billboard's Top 100 Chart with his irreverent and funny "Hello Mudda Hello Fadda." But the song that poured from everybody's radio, record player, juke box, and lips that September was the Angels' infectious "My Boyfriend's Back." The number one song in the country was everywhere, including on Amy's sweet lips—*especially* Amy's sweet lips.

It was as if she were trying to tell me something.

The angry skies had cleared somewhat after last night's thunder storm, as I trudged up Cornwall Hill on first Wednesday. Today's *Delaware County Daily Times* front page headlines declared, "3-Inch Deluge Drowns Delco." The violent thunder and lightning storm had kept me company as I lay in bed awake, listening to Jerry Blavat go on about young teenage love. Okay, I was young... and as far as I could tell I was in love... that was two out of three... But his advice didn't help, leaving me to my own confused thoughts. The rains may have drowned Delaware County, but they did little to dampen Amy's enthusiasm.

The night I gave Amy the silver plated friendship ring from Woolworths I had made it official: Amy and I were boyfriend-girlfriend—going steady. She hugged and kissed me like I had returned home from the war. So far so good... that *was* more like the reaction I was expecting and hoping to receive.

But the next morning I awoke to a ringing telephone. It was Amy. Amy never called me. But when you stir up female emotions with a cheap, silver-plated, five-and-dime ring, you never know what is going to float to the top. Amy's voice chimed brighter than a chromed teardrop spotlight on a custom Merc as she explained to my mom all about the ring, and the Ferris wheel, and the bumbling, romantic way I had presented it to her. By the time I was handed the phone, Mom was grinning like the Cheshire Cat. Amy chatted and squealed and squealed and chatted, exactly like the girls I tried my best to avoid, the ones Chris had warned me about, all gushy and girly. I barely got in a hello. The decidedly one-sided conversation ended with my new *steady girl* announcing she intended to call everyone she knew and tell them the news.

I had wanted Amy to know how I felt about her. I wasn't expecting the whole world to be in on it. Perhaps that was something else I should have thought out beforehand.

For the next few days I avoided seeing Amy—why, I'm not really sure. By the weekend I had run out of excuses. Sunday night before first Wednesday, I sat at the Johnses' dinner table. The tension was harder to slice than the steak, and thicker. The ring hanging from the chain around Amy's neck screamed aloud, "Look at me everyone, look and see!"

Mr. Johns avoided eye contact with the ring, and his daughter, and me, as well as all unnecessary conversation. Amy's mom rose above the silent cries for attention, making small talk about seventh grade and their vacation and my work at WIBG and nothing in general. I knew full well Amy had told her everything. Amy shared everything with her mom. And now mother and daughter wore the same unsettling, sagacious Cheshire grins. I found it disconcerting to look her mother in the eye. With one simple, innocent act, I had managed to turn her from Amy's mom and my friend, confidant, and ally, to Amy's mom, *Mrs. Johns*, *parent*.

That night I phoned my friend Hy Lit during his Sunday Night Hall of Fame Program. Hy listened patiently and offered up some tired words of encouragement. Five minutes after hanging up he switched open the mike and announced my predicament to the entire teen population of Philadelphia, the Delaware Valley, and South Jersey.

"And now, going out to my main man Billy—that's right, Billy the Kid, my right hand man... all you groovy gals out there know him as the happening cat who spins the platters at Hyskie's record hops. For Billy and his new steady kitten Amy, on the Big 99... WIBG... here's Jimmy Charles."

Thanks, Hy.

Jimmy Charles began his touching peon to teenage angst.

"A million to one, that's what our folks think about this love of ours"

Thanks a lot, Hy.

That night I sank back into my bed, hoping the mattress would swallow me up whole, then spit me out, depositing me into some universe where there were no such things as feelings and emotions.

Now, as I slogged up the old Widow Maker hill on first Wednesday, I could imagine the taunts and jeers from the usual boneheads, male and female alike. By now the whole school would be a-buzz with the news: Billy and Amy were going steady.

I cranked up my radio. Frankie Valli's falsetto urgings to "Walk like a Man" did little to placate my rampant thoughts.

The effects of the March on Washington were still being felt in the nation's capital on first Wednesday, as well as across the rest of the country. A new, positive energy seemed to permeate the battle for civil rights. Peaceful protests and quiet sit-ins were quickly becoming the demonstrations of choice. But not everyone was willing to accept the new order.

By September 2, Alabama's governor, George Wallace, was up to his old tricks. This time the southern segregationist ordered state troopers to surround Tuskegee High School to prevent its integration. The standoff lasted a week, prompting demonstrations and claiming national headlines. Finally, on September 9 the governor was served with a federal injunction to remove the officers encircling the building. The following day, with President Kennedy once again utilizing federalized National Guardsmen, twenty black students entered public schools in Birmingham, Tuskegee, and Mobile.

But violence continued to challenge the Reverend Martin Luther King's call for peaceful resistance. September 15 would be the day when four young girls were killed as they prepared their Sunday School lessons on "The Love That Forgives"—killed when a bomb exploded in their church. It would take four decades before all of the murderers were brought to justice.

The same day as the church bombing, two young black brothers, James and Virgil Ware, were shot at as they rode their bicycles home. Virgil died, spurring further statewide protests. In Birmingham, vicious police attack dogs were turned loose on the peaceful demonstrators.

Later in the month, President Kennedy spoke before the UN General Assembly in New York City. Drawing on the success of his negotiating a nuclear arms test limitation treaty with England and the Soviet Union, the president proposed a joint U.S.–Soviet expedition to the moon. The motion was initially met with enthusiasm but failed to gain much momentum in either country.

Meanwhile, my Phillies were having a typical roller-coaster year. Manager Gene Mauch piloted his team to an 87–75 record, finishing the season in fourth place, twelve games behind the National League Champion LA Dodgers. The Dodgers would sweep the defending New York Yankees in four games to capture their second World Series title in five years.

But it was the music news coming out of Philadelphia that would have a drastic and far-reaching effect on teens across the country.

Dropping the Monday thru Friday format it had followed since 1952, on September 7 *American Bandstand* began to air once a week on Saturday afternoons. Rumors of the show's ultimate demise were finally put to rest the following February, when the long-running Philly favorite left town forever to set up operations in Los Angeles. *American Bandstand* would continue as a Saturday afternoon staple for two more decades. Ironically, the switch to Saturdays came as a welcome blessing to teens in Texas. ABC TV affiliates WFAA in Dallas and KTRK in Houston, which had long refused to air the popular rock 'n' roll show, finally added the music and dance program to their line-ups.

Perhaps even more telling of the changes that would soon shake rock 'n' roll and the entire music industry to its core were two incidents that took place with very little fanfare. On Saturday, September 7, the same day that *American Bandstand* went weekly, a little-known group from England made its American TV debut on ABC's *Big Night Out.* In a pre-recorded segment from Didsbury Studio Centre in Manchester, England, the Beatles sang two original songs: "From Me to You" and "She Loves You," as well as a cover of the Isley Brother's "Twist and Shout." The performances, although energetic and noteworthy, were soon forgotten, along with the short-lived variety program.

And then, on September 28, popular New York DJ Murray "The K" Kauffman played "She Loves You" on his nightly WINS Radio program. Kauffman had moved to WINS-AM in 1958 with an all-night music show he called the "Swingin' Soiree." After Alan Freed was forced off the air as a result of the payola scandals, Murray The K took over his 7 to 11 p.m. time slot. But the post-modern style of the Beatles' recording received a very lukewarm reception with greased-back New York rock 'n' rollers. In another six months, as American teens began to warm to the new sounds from across the pond, Murray The K would bill himself as the Fifth Beatle.

My only thoughts on first Wednesday were of Amy and my friends and what lay ahead. Seventh grade at St. Pius X started out well enough. Most of the gang once again landed in the same class, and our new teacher, Sister Alverez, actually seemed to be pretty cool, for a nun. I found myself in a seat over by the windows, which didn't help my attention. Amy was stuck in the back of the second row. No more passing notes and whispering secrets. We'd have to make do with seeing each other in the schoolyard.

I had entered the schoolyard cautiously. Looking around, everything seemed normal. Girls gathered and chatted about vacations and summer romances and personal changes, although it was obvious some had changed more drastically than others. On the boys' side it was business as usual: games of tag; flipping, trading, and comparing baseball cards; good-natured name calling; and rough housing. I still found myself searching for my friend Chris. For over six years he'd been the first person I sought out every school morning. Although I would deny it to myself and anyone who bothered to ask, I still missed him badly.

First Wednesday of seventh grade, the first person I found was Amy. Or, more correctly, she found me.

"Hey, Delinquent—over here!"

I swallowed hard, trying to ignore my fears and calm my emotions. How was I going to play this? Better yet, how was she going to act? I didn't like the thoughts or feelings racing out of control. Being with Amy had always been fun, easy, natural. Now everything had changed.

I didn't know what to do.

I didn't have to decide. Waving wildly and smiling like she'd slept with a coat hanger in her mouth, Amy raced across the schoolyard. Luckily, no one seemed to notice.

No yet anyway…

Landing in my arms, Amy hugged me tightly. "Oh, it's so good to see you!" she exclaimed aloud. I was certain the declaration was more for the benefit of the school. Jump ropers stopped jumping; gossipers stopped yakking; card players stopped flipping. All now stared at the couple standing in the middle of no-man's land.

It was then Amy chose to kiss me.

I wasn't exactly a stranger to public displays of affection. Ronnie and I had shared some steamy moments on the Little League bleachers. But those around had been strangers or neighbors I couldn't care less about. Even Amy and I had had our amorous public moments.

This was different.

Amy pulled me closer, standing on tiptoes and pressing her lips to mine. I returned the kiss, keeping my eyes wide open, wondering what I should do next. Again, the decision was made for me. A resounding chorus of "Oooooooo!" rose up in unison from both sides of the schoolyard. While I turned a crimson shade of shame, Amy started to laugh, burying her head in my chest. The next thing I knew a pale white, bony hand was clawing at my shoulder. I turned.

It was Sister Alverez.

"All right now, that's enough of that. The schoolyard is no place for that sort of thing." She looked me in the eye and then winked. "At least not on first Wednesday."

ᴄ✐Chapter Nineteen✎ᴐ

According to Webster's, the definition of the word "boring" is, "Seventh grade at St. Pius X Catholic Grade School." Sister Alverez turned out to be sweet, kind, and understanding—and so boring you wanted to shove a number two pencil into your ear until it came out the other side. By mid-October I would have welcomed even a sharp rap across the knuckles from Sister Tres-Martin's stiff wooden pointer. At least it would have been something. As it was we were trapped; trapped in the mind-numbing hamster wheel of multi-syllabic, mixed metaphor, decimal dividing, state capital, I before E except after C, Western expansion. You could read the misery in the painful expressions of the sad inmates.

At least I could look out the window. A beautiful Indian summer had settled over the Delaware Valley, and there were plenty of autumn blossoms and foraging squirrels to keep me entertained. Poor Amy cast hopeless, forlorn looks to me from her seat on the far side of the room. Surprisingly, I found her distance—and the resulting absence of gentle pats and subtle remarks and teasing taunts—strangely refreshing. I did, however, catch myself from time to time missing the ever-present, alluring scent of orange. But more and more my thoughts wandered to Ronnie.

Since first Wednesday, Ronnie and I had seen each other only a couple of times. I found I missed her company, wondering what it was like for her at Paxon Hollow Junior High. In my usual hurry to grow up, seventh grade couldn't end soon enough. Then it would be eighth grade and finally I'd be done with St. Pius forever. I couldn't wait to move on to public school.

I'd be joining Ronnie at Paxon Hollow in the ninth grade.

But Amy would be going on to Cardinal O'Hara. And so would the rest of the gang.

Change, the one thing that seemed most constant in my life, was also the one thing I hated the most. Why did things have to change? Then again, I was looking forward to changing schools, and leaving the nuns behind, and being old enough to drive.

As usual, I buried my confused feelings in alcohol. I didn't know how to handle the changes happening in my body, my emotions, and my life. No one bothered to tell me this was all a perfectly normal part of growing. Weekend evenings often found Tommy and me and the rest of the guys talking over such things at our meeting spot in the woods.

But none of us could offer up any answers.

And so we drank and got high and got into trouble and did our best to mask the pain of change—of growing up.

My internship at WIBG had all but ended with the start of school. After a few back-to-school record hops with Joe and Hy, I was back to being just plain Billy. But my last gig with Hy Lit would prove to be a memorable one.

The hottest song of the summer had been "My Boyfriend's Back" by a group of girls from Orange, New Jersey. Reaching the top of the charts, the infectiously happy tune turned out to be the biggest hit for three girls known as the Angels.

But it wasn't their first.

The trio's first release back in 1961, a tender ballad titled "Till," had featured the silken, plaintive vocals of Linda Jensen. Thanks to heavy air play on WIBG and numerous appearances at Hy Lit's record hops, "Till" broke out of the Philadelphia market, reaching number 14 on the national charts. Their next release, another ballad, "Cry Baby Cry," also made the top 40. But by 1963 Linda Jensen had left the group to be replaced by Peggy Santiglia. The personnel change and a label switch to Smash Records revived their faltering careers. By September of 1963, "My Boyfriend's

Back" was a million-seller, riding comfortably atop Billboard's charts. The Angels were international stars. But the ladies from New Jersey hadn't forgotten their roots. In late September, while in town to film a segment for *American Bandstand*, the Angels appeared at a Hy Lit record hop.

Sisters Phyllis and Barbara Allbut were sweet and friendly, making a point to talk to me and sign autographs. But it was lead singer Peggy Santiglia who captivated my young heart. Closing the dance with their latest release, "Thank You and Goodnight," she seemed to sing the touching ballad directly to me. By the time she placed a tender parting kiss to my cheek, I was sure I was in love with the beautiful, nineteen-year-old songstress.

I never forgot that evening, and, interestingly, neither did she.

During the summer of 1975 I was hosting an oldies concert at a local night spot. The Angels were headlining. The three girls were as sexy and beautiful as I remembered. But Peggy seemed to recognize me immediately. Eyes wide and smiling sweetly, she hugged me, kissing my cheek.

"Hey, Billy, it's you! From the Hy Lit record hops…"

That was another night I would never forget.

While guests on *American Bandstand* continued to lip sync to their hits, record hop appearances called for a different approach. Minus tracks were 45 RPM records identical to those commercially available but lacking the vocals. Performers sang live into the classic Shure 55 microphone with music provided by the minus track spinning on the turntable. Over the summer I managed to talk Hy out of several of the radio station's spare minus track recordings. Now it was time to put them to good use.

In October the gang's monthly parties resumed, and it was my turn to host. On Tuesday, October 15, I passed out envelopes before class. They weren't invitations exactly. Aside from informing the recipient of the time, date, and place of our next get-together, each contained a couple of 45 RPM records—minus tracks. In lieu of costumes, those attending the Halloween night party would be required to perform. Sing a song. I thought my idea was clever, funny. At first the others weren't so thrilled with having to sing, but they played along.

The night of the party my sister had a date, and Mom and Dad made themselves politely scarce. We had the den all to ourselves. By 10:30 Tommy's flask was empty and the party was in high gear. Dimming the lights, we each took our turns.

Totally ignoring my suggested script, Frankie ruffled his hair, pulling a single, curly bang across his forehead. He rendered up a cool version of Gene Vincent's "Be Bop a Lu Lu." Next a reluctant Nick and Bob teamed up to perform the Kalen Twins' bouncy "When." As could be expected, the gang's resident lover boy had other things on his mind. With Connie seated on a bar stool next to him, Tommy presented a soulful, if slightly off-key, version of Earth Angel.

Then it was my turn.

Not to be outdone, I downed a shot of my dad's bourbon and fetched my guitar. With Amy at my side, I strummed and sang along to one of the first songs I'd learned to play, the Royal Teens' "Believe Me." I'd sung the old doo-wop standard a dozen times with my older buddies. Now, fortified with more Canadian Club, I belted it out with shameless abandon. My strained performance elicited peculiar looks from my father the next morning over the breakfast table.

But it was the girls who surprised everyone. It was the height of the girl group era, and Amy, Connie, Marianne, Marlena, and Sherry took up their positions. They had been secretly practicing for a week. With Sherry remarkably good on lead, our girlfriends performed a sugary, sexy version of the Donays' "Devil in His Heart," complete with wavering choreography and intentional innuendos.

It was a performance for the ages.

Around 11:30 Amy and I slipped out the back door. A bulbous witch's full moon peeked from behind wispy clouds of sullen grey. Amy fell into my arms and immediately began to cry.

"Hey, what's the matter?"

"Why did you give this to me?" She looked up, the friendship ring in hand.

"What—what do you mean? I..."

"You what, Billy? You like me, you love me? What—what about... Ronnie?" She buried her face in my shoulder and continued to cry.

I felt my heart cease its beating. I had no idea what I should say, what I should do. Images of making out with Ronnie in the dugout filled my mind. I loved this sweet girl softly crying in my arms, there was no doubt. But thoughts of Ronnie excited me, made me feel good. A sudden burst of young male testosterone raced through me.

"What about you? You gonna tell me you didn't fool around in Wildwood?"

I have no idea why I said that. The words were out before I realized. Amy looked up again, hurt and confusion twisting her pretty face. Her moist hazel eyes sparkled in the pale moonlight. Again I found myself lashing out without cause. "Well? How about it? Tell me about *your* summer."

Clutching the silver friendship ring, she headed toward the door. "Please—take me home."

As we pulled up in front of Amy's house, Dad turned in his seat. He didn't have to speak. The look on his face cried out, "You need to make this right."

I got out of my side of the car; Amy got out of hers. Before I could say anything, we were met at the front door by her mother. Amy forced a smile. "It's okay, Mom. Can we have a minute?"

Mrs. Johns looked at me and then at her daughter. "Okay sweetheart, I'll be inside." The door closed, leaving us alone.

"I—I can't be with you right now, Billy."

With that, she was gone.

I don't think I slept all weekend. I was angry: angry with Amy for the way she had left things; angry with myself for the way I had treated her; angry, hurt, and confused. I remember at one point flinging my radio across my bedroom. I had been listening to it under my pillow when Little Anthony and the Imperials came on with "Tears on My Pillow," our first slow dance. Amy had cried as we moved across the dance floor, as if she knew, knew even then, that I would hurt her. The tiny transistor struck the wall squarely. Only the good grace of God kept it from shattering into a million pieces.

That weekend I sought consolation with my older buddies. Singing and carousing with them always seemed to make everything better. As we sang and passed the bottle, the cares and problems of the world disappeared into the chilled night air. But even as we broke into a chorus of the funny and racy "Work with Me Annie," I realized most of these guys would soon be gone, heading off to college or the service. In a little over a year everything would be different... surrendered to the fickle winds of my old nemesis, *change*.

I don't remember a lot about the next few weeks. Withdrawing into my own fears and confusions, I became inconsolable. I shied away from my friends, keeping the gang at a distance. Amy and I exchanged uneasy glances at school but found no common ground to speak. Sometimes hurt clouded her pretty eyes, at other times, sorrow. All I could do was turn away. Even drinking didn't ease my deepening depression. I tried, but found I had no desire to get drunk or high.

In spite of all of this I continued to see Ronnie. We met up a few times at the now closed Little League field. But even that wasn't the same anymore. We spoke very little, went through the motions, and then sat in total silence until it was time to go home.

I withdrew further into myself, setting up a thick wall of isolation. Aloof, dark, and mysterious, perhaps even non-social became my unofficial brand. I had become the total loner I admired in Ronnie. The mask felt good, comfortable, like a familiar pair of jeans. On the surface I would continue to make friends and have numerous relationships and, as always, play the part. But it would be a long time before I allowed anyone inside.

Friday, November 22, 1963. The Delaware Valley was still enjoying a mild Indian summer. Temperatures continued to reach ten degrees above average, with plenty of sun. WIBG's weather forecast called for a high in the mid 60s and mostly fair skies. In Philadelphia the large department stores took advantage of the agreeable weather to gear up for their pre-holiday sales. Meanwhile, the Lawrence Park Shopping Center was gaily festooned with strings of lights and garlands in anticipation of Christmas.

Bright sunshine reflected off the two large, chrome fenders of my hefty Columbia two-wheeler as I pedaled up Cornwall Hill. Parking my bicycle in the rack, I grabbed my Army bag and radio and headed across the schoolyard. With the warm weather, there would be no cute pink stocking cap with a pink pom-pom to search for today. It didn't matter. Amy and I still weren't on speaking terms. We had exchanged glances and polite, albeit curt, greetings a few times. And she still wore my ring around her neck. But neither of us seemed willing to initiate conversation, let alone apologize. I had long since come to terms with my rash and hurtful outburst, but stubbornly refused to admit to it publicly.

At 12:40 I sat in the St. Pius X auditorium-cafeteria. I'd traded my peanut butter and jelly sandwich to Tommy for a second dessert of Tastykake Krumpets. Washing down the butterscotch pastry with a pint of Sealtest chocolate milk, I pumped Nick and Frankie for details on the history chapter I'd neglected to read for homework. Rumor had it that Sister Alverez was planning a pop quiz. But my interrogation led nowhere. My friends were as clueless as I was. Later, in the schoolyard after lunch, I managed to lose a

Don Clendenon and a prized Yogi Berra baseball card in a fast game of match.

By 1:29, Miss Keaffer had our class deep into a boring, repetitive period of spelling drills while Sister Alverez taught her class religion. Pretending to follow along, I divided my time between looking out the window and looking at the young lay teacher's shapely legs. A minute later the bell rang, mercifully bringing the mind-numbing session to an end.

We had a short afternoon bathroom break, returning around 1:38. As I took my seat, I gave Amy a smile from across the classroom. Surprisingly, she returned the gesture, flashing her killer smile and melting my heart in the process. Maybe things would be okay after all. I glanced up at the clock: 1:40. If I could time it right, I might manage to steal a few minutes with Amy in the coat closet before she headed out to catch her bus.

Two o'clock p.m. on Fridays had been set aside for some sort of cultural class. St. Pius X was never very big on teaching the arts. Once a week for one full period, we suffered through an anemic lesson on music or literature or poetry. Today it would be Sir Walter Scott's *Young Lochinvar*.

By 2:33 I was fighting hard to stay awake. Five minutes later, as the smell of fresh ink filled the air; I was wishing we were still reading about the exploits of Scott's noble knight. "All right now class, please clear your desks." Sister Alverez began to hand out mimeographed papers. "Please, take one and pass the rest back. And no talking, please!"

Friday, November 22, 1963. The light rain that had been falling in the Dallas–Fort Worth area started to let up. As the skies began to slowly clear, Dallas radio station KLIF promised its listeners a mild autumn day with temperatures in the mid 70s. While area newspapers ran full-page ads for the upcoming holiday shopping season, headlines reported on President Kennedy's visit.

By the fall of 1963, Kennedy and his political advisors were gearing up for the next presidential campaign. While he hadn't formally announced his candidacy, the popular young president seemed destined for a second term. In September, Kennedy traveled west, making speaking engagements in nine different states in just a week. The trip helped to pinpoint topical themes—including education, national security, and world peace—he would highlight during his run in 1964.

In October, JFK spoke before Democratic gatherings in Boston and Philadelphia. Then, on November 12, he held his first political planning session, stressing the importance of winning Florida and Texas. Kennedy was aware of the rift developing between Democrats in Texas. A feud among party leaders could jeopardize his chance of carrying the state in 1964. With his Civil Rights Bill mired down in Congress, it would be imperative to secure the southern stronghold. Finally a trip was planned for a two-day, five-city tour through the Lone Star State.

On Thursday, November 21, President and Mrs. Kennedy arrived in San Antonio, welcomed by Vice President Johnson, Texas Governor John Connally, and Senator Ralph Yarborough. Following a visit to Brooks Air Force Base, the group traveled to Houston, where Kennedy addressed a Latin American citizens' organization and spoke at a dinner for Congressman Albert Thomas. The first day's activities concluded in Fort Worth.

On Friday morning, JFK greeted a crowd of several thousand outside of his hotel. With no protection against the dissipating drizzle, he addressed the gathering.

"I appreciate your being here this morning. Mrs. Kennedy is organizing herself. It takes longer, but, of course, she looks better than we do when she does it." He then went on to talk about the nation's need to be "second to none."

After he spoke at a breakfast for the Fort Worth Chamber of Commerce, the presidential party flew to Dallas's Love Field, arriving at 11:40 a.m. President and Mrs. Kennedy took time to greet and shake hands with a crowd of well-wishers. Jacquelyn looked stunning in her pink suit as she accepted a bouquet of roses from a supporter. Leaving the airport, the motorcade was scheduled to travel a ten-mile route through downtown Dallas to the Trade Mart, where Kennedy was to speak at a luncheon. During the thirteen-minute flight from Fort Worth, with the weather clearing, some reports say the president expressed his desire to have the protective plastic bubble removed from the presidential limousine.

At 12:29 p.m. the presidential party entered Dealey Plaza. A minute later, as the limousine made the turn from Houston onto Elm Street, passing the Texas School Book Depository, gunfire was heard. Witnesses recalled hearing three distinct shots, the last two coming close together. President Kennedy was struck twice, once in the throat and once in the back of the head. Governor Connally, who was riding in the limo's jump seats with his wife, was struck also but would recover from his wounds. As Mrs. Kennedy cradled her mortally wounded husband in her arms, the driver turned on his sirens and sped to nearby Parkland Hospital, arriving about 12:38 p.m.

CBS was the first to break the news of the shooting via television. At 12:40 CST, the network interrupted a live broadcast of *As the World Turns*. With no camera available, Walter Cronkite filed an audio report, saying shots had been fired in Dallas, Texas, and first reports said that President Kennedy had been seriously wounded.

Meanwhile, at Parkland Hospital, a team of doctors and surgeons gathered, working frantically to save the president's life. But Kennedy's wounds were too great, and a Roman Catholic priest was called to perform the last rites. At 1:00 p.m. CST, Kennedy was pronounced dead.

At 1:33 p.m., White House Assistant Press Secretary Malcolm Kilduff addressed a stunned press corps at Parkland Hospital, making the official announcement.

"President John F. Kennedy died at approximately 1:00 CST today, here in Dallas. He died of a gunshot wound to the brain. I have no other details regarding the assassination of the president."

At 1:38 p.m., appearing live on the CBS television network and reading from an Associated Press news ticker, a visibly shaken Walter Cronkite broke the news to the country and the world:

"From Dallas, Texas, the flash apparently official, President Kennedy died at 1:00 p.m. Central Standard Time, 2:00 p.m. Eastern Standard Time, some thirty eight minutes ago..."

It hadn't been the best of days, or the worst of days for that matter; just another overly long day at old St. Pius X. But it was a Friday. Why anyone would choose to end such a beautiful autumn Friday with a history quiz was beyond me. Accepting a stack of papers from the guy in front of me, I pressed a page to my face, inhaling deeply, and passed the rest back. I wondered if it was possible to get high off mimeo ink. Scanning the page, I decided to get it over with as quickly as possible.

I didn't have the chance.

About 2:40 p.m. the door to the classroom flew open. It was Mother Superior. The head nun whispered frantically to Sister Alverez and then disappeared. Our teacher turned to the class. She wore a pale, stunned expression. "Children," she began in a forced, nervous tone, "something has happened. Please gather up your books and get ready to be dismissed."

I glanced toward Amy at the back of the classroom. She looked as confused as the rest of us.

School at St. Pius X let out at 3 p.m. sharp.

By 3 p.m., Friday, November 22, 1963, I was already home and changing out of my school clothes.

I hadn't bothered to switch on my radio during the brief ride home. Around 3:15 the phone rang. It was my father. He told me he was leaving work. He was picking up my sister from high school and would be home soon, and that Mom was on her way as well. Then he told me to turn on the TV and not to leave the house. It was an odd request. Minutes later I stood frozen in the middle of our den. Mixed feelings of emptiness, betrayal, disbelief, and confusion accompanied the frightening sounds and images coming from our television set.

By 4 p.m. the family was gathered around our 19" black-and-white Zenith. Like the rest of the country, we would remain there for the next three days.

The president was dead, cut down by an assassin's bullets as he drove through downtown Dallas in his open limousine. Pronounced dead at Parkland Hospital, his body was placed in a casket by Secret Service agents for return to Washington. Aboard Air Force One, with the late president's widow in attendance, at 2:38 PM CST, Sarah T Hughes swore in Lyndon B. Johnson as the thirty-sixth president of the United States.

About 6 p.m. EST, Air Force One arrived at Andrews Air Force Base. Robert Kennedy boarded the plane, and the late president's casket was removed to Bethesda Naval Hospital. The emotional events were covered by the three major television networks. President Johnson had requested that the arrival be broadcast live. One of the evening's most striking images was captured when Jackie Kennedy emerged from the plane with her brother-in-law Robert. Her pink suit and legs were stained with her husband's blood. Throughout the trying and tragic day, Mrs. Kennedy had refused to leave her husband's body or change out of her blood-stained suit. Later, Lady Bird Johnson would recall Mrs. Kennedy as saying, "I want them to see what they have done to Jack."

On Sunday, Kennedy's body was moved to the Capitol Rotunda, where it lay in state, viewed by more than 250,000 mourners. On Monday, November 25, Kennedy was laid to rest in Arlington National Cemetery. Graveside, Mrs. Kennedy, along with Robert and Edward Kennedy, lit an eternal flame.

The president's murderer was Lee Harvey Oswald. At the time, little was known about the twenty-four-year-old former Marine who had briefly defected to the Soviet Union. After firing the fatal shots from the Book Depository window, he fled into the streets, where he later confronted, shot, and killed Dallas police officer J. D. Tippit. Oswald was finally arrested inside the downtown Texas Theatre.

In 1964, a Presidential Commission, ordered by President Lyndon Johnson, found that all three shots fired at Kennedy and Governor Connally had been fired by Oswald. In its 888-page report, the Warren Commission concluded that Lee Harvey Oswald had acted alone in assassinating the president. In 1976, the House Select Committee on Assassinations reached the same conclusions.

Ironically, on Sunday morning, November 24, while the president's body lay in state, Lee Harvey Oswald was shot and killed in the basement of the Dallas Police headquarters by local nightclub owner Jack Ruby. The murder was witnessed live by millions on national television.

The only man who could have answered the many questions surrounding the assassination of President John F. Kennedy took those answers with him to the grave.

244

⸎Chapter Twenty⸎

On November 28, the Space Center at Florida's Cape Canaveral officially became known as the John F. Kennedy Space Center. By the end of the year, New York's Idlewild Airport—along with thousands of schools, community centers, and boulevards across the country—had been renamed after the late leader. President Lyndon Johnson declared November 25 as a national day of mourning, and then on the 29th he appointed Supreme Court Justice Earl Warren to head up the official investigation of the assassination. There was little for which give thanks and much to reflect upon as Thanksgiving 1963 came and went, virtually unnoticed. Meanwhile, flags remained at half-staff through the end of the year in honor of JFK.

My father seemed reluctant to talk about the events unfolding on our TV. I awoke late Sunday morning, surprised to find him sitting silently by himself in the living room. I could tell he didn't want to be bothered, so I headed down to the den. Turning on the television, I noticed the cabinet was warm. Dad had been watching. The three networks were switching frantically between coverage of the president as he lay in state in the Capitol Rotunda and the news of Lee Harvey Oswald's murder in Dallas. On Monday, after Kennedy had been laid to rest, my father rose and switched off the old Zenith.

He looked at my mom. "Well…"

I never heard my father speak of the assassination again.

The gang's monthly party that had been scheduled for Saturday the 23th was canceled. Instead, the guys gathered at our meeting place in the woods behind Tommy's house. After a few insightful moments of conversation about Kennedy and the events of the previous day, it was business as usual. There wasn't much else for us to say. The young, charismatic leader, whom we admired and looked upon as a friend and savior of an increasingly troubled future, was gone. He'd been taken from us, like so many others. Now, the country and the world were back in the hands of the older establishment: the war mongers who despised rock 'n' roll, who were fearful of the younger generation and suspicious of change.

Camelot was dead.

And so we drank and smoked and got high on glue and a few rolled joints.

Tommy said that Amy and Connie had been talking in the schoolyard. Amy confided she wasn't mad at me but upset about our being apart. She told Connie that she wanted us to talk, she just wasn't sure if I'd be willing. I did my best to pump Tommy for more information. But soon the conversation deteriorated into exaggerated locker-room boasting of our limited sexual experiences. Passing around a fifth of Four Roses and a re-fired blunt, the guys listened eagerly as I recounted my exploits with the enigmatic Ronnie.

In keeping with the tone of a nation in mourning, winter arrived on bone-chilling wings out of the northeast. High temperatures barely topped the twenties, while nights fell to near single digits. For the most part, the skies remained a dark but snowless gray.

On Friday, December 20, the last half day of school at St. Pius X, I managed to once again sneak onto Amy's bus. We'd spoken briefly in the schoolyard and she invited me over, saying we needed to talk. Mrs. Johns was courteous but not overly friendly, offering me hot chocolate. We sat in an awkward silence while Amy changed out of her uniform. With my father remaining mute on the subject, I longed to talk with someone about the murder of the president. Even St. Pius had been relatively quiet on the matter, offering up a few meaningless words of encouragement and a lot of ominous prayers for our slain leader and the country's future. I could tell Amy's mom wanted to talk, to go back to the close relationship we had forged. Neither of us found the ground or the words to begin. A half hour later, Amy and I faced each other as we shivered in her back yard play fort.

I found it hard to look into her eyes. "So... been a weird couple of months, huh?"

Amy half-smiled, pulling her pink knit stocking cap with the cute pink pom-pom low over her ears. "Yeah, crazy... that day, the day it happened, I wanted to—to—"

"Yeah, I know. Me, too. Your parents say much?"

"No, not really. They don't talk about it." She cupped her hands and blew into them. Instinctively I pulled her close, trying to keep her warm. It felt good to hold her again.

"I know. My dad has barely spoken since it happened. It's like adults think if they don't talk about it, then maybe it will go away or something." I waited. A long period of silence passed between us; I didn't think Amy had heard a word. I could feel her softly crying against my chest. I thought she was just releasing bottled-up feelings from the trying and confusing events of the past month. I found my own eyes getting damp.

"Billy, I—" Amy looked up at me. Her hazel jewels were clouded and dark. "I hate the way things have been—what happened between us."

This was the conversation I had been dreading. Since that night at the carnival, little else had been on my mind. But no matter how many times I went over it, no matter how many ways I looked at it, how many spins I could put on it, I still had no idea what to say. I liked Ronnie and had done things with her, enjoyed being with her. But my feelings for her were different from what I felt for

Amy. Exactly what those feelings were, I wasn't sure. I was still struggling to understand it myself.

Amy trembled in my arms. I thought it was from the cold. "Hey, we're not them. We're not our parents. We can talk about things." I forced a smile, and my fallen hero's words returned to me. "Remember...? ' *The torch has been passed to a new generation of Americans.'*"

It was at that very moment, recalling something I'd heard just once, years ago, that I became aware of how deeply and permanently our youngest president's words and actions had influenced me. Blinking back the tears beginning to puddle in the corners of my eyes, I summoned a deep, cleansing breath. "Well, I—"

Again Amy buried her face into my chest, interrupting me. "I'm so sorry, Billy. I'm so, so sorry. It wasn't anything, really..."

"What—what do you mean? What are you talking about?"

"When I was in—in Wildwood—over the summer..." She sniffed back more tears, trying to catching her breath. "I met someone, Billy, on the beach."

More feelings than I could count began to take up sides in my mind. Despite the shock and confusion, I could feel anger and jealousy bubbling inside of me. Selfishly, all thoughts of a confession about Ronnie disappeared. But at least this time I was able to control my emotions. I steadied my voice. "What? You— you what?"

By now Amy had calmed down somewhat. Wiping her tears, she took a step back, looking down at the ground. "This guy, we met on the beach... I'd seen him around before, and he started to talk to me. I don't know." Amy sniffed, wiping her nose on the sleeve of my denim jacket. She looked up, trying her best to smile. "I missed you so much. I hated it, being away from you. But it was nice to be with someone, to have someone there. It really didn't mean anything, honest. It was just—just *different*."

Just different. It was the same reasoning I'd used to justify being with Ronnie. *It was different and didn't mean anything.* But I had felt something with Ronnie. In my limited experience, I failed to recognize the physical attraction for purely physical pleasures.

Amy and I talked for another hour. We never really said much, or reached any sort of settlement, but it felt good. By the time Mrs. Johns drove me home, Amy and I had agreed to forget the past. We'd take a break over the holidays. When school resumed in January, we would meet and talk some more. It seemed like a good plan, one I'm sure JFK would have approved.

That evening, with WIBG keeping me company from beneath my pillow, I decided a break from all relationships, regardless of who, or what, or why, might be a good idea. I was through with girls, at least for a while.

My older buddies had other ideas.

On Saturday night, December 21, with temperatures plummeting, we huddle around a flaming can of Sterno, trying to keep warm. Don Rondo passed over a brown bag containing a bottle of rum. I took as long a pull as I could handle, the spicy brown liquor burning my stomach, and passed it on. Don, Joe Capone, Johnny and Timmy Mancuso, and I had been trying our best to harmonize the Elegants' "Little Star." It was just too damn cold.

I was seriously considering calling it a night when Larry Cartelli spoke up. "Hey, Billy, isn't it your birthday or something?"

"Not yet, it's on the twenty-fourth."

"Oh, yeah, that's right—you're a *Christmas baby.*" The exaggerated comment brought on laughter from the others. I was surprised any of these delinquents had taken notice of my birthday. I was about to find out why.

Allan Sarafino ruffled my hair as if I were a little kid. "Not only that, but he's gonna be thirteen… a *teenager!*"

That comment elicited harder head scrums and several rounds of birthday punches. By the time the group was through, both my arms ached. Next I was handed the paper bag. The bottle still contained about four inches of rum. I tipped it back to a chorus of *chug it, chug it, chug it*. Forcing down the last swallow, I felt it all starting to come back up.

Larry eyeballed me curiously as I gagged hard and swallowed again. "Hey, you know, he's never been properly initiated!"

What the hell? What was all that I'd just suffered through?

A collective smirk appeared on the devious faces of my older friends. "We can't have no kid who ain't been properly initiated hanging around us, now can we?" someone cried. The others nodded their agreement.

Louie shot Don a wily glance. "Well, no time like the present." He turned to me. "Up for a little initiation? I mean, you *do* want to continue to be a part of the group, don't you?"

Finally managing to keep the rum in my stomach, I nodded.

"Okay, good. You go down to the baseball field and wait in the home team dugout."

Everyone laughed at the private joke. "Good idea," Larry added. "We can kill two birds with one stone." He slapped Louie on the back and the laughter grew.

"Okay." I wasn't sure what I was agreeing to do. But I knew I wanted these guys' approval; to be *in* with them. "But what do I do?"

There was more laughter, "Oh, don't worry, you'll know what to do to..."

"He'd better!"

It was freezing in the dugout. My *friends* let me sit there for almost an hour. I was just about to leave when I heard her voice.

"Oh, so it's you."

It wasn't unusual for girls to be at the public school where we hung out. Often one or more of the guys brought their girlfriends along with them. They all smoked and drank, some even harmonizing along with us.

And then there were the *others*.

Most of the guys referred to them as *fish*, girls who hung around, usually uninvited. Most didn't have boyfriends but wanted to be a part of the group. They were fair game for anyone and anything.

I'd seen her around a few times. Her name was Sheila. She was sixteen, with long raven hair, big breasts, and a mole on her cheek. She was a fish. "You know, you're kinda cute. What are you, like 15 or something?"

She didn't wait for my answer. I watched with my mouth ajar as she took off her coat and began to unbutton her tight white blouse. In no time she'd removed her bra and wiggled out of snug jeans, slipping back into her overcoat. "Well—you just gonna stand there? It ain't getting' any warmer in here."

Through a suddenly dry mouth I managed to speak. "Thirteen— I'm thirteen, almost."

Sheila smiled, spitting out a thick wad of gum. "Okay, whatever. Come over here. Its Billy isn't it? Come on over here, Billy, I promise I won't bite." By now the rum had ricocheted throughout my entire body, coming to a violent halt inside of my head. I teetered forward, almost falling into her outstretched arms.

She smelled of stale cigarettes, rum, and roses.

She didn't bite.

She felt good.

Twenty minutes later I stumbled home, finding my parents in the den. I wavered uneasily on the second step. Experience had taught me this was as far as I needed to go. From here Mom could see I was home safe and Dad couldn't smell the booze.

"I'm home," I announced much too loudly.

Dad grunted something. Mom looked up from the play book she was studying. "That's nice, Billy. Did you have a good time with your friends?"

Pictures of Sheila lying naked on the home team bench, light from the pale quarter-moon shimmering on her olive skin, flooded my brain. I laughed, again much too loud and obvious. "Yes. Yes I did."

Dad continued to stare at the TV. "That's nice, Billy," Mom repeated.

Holding tight to the railing, I started up to bed. But then I turned, nearly falling down the steps. "Tonight," I declared at the top of my voice, "I am a man!"

This time Mom didn't bother to look up. "That's nice, Billy."

As I mounted the top step, my father finally spoke, "I thought his birthday wasn't until Tuesday?"

᎒᎐Chapter Twenty-One᎒᎐

C hristmas 1963 was quiet and uneventful. Mom made a big deal about my turning thirteen. Dad just gave me the look, probably contemplating additional chores I could handle now that I was a teenager. And my presents reflected a disturbing trend toward more grown-up gifts. I did receive a nice selection of the latest car models, and my sister came through with some cool 45s, but the bulk of my Christmas–birthday haul turned out to be clothes.

I didn't *feel* any older. I remember thinking something should be different—what, I had no clue. But I was older, a teenager, and... I'd had sex. To my surprise and dismay I still walked and talked and looked the same as before. Images of the night in the dugout with Sheila began to haunt my dreams. We had spent maybe a total of twenty minutes together, most of which I didn't even remember. Yet I couldn't get her out of my mind. I found myself comparing her to Ronnie and even to Amy. Once again the word *different* surfaced. I tried to forget the matter. But memories of Sheila and that cold night in December would continue to be part of my maturing for some time to come.

We returned to Sister Alverez's seventh grade on January 2, a Thursday. Why on Thursday, why not just wait until Monday? Another question unanswered. If there was one thing I noticed about growing up, it was that the questions increased, while the answers didn't. Things were changing.

At times it seemed like everything was changing—even me. I could feel a restlessness slowly growing inside of me. But I had no clue what it might be or where it would lead me. One morning before school I tried to talk about it with my father over breakfast.

I'm sure I did a poor job of explaining my feelings. His voice was slow and steady, while his expression showed concern. I know he did his best. But I came away from our conversation with little more than I knew before.

"It's nothing to worry about," he'd said. "It's perfectly normal, just all a part of growing up."

In reality I understood at least partly what was going on within my rapidly maturing young body. I wanted things to be right with Amy, the way they were before I gave her the ring: simple, fun, and uncomplicated. But I also wanted to keep seeing Ronnie and to return to the dugout with Shelia. At the same time I wanted the gang to continue, to keep drinking and partying and having fun. I wanted to keep singing with my buddies, and to drive a car, and go on real dates, and work with Joe Niagara and Hy Lit at the radio station. More than anything, I wanted to feel special and important again, the way the crowds at the dances and record hops made me feel; the way I felt sitting behind the on-air console at WIBG.

I wanted it all. It was a feeling and desire that would refuse to be sated, one that would fuel a life-long journey.

But the sad reality of it all was that I was lonely. With a wonderful, loving, supportive family; friends who admired and looked up to me; a girlfriend who cared deeply for me; and adults willing to mentor, guide, and help me, I still felt alone. Lying in my bed at night I felt alienated from a changing world I could no longer understand. If this was *normal*, just a part of growing up, as my father had said, I wanted nothing to do with it.

It wasn't long before I found my questions turning to *who cares*, my caring becoming *why bother*, and my attitude hitting an all-time low.

I knew I'd probably never see Sheila again, at least not under the same circumstances. And with Ronnie attending Paxon Hollow Junior High, it would be summer before we would meet again. I also knew there were a lot more girls out there, girls who wanted to be with me, or at least wanted to be with the cool guy on stage spinning the records. Working the hops with Hy had proven that. With temperatures warming into the upper 30s, Amy and I met up in the schoolyard and talked. As it turned out I did my best to listen while she did most of the talking. Again nothing much was said or settled and we continued to coast through whatever it was we were doing. Actually, that was fine with me. After almost two years, I was discovering being in a one-on-one relationship wasn't my strong suit. To my surprise and bewilderment, I realized Amy seemed to feel the same.

I also soon discovered that I wasn't the only one in the gang who was frightened by change. The girls especially seemed worried about what the future might hold. The ten of us talked often, trying our best to figure things out and make some sense of the ever-changing world around us. While it felt good to know others shared some of my fears and feelings, inside I continued to grow more restless and bitter.

Amy was the first, but not the only one, to notice the painful, inexplicable transformation I was going through. The beautiful hazel eyes I'd come to love began to show traces of concern and even fear. My increasingly sullen attitude gave her just cause, as my fuse grew shorter and I began to lash out at anything I didn't agree with or couldn't understand.

But I wasn't alone.

The gang tried its best to continue on as always, again joining the winter bowling league at the Lawrence Park Lanes. We returned to our familiar routine of bowling, hanging out, and going to movies. One Saturday afternoon we wandered over to the drug store lunch counter. Taking our places on the vinyl and chrome stools, we were greeted by an ugly, tattooed snarl.

"Wha' da you kids want?"

What we wanted were fries and cherry Cokes and a friendly face. Tommy was the first to find his voice.

"Where's Curtis?"

The harsh gray eyes narrowed and the snarl deepened. "That lazy ass nigger? He's gone and good riddance, too."

Nick and I nearly came up over the counter. The others held us back. Our host turned, pretending to busy himself with a coffee pot.

"Stupid ass kids!"

We left and never returned.

On Friday, Valentine's Day, we gathered at Marlena's house. I presented Amy with a sappy card and some cute hair clips I had noticed her admiring in Lit Brother's department store. Tommy and Connie chose the romantic date to announce they were officially going steady. As he proudly placed his gold tie clip on the lapel of Connie's blouse, I wondered what the snobbish Mrs. Grant would think of her son hooking up with a girl from the wrong side of Lawrence Park.

That night we danced and talked and ducked outside a few times to sample Tommy's flask and drink a toast to him and Connie. But along with everything else, our monthly parties were changing. Around 11 p.m., the lights had lowered and we were slowly grinding to the Mellow Kings' "Tonight, Tonight." Suddenly the music stopped.

"Hey guys, check this out!" It was Bob.

He replaced the classic 45 spinning on the record player with another. A strange yet strangely familiar sound filled the room. Amy and I looked at each other with puzzled expressions.

And then it hit me.

By now we had all heard of the Beatles. It was nearly impossible to turn on a radio without hearing something about the group of mop tops from England. Even the nightly news had started reporting on the "British phenomenon." The group that Joe Niagara predicted would find acceptance had finally established itself firmly on the American air waves.

"Ah, c'mon, take that crap off, will ya?" Still holding Connie by the hand, Tommy headed across the den. "C'mon, man, we wanna dance."

Bob stood his ground. "We're dancin' to this, fool!"

Tommy and Bob stood toe to toe while the Beatles continued to shout out their "Yeah, Yeah, Yeah." Amy shook her head, and I prepared to jump between the two friends. Thankfully it wasn't necessary.

From a corner of the den Frankie called out, "With the way Tommy dances, what frickin' dif does it make what you play?" The comment eased the tension, and we all laughed.

Red faced, Tommy slapped his friend's shoulder. "At least play somethin' slow, dude." The record ended and the next one dropped. The Beach Boys began to sing about the joys of being "In My Room."

"There ya go, Twinkle Toes."

"Oh, for the love of—" This time it was Nick's turn to complain. "You gotta be kiddin' me, man! Surf music?"

"Hey, it's slow ain't it?"

The rest of us returned to our corners and our girlfriends and our slow grinding. I held Amy close, finding it easy to dance to the deliberate, rhythmic melody.

"You like it, don't you?" Amy asked, sweetly whispering into my ear in the way she knew always drove me crazy.

"Yeah, yeah, I guess I do. It's cool, and the harmonies are really great, nice and tight." My own comments surprised me. I wondered what my greaser singing buddies would say if they heard me praising the new music.

Amy nestled tighter into my arms. "Well I like it, too, but not as much as the old stuff."

I kissed her forehead tenderly. "That's why we're so good together."

And so it went the rest of the night, from doo-wop to beach to Beatle; from New York street corner to Motown soul to the California sand. We listened and argued, debated and danced. The only thing agreed upon that evening was that good music was good music, no matter where it came from. Musically, the times were indeed changing, and perhaps... maybe... just maybe... it wasn't all that bad.

By spring our differences were meaningless. The Beatles had more than proven themselves. On April 4, 1964, the Fab Four held down the top five spots on Billboard's Hot 100 Chart, a feat that's never been equaled. Year's end found nine of the top twenty songs for 1964 coming from Motown, the Beatles, and the Beach Boys. The American music scene would never be the same, nor would it ever fully recover. By 1965 only four American acts with number one hits before the Beatles arrived would survive to top the charts again: the Supremes, the Four Seasons, the Beach Boys, and Elvis.

WIBG was in trouble. It was the same trouble facing rock 'n' roll radio stations everywhere. Since the late fifties, as rock 'n' roll struggled to establish itself as a viable music format, and stations and DJs managed to survive the payola scandals, rock radio had grown into big business. By 1964, rock 'n' roll was recognized as the number one radio format across the country, and stations programming the unpredictable, youth-driven sound found themselves market leaders. But by 1964, rock 'n' roll was changing. To many, the tried and true four-chord rhythms and five-part harmonies had grown stale and tired.

First to challenge the old sound was Motown, an upstart company begun by ex-prize fighter Berry Gordy, Jr... Growing up in Detroit, Gordy was familiar with the strong blues and gospel influenced sounds that flowed from the numerous clubs in the city's predominantly black neighborhoods. In 1957, he was introduced to singer Jackie Wilson. The two became friends, and Wilson went on to record several songs written by Gordy, including "Lonely Teardrops."

Reinvesting his songwriting profits into production work, Berry Gordy discovered the Miracles, adding them to a growing portfolio of local artists. Then, borrowing $800 from his family, Gordy formed his first label, Tamla Records. The talented producer had several minor hits, including "Money" for Barrett Strong, and "Shop Around" and the lush ballad "Bad Girl" for the Miracles.

In 1961 Gordy struck gold as the Marvelettes' "Please Mr. Postman" climbed to the top of Billboard's charts. It was the start of a musical empire. By 1964 Motown, along with its several subsidiary labels, had become a major player in the music industry, with artists including the Supremes, the Four Tops, Mary Wells, Martha and the Vandellas, Marvin Gaye, Kim Weston, the Marvelettes, and Smokey Robinson and the Miracles.

About the time Motown was finding its sound, several friends from the beaches of southern California were developing their own musical style. Jan Berry and Dean Torrence met at Emerson Junior High School in Westwood, Los Angeles. The duo found a common interest in music, winning several school and local talent contests. In 1959, with the help of record producers Herb Alpert and Lou Adler, the pair, now known as Jan and Dean, scored a top ten hit with the bouncy, nonsensical "Baby Talk." The song included early elements of what would become the California sound: tight harmonies, careful use and blending of major and minor chords, and doo-wop style falsetto. Playing local clubs and dances, the pair met and became friends with a musical singing group from Hawthorn, California.

Originally known as the Pendletones, the Beach Boys formed in 1961. Unlike most vocal groups of the time, brothers Brian, Carl, and Dennis Wilson, along with cousin Mike Love and friend Al Jardine, all played their own instruments. Their smooth, close harmonies, combined with frantic, twangy guitar work and lyrics extolling the California beach lifestyle, caught on with DJs and listeners alike. The Beach Boys, along with Jan and Dean became the first and chief purveyors of surf music.

While the beaches of Southern California became home to the West Coast sound, four guys from Belleville, New Jersey, were pushing rock 'n' roll into new directions. Like the Beach Boys, Bob Gaudio, Tommy DeVito, and Nick Massi were musicians, playing their own instruments. But in contrast to their West Coast counterparts, Frankie Valli's strong falsetto lead, backed by the group's multipart harmonies, was pure doo-wop. The combination of classic vocals and modern musical styling would propel the Four Seasons to numerous top ten hits.

In 1958, Danny and the Juniors had loudly proclaimed, "Rock 'n' Roll Is Here to Stay." No one ever said anything about its remaining static. From doo-wop to rockabilly to teen idols; from Elvis to Bobby Darin to Frankie Avalon; rock 'n' roll was constantly evolving. The music of the Four Seasons, the Beach Boys, and Motown were logical progressions in the development of rock 'n' roll. Radio took full advantage of the musical evolution, spinning the new sounds along with the old. Battles of the Bands became a popular programming gimmick, pitting doo-wop against Motown; surf against city and old against new. While listeners were encouraged to call in and vote for their favorite, in the end it was a win-win situation for all as the new music found acceptance and popularity alongside established artists.

In 1964, evolution turned to revolution when the radically different Beatles finally arrived.

Like the jocks at WIBG, radio stations country wide found they could ignore the unusual sounds coming from across the Atlantic for only so long. When Murray the K first played "She Loves You," proclaiming to his disbelieving New York audience that the group was the greatest thing to come along since Chuck Berry, the writing was on the wall. In the ultra-competitive world of radio broadcasting, programmers were constantly on the search for the next big thing, hoping to cash in on anything that would attract listeners and boost ratings.

Throughout the winter of 1964, stations continued to test the waters, slipping in a Beatles song here and there, even labeling the new release as a "pick hit of the week." Rock 'n' roll was celebrating its first decade, and a new generation had grown up listening to the beat. The Beatles' music spoke directly to these young enthusiasts who were ready to claim a sound of their own.

Most cities and towns in 1964 had but one radio station playing pure rock 'n' roll; to many adults, one was more than enough. With a younger generation poised to spend their allowance on 45s and music-related products, rock 'n' roll radio found itself at a crossroads: continue to play the old sound and ignore a growing demographic, or add the Beatles to their rotation and risk alienating older listeners. At WIBG the decision was reluctantly made to program the new music along with conventional American rock 'n' roll. But the DJs at the station, like the music they loved, were from another era. It was often obvious by their stilted patter that the jocks didn't really care for the new music.

In September 1966, ABC-owned WFIL began playing Top 40 rock 'n' roll using the Boss Radio format, programming what was now referred to as the British Invasion almost exclusively. Philadelphia became a city musically divided. Long-time favorite WIBG began a long, painful slide into oblivion. As the number and popularity of British acts steadily grew, and rock 'n' roll continued to evolve, station after station faced the same fate as my beloved WIBBAGE.

Like most of the country, the gang was fairly evenly split. Long hours of heated debate were spent discussing the future of rock 'n' roll. We were all greased-back, first-generation rockers who still loved the simple beauty of a doo-wop ballad. But the infectious appeal of the Beatles was hard to ignore. Just as I had wondered what JFK thought of rock 'n' roll, I found myself daydreaming of legislation, spearheaded by my political hero, limiting British airplay on American airwaves.

But it was just fanciful reverie. Those days were behind us now. With the flash of rifle fire, the world had changed forever. Like it or not, we were forced to change as well.

I seriously doubt our new president had any kind of feelings toward rock 'n' roll. Even if he did, he had little time to express them. Foreshadowing his entire presidency, President Lyndon B. Johnson's first months in office were busy and troubled.

On January 8, in his first State of the Union address, Johnson announced a "War on Poverty." Over the next several months, bills aimed at easing the burden for the middle and lower classes were drawn up. But growing international problems would soon divert the new president's attention.

Two days after his State of the Union address, the president held a meeting with Defense Secretary Robert McNamara. Johnson granted approval for covert operations against North Vietnam, later transferring responsibility for the actions from the CIA to the military. By summer, developments in Southeast Asia would force the president to take further and more controversial steps. On August 2, the U.S. destroyer *Maddox* engaged three North Vietnamese torpedo boats in the Gulf of Tonkin. The outcome of the incident was passage by Congress of the Gulf of Tonkin Resolution. The act granted the president authority to assist any Southeast Asian country whose government was considered threatened by communist aggression. While civil and domestic problems grew, our thirty-sixth president soon found the country mired in an escalating and unpopular war.

On January 23, the 24th Amendment to the Constitution was ratified, ending the century-old poll tax in federal elections. Three days later, eighty-four people were arrested in a segregation protest in Alabama as the struggle for equality continued to grow. On May 2, black teens Henry Dee and Charles Moore were beaten and killed by members of the Mississippi Ku Klux Klan. Once again a racially motivated murder would go unpunished.

But a few major milestones were achieved by the Johnson administration. On May 22, in an address at the University of Michigan, LBJ delivered his Great Society speech, outlining his legislative agenda for widespread social reform. Then on July 2 he signed into law the Civil Rights Act of 1964, the long-awaited legislation begun over a year earlier by President Kennedy. Other domestic legislation that summer included the Economic Opportunity Act, the Food Stamp Act, and the Wilderness Act.

The Cold War also continued to make headlines and plague the president. On May 19, the State Department announced that the U.S. Embassy in Moscow had been bugged. A network of some forty microphones was discovered embedded in the walls of the "secure" building.

As the year progressed, the country did its best to return to normalcy. In February, Indiana Governor Mathew Walsh tried to ban "Louie Louie" from the airwaves. The Kingsmen's popular tune caught the attention of the FBI, who investigated the song for containing possibly obscene lyrics. The agency found no basis for the allegations, but the controversy dramatically increased record sales.

The same month, the Beatles began their first American tour, including their first of four appearances on the *Ed Sullivan Show* on February 9. But not everyone was ready to accept the new rock 'n' roll. Typical of groups popping up across the country, a faction from the University of Detroit began a movement called "Stamp Out the Beatles."

The first Ford Mustang was introduced in the spring of 1964. The iconic muscle car would go on to become one of the most popular American cars ever produced, rivaling the company's own Model T. Meanwhile, Chrysler was busy showing off its futuristic Turbine car. Fifty of the beautiful vehicles, engineered by Chrysler and styled by Ghia of Italy, were built to gauge people's reactions to alternative fuels and power plants. The 130-horsepower gas turbine engine could run on almost any combustible liquid, from peanut oil to perfume. Tommy's father received one of the test vehicles for a month's use. I got to take several eye-popping, awe-inspiring rides in what Chrysler touted as the "Transportation of the Future."

At the movies, Sidney Poitier became the first black performer to receive an Oscar in a leading role for his performance in *Lilies of the Field*. The Best Picture Oscar went to the movie *Tom Jones*. TV Emmy Awards for 1964 went to Dick Van Dyke, Mary Tyler Moore, and the *Dick Van Dyke Show*.

On April 22, President Johnson took time out from his busy schedule to open the 1964–1965 New York World's Fair in Queens. This time around, my nagging persistence was rewarded, and the Neblett family spent four days in the Big Apple visiting the Hemisphere and other futuristic exhibits. Like many, I came away from the fair with wondrous, wide-eyed visions of a modern, peaceful future.

Closer to home, my Phillies began the 1964 season as strong contenders for the National League pennant. Behind the fielding and batting talents of Tony Taylor, Dick Allen, Johnny Callison, Bobby Wine, Cookie Rojas, and Tony Gonzalez, the Phillies soared into first place. Punctuating their winning season, on Father's Day, Jim Bunning pitched a perfect game against the Mets at Shea Stadium. It was the first perfect game thrown in the National League since 1880. The feat became the high point of what would turn out to be a typical Phillies heartbreaking season.

With only twelve games to go in the regular season, and holding a commanding six-and-a-half game lead in the National League, World Series tickets were printed and distributed to season ticket holders. Then the Phillies lost ten straight games, the first seven at home, and fell to second place. They would end the season tied for second with the Cincinnati Reds, just one game behind the pennant-winning St. Louis Cardinals. The Cardinals would go on to defeat the heavily favored New York Yankees in seven games to claim the World Series title. I would have to wait another sixteen years to celebrate a Philadelphia Phillies Word Championship.

৫৯Chapter Twenty-Two৯৩

Things may have been changing. But one thing remained constant: my buddies and I still managed to find ways to get into trouble. The annual Philadelphia Auto Show arrived in town, and the ten of us made plans to attend. That was fine for a Saturday afternoon date. But being certified car nuts, the guys looked forward to spending hours peeking under hoods, inhaling new-car aromas, collecting new car brochures, and wearing out salesmen with endless questions. None of us cherished the idea of having to entertain our girlfriends in the process. Tommy came up with the solution.

The show at the Philadelphia Convention Center was scheduled to open Thursday night and run through Sunday. A private show, reserved for auto industry VIPs and their families, was held Thursday afternoon. Tommy "borrowed" his father's passes, and he, Bob, Nick, Frankie, and I skipped school and headed down to University City and new car nirvana. We bluffed our way in, and everything was going fine until we got to the Ford exhibit.

The Philadelphia area Ford Dealers were giving away a new car. The lure was just too great. Naturally the contest was open only to licensed drivers, so while Tommy, Nick, and I distracted the salesman on duty with pointless questions, Bob and Frankie stuffed their pockets. We made our way to the food court where, for the next hour or so, we filled in hundreds of entry forms. Returning to the scene, we found the salesman had been replaced by an attractive, sexily attired young woman, one of the auto show bunnies hired to dress up the merchandise. Tommy turned on the charm while we stuffed the ballot boxes.

That night the VIP passes were returned to Mr. Grant's desk drawer, and we returned to class the next day, no one the wiser. On Saturday the entire gang boarded a SEPTA bus, transferred to the subway train, and spent the day checking out the automotive world's latest offerings.

On the way home from the auto show, Tommy and Connie and Amy and I stopped at the 69th Street White Castle for hamburgers and shakes. It had been obvious to everyone for some time that all was not well with St. Pius' hottest couple; obvious to everyone except the couple. Tommy and Connie were arguably a match made in heaven. But familiarity sometimes breeds contempt, and Tommy and Connie couldn't get any more familiar with each other. No one doubted the couple cared for one another. Everyone assumed they would be married right after graduation, as did Tommy. But as time passed, Tommy grew more possessive and jealous. At the same time, Connie was discovering her own identity. As the *Father Knows Best* mindset of the fabulous fifties began to fade from memory, women the world over were starting to find their own voices. It was the early dawn of the feminist movement, and Connie jumped in with both feet. She loved Tommy and wanted to be with him, but on her own terms.

Half way through the French fries, the same old argument resurfaced. The first salvo came from Connie.

"What do you mean?" The question, directed at Tommy, was less than cordial. "Amy, tell this—this *boy* that a woman can be anything she wants."

Amy and I looked at each other. We'd both seen this rerun before.

Tommy countered. "I never said a woman couldn't do what she wants—"

Right on cue, Connie interrupted. "I didn't say a woman couldn't *do* what she wants, I said *be* whatever she wants."

"What's the dif?"

"There's a lot of *dif,* you just refuse to understand."

"So school me, cutie pie."

Connie nearly screamed out loud in frustration. If this was how they discussed things in public, I wondered what their private life was like.

I took Amy's hand, and we slid out of the booth. "C'mon, sweetie, let's see what the jukebox has to say."

"You see? That's exactly what I mean!" By now Connie was red-faced and breathless. "Men think all they have to do is call us 'sweetie' and everything is fine and peachy." She hopped up, pushed past us, and headed for the ladies room.

Amy gave me an exasperated look. "I guess I'd better go see if I can calm her down."

I returned to our table and Tommy. "What is it with you, man; can't you just let it be?"

Tommy propped his head in his hands, slurping the last of his chocolate shake through a straw. "What da *you* know? You and Amy are perfectly compatible. Connie wants to be an astronaut or something."

Perfectly compatible? It was a thought I would do well to remember. Of course I wouldn't. A few minutes later the girls returned. Tommy almost had an epiphany right there in the middle of White Castle—almost. I'm sure he was just about to apologize when the jukebox kicked on and Lesley Gore's voice filled the dinner:

"You don't own me/I'm not just one of your many toys"

The expression on Connie's face read like a neon sign. I felt sorry for Tommy. But then Amy whispered into my ear, "Maybe you should listen, too, *sweetie*."

The ride home was an amicable, albeit quiet one. By the time of our monthly party, each couple seemed to have adopted a song exclusively their own, although I doubt any of the guys had much of a voice in the matter. To no one's surprise, Tommy and Connie's became "You Don't Own Me." And I should have been paying closer attention the second time Amy pulled me to the dance floor, singing along to Dionne Warwick's "Don't Make Me Over."

Years of experience ducking trouble tends to heighten a young boy's inner sense of doom. With uncanny accuracy, he can usually tell when danger is close at hand or when he should probably be somewhere else. For example, a parent calling you by your full name never leads to anything good. In the Neblett house, the phone ringing at dinner time always spelled disaster. One warm evening in late spring, we had just sat down to dinner when the phone rang.

Immediately my father looked at me. My mind raced. I hadn't done anything to warrant a dinner-time phone call in months. I had actually been behaving myself pretty well lately... as well as I ever behaved myself, anyway. Nothing came to mind.

My father rose, cleared his throat, and lifted the receiver. "Hello? Yes, yes, this is Mr. Neblett." There was a long pause during which my dad's expression grew increasingly puzzled. "No, no, I'm sorry—there must be some mistake." Once again his stern gaze landed on me. "Yes, but..."

My sister began to grin as my father's expression slowly turned in the other direction. It had been months since the auto show. In my mind I could easily hear both sides of the strained conversation.

Man: "Congratulations Mr. Neblett, your name has been selected from the thousands of entries!"

Dad: "What?"

Man: "You won, Mr. Neblett. That's right, you're our big winner!"

Dad: "But I don't understand."

Man: You've won the grand prize! Mr. Neblett, you are the lucky winner of a brand new Ford Mustang!"

Dad: "There must be some mistake. I—"

Man: "No mistake, Mr. Neblett. Your name was chosen from the thousands and thousands of entries received at this year's auto show. You have just won a brand new 1964 ½ Ford Mustang, compliments of your local area Ford dealers! Congratulations, Mr. Neblett!"

For a moment I felt sorry for the man on the phone. He'd have to explain to his bosses how the big super grand prize had been refused by the overly serious-sounding Mr. Neblett. The moment passed quickly; I had bigger problems of my own. It took some doing, but somehow Dad managed to convince the overzealous caller that he wasn't interested. He appreciated the call and certainly recognized what an honor it was, and what a great opportunity, but no, he would not accept the new car. At least Dad didn't rat me out—the poor guy probably would have lost his job.

That evening my father and I had a long father–son talk. He talked, I listened. Not wishing to stir the pot any further, I didn't ask, "Why?"

But throughout the conversation, I couldn't help but think my dad was trying desperately to suppress a grin. My father never spoke of his childhood. Aunt Millicent, Dad's kid sister, was the Neblett family historian. On more than one summer visit to Joplin, my sister and I were entertained by tales of the exploits of the young William I. Neblett, or Inlow, as his family called him; stories that I'm sure my ultra-conservative father would deny to his grave. It was at times like this that I recalled those stories. It helped me to suffer through the lectures, to say nothing of the punishment, knowing that Dad was, after all, only human.

I was grounded for a month. Within a week I was back on the streets.

Who needed a brand new 1964 ½ Ford Mustang? I still had Princess, my '54 Dodge Coronet. School ended, and we graduated to eighth grade, kings of St. Pius X Catholic Grade School. I openly bragged to the gang that come September it would be my last run with nuns and suit coats and blue ties, never noticing the hurt and sadness in Amy's eyes.

During the summer of '64 I experienced freedom as never before—freedom granted as well as stolen. My curfew was all but eliminated. My dad's take on the matter was simple: I was old enough to know better and old enough to act responsibly. If I didn't, I'd pay the penalty. I didn't need to be home at any particular hour, just a "reasonable and responsible hour." But it was all academic anyway. Mom had landed important roles in local plays. She had even somehow talked Dad into taking on lighting and staging duties for the theatre. And her modeling and acting careers were in high gear. By the end of the summer it was nearly impossible to turn on a TV or ride public transportation without seeing Mom's face hawking some local product. Between plays, rehearsals, parties, and a two-week vacation with friends in Cape May, New Jersey, my parents were rarely home. And my sister, who was now a junior in high school, was dating regularly. I had the summer and the house almost all to myself, and I intended to enjoy every minute.

Lawrence Park couldn't have been more perfectly laid out for a clever teenager. With the new build-out, our house on North Central lay right in the middle of the development. Beyond the new section, a large track of undeveloped wooded land was crisscrossed by dozens of roads leading nowhere. The area was a popular parking spot for amorous couples seeking a little privacy. Exploring on my bicycle, I had long since discovered I could navigate my way to the shopping center, the local swim club, all of my friend's houses (save for Amy's), Loomis Public Grade School (where we hung out and sang), and Cardinal O'Hara High School—without ever leaving the neighborhood. With my parents and sister mostly out of the picture, I took full advantage of the situation. Perhaps my father hadn't been as clever as he thought in selecting the unassuming little brown house located just inside of a mile from St. Pius X.

Eager to exploit my new freedom, I didn't return to WIBG as an intern, instead choosing to work a few dances with Hy Lit. Amy was once again away in Wildwood, New Jersey, and my days were spent playing with my car or playing with Ronnie. Evenings

I'd wander up to Loomis School and join what was left of my older friends for a few rounds of bourbon and doo-wop. I also secretly hoped I'd run into Sheila again. Plus, Tommy, Frankie, Bob, Nick, and I still hung out together and did our share of drinking and getting high.

It wasn't long before I decided I needed some better transportation. Once or twice every couple of weeks, with my parents and sister gone for the night, I quietly snuck Princess out of the garage for a joy ride. Picking up my friends, we'd head up to the shopping center, being careful to park the old Dodge discretely out of sight. More than once Ronnie and I found ourselves snuggled in the spacious back seat, parked along one of the lonely, undeveloped roads.

Amy returned in August. Our initial awkwardness spoke volumes of what the both of us had been up to while apart. Neither of us asked, nor did we volunteer any information, and soon things were pretty much back to normal. Often Mrs. Johns would drop Amy off at my house. Cardinal O'Hara was holding weekly dances, and we'd hop into Princess, pick up Tommy and Connie, and head over to the Catholic high school. Amy enjoyed my driving her and the gang around, but she gave me hell about driving while drinking or high. Afterward, we'd often make our way to one of the deserted back roads. I like to believe that was one thing she never shared with her mom.

For some strange reason I couldn't wait for first Wednesday of eighth grade. Perhaps I was looking forward to being part of the senior class. Or maybe I figured the sooner eighth grade started, the quicker I'd be done and finished with old St. Pius X Catholic Grade School. Or it could be simply that I was just looking for some sort of stability in my scattered life. Whatever may be the reasons, the anticipation and expectation fell far short of the reality.

I landed in the class taught by Sister Joanna, a nun well known for her short temper, painful head thumps, and heavy homework assignments. To make matters worse, St. Pius finally managed to break up the gang. Tommy, Nick, and Bob were assigned across the hall, while Frankie landed in class with me. Adding insult to injury, we were all split apart from our girlfriends. We could continue to meet in the schoolyard before class and during lunch break, but I knew I'd miss the reassuring, killer smile lurking somewhere in the back of the classroom.

As if things weren't bad enough, more changes lay ahead. In an attempt to modernize the outdated curriculum, and bowing to outside pressures, our school made a token attempt at two new subjects. Earth Science turned out to be little more than a joke, as the clueless nuns showed just how little they knew and understood about the world just beyond their cloistered halls. Plus, I had taught myself this stuff when I was nine years old and became interested in space and the solar system and how our own planet worked. Our colorful text book became little more than a paperweight, as even the most remote mention of anything sounding like evolution was completely ignored.

But it was the course in civics that vexed me most throughout eighth grade. At St. Pius, civics seemed to mean current events. Our text book became the front page of the daily paper and stories from the six o'clock news. About once a month we were required to bring in timely news articles or report on something we had seen on TV.

It wasn't long before ultra-conservative, lily-white St. Pius X showed its true colors. In late August there had been race riots in Philadelphia. Blacks were tired of what they considered to be harsh and unfair treatment at the hands of the police department. Peering over the top of her wire-rimmed glasses, Sister Joanna scratched a large red D atop the Philadelphia Tribune article I had brought in, claiming it wasn't timely enough. A second column from the black-owned newspaper was likewise dismissed. A few weeks later I was refused permission to read aloud a *Time* magazine story on the struggles in Vietnam because it was too long. It became obvious that our school's idea of current events meant only things that had to do with our new president—as long as it wasn't too controversial. I also discovered that I enjoyed rattling our nun's cage with unacceptable material. Hey, with Amy and the guys across the hall, I had to do something to make eighth grade interesting.

Civics class actually salvaged my waning interest in what was going on in the world. After JFK's death I had lost all desire to keep up with the news. The less I knew about the changes going on around me, the better I liked it. I retreated into myself, ignoring anything that didn't fall directly into the comfortable life I'd fashioned. If I didn't accept the changes, then maybe they wouldn't affect me. I had actually made an honest attempt to follow our new president and his policies. I just couldn't relate.

President Johnson was making the best out of a difficult situation. And he was doing much for the civil rights movement. But by now the presidential campaigns were in full swing, and the inevitable mudslinging was in high gear.

At their convention in San Francisco, the Republicans had nominated Arizona senator Barry Goldwater as their presidential candidate. Goldwater immediately attacked the administration for not doing enough to guarantee the continued freedom and security of the country. Taking a direct shot at President Kennedy's voluntary removal of ICBMs in Turkey during the Cuban Missile Crisis, Goldwater proclaimed, "Extremism in defense of liberty is no vice."

In a bit of political irony, President Johnson attempted to portray Goldwater as an extremist, while at the same time steadily increasing the presence of U.S. advisors and military personnel in Vietnam. Like most young people, I found myself suspicious and distrustful of our senior establishment president. It was a feeling that many would carry through their teens and on into adulthood.

The forced separation at school didn't help matters as the gang struggled on. Over the summer, Nick and Marianne began having problems, something about her plans to go to a private high school for girls. Connie's constant urgings for Marianne to "find herself" didn't help. And Connie's well-intended advice didn't help her strained relationship with Tommy. But they weren't the only ones whose relationship was changing. Since her return from Wildwood, an unspoken tension had wedged itself between Amy and me. We were aware of each other's summertime dalliances, we just didn't mention them.

One night at the shopping center's back-to-school carnival, while Amy and I strolled hand in hand, I spied Ronnie walking toward us. I tried my best to stay calm. I'm sure my body language gave me away to both girls. Ronnie brushed past, first looking toward Amy and then flashing me a coy smile. I could feel Amy's hand tightening around my fingers. We continued to walk, staring straight ahead, looking at nothing.

"So... that's her?"

Amy's comment was nearly lost amid the din of the midway. I wasn't sure how to respond, or even if I should. We shared a hot dog and lemonade and played a few games, mostly in silence. By the time we snuggled together on the carrousel, things were back to normal and the incident was forgotten—until October.

Our monthly party was back at my house. Around eleven I held Amy tightly as we slowly moved to the Shirelles' "Baby It's You." A tear escaped from Amy's hazel jewels as she looked up at me. "Did you dance with her?" she asked.

I didn't understand. "What?"

"Did you... dance with her?" Amy repeated, the words catching in her throat as she swallowed more tears.

I thought of the time I spent with Ronnie. We'd done many things, but we had never danced. Slowly, the clouds began to clear. Chris had been right about girls being different. Amy knew Ronnie and I had kissed, been close, even touched. She also understood that it had meant nothing; we were both just young and exploring, learning, growing. It was the closeness, the special and private things Amy and I shared like dancing that were important to her. I can't say I fully understood. In my inexperience, sex and intimacy were one and the same. As I grew older the lines would continue to blur. A large part of my life would be spent moving from one

274

unfulfilling relationship to the next; from one-night stands to nameless, impersonal encounters.

Amy's jealousy was a new experience for me. For some reason it felt good to know she was envious of my time with another girl. I looked into her beautiful eyes and melted. "No—you're the only one I want to dance with."

At the time I'm sure it was true.

It was obvious to everyone that we all cared deeply for one another. Yet at the same time as we were growing and learning about relationships, the very nature of relationships was changing. Women were beginning to find themselves, taking their place in the world beyond the kitchen. Having a career woman for a mother, it was one change with which I found myself comfortable.

The remainder of 1964 proved boring and uneventful. Once again the Philadelphia area enjoyed unseasonably mild temperatures. I took full advantage of conditions, riding my bike to school daily, arriving early to spend time with Amy in no-man's land. Once or twice a week I pedaled over to her house. We enjoyed each other's company—talking, sharing a bowl of ice cream, going for walks or bike rides, and fooling around in the back yard play fort. But it was beginning to seem all too predictable and mechanical. I still loved and cared for Amy, but routine was never my strong suit. The old, familiar restlessness returned.

Even my birthday and Christmas held no surprises, no excitement. I told myself to just tough it out, things would be better after St. Pius. But I never managed to grasp the irony. The very thing I distrusted the most—change—would be the one thing I'd continue to pursue throughout my adult life. There would always be something better, someone better, just around the next corner.

Both Amy and Connie's birthdays were coming up. A combination of boredom and guilt about Ronnie brought me to the conclusion that we should mark the occasions with something special. Tommy agreed. He and Connie had been going at it fairly regularly, and he was hoping to smooth things over. By now the Motown sound was firmly established on the American music scene. As I rode up Cornwall Hill, listening to the Contours' "Do you Love Me," I had an idea.

The Uptown Theatre was located at 2240 N. Broad Street, a juncture where predominantly black North Philly and the expanding Great Northeast came together. The theatre had long been a popular stop on the Chitlin Circuit, featuring blues, soul, and gospel performers. With the rise of rock 'n' roll and rhythm and blues, the venue became an important stop for black artists, with shows rivaling those at Harlem's Apollo Theatre. Popular WDAS radio personality Georgie Woods, "the guy with the goods," often hosted shows featuring as many as ten different acts. In February, the Motown Review would be coming to the Uptown.

Tommy liked the idea. The rest of the guys thought we were nuts. The neighborhood around the Uptown could be dangerous. And we'd have to ride the subway through some of West Philly's toughest areas. Plus, there was still plenty of lingering tension following last summer's race riots. No parent in his right mind would give their permission. Fortunately the show ran for two weeks, including a Sunday matinee on Valentine's Day. And I was a veteran of riding Philly's infamous elevated subway trains.

The gang had returned to the Lawrence Park Lanes for the winter league. One morning, after convincing our parents we would be doing the usual Saturday routine, and appeasing our girlfriends with promises that we were doing it *for them,* Tommy and I skipped bowling and headed into town. The ticket run was perfect for getting our timing right. We'd make some excuse about a Valentine's get-together, catch the early show, and be back before sundown.

It was perfect.

The surprised look on the face of the woman at the ticket window was worth the trip. "You kids want what?"

Once more Tommy turned on the charm. I wished I could have filmed the encounter and shown it to his parents. "Yes, ma'am, we'd like four tickets to the Motown Review show."

She almost fell off her seat. "You mean, here? You want to come here to see a show?" While white patrons were rare at the Uptown, this was starting to get a little ridiculous.

Tommy turned and winked at me, producing a thick roll of bills. I could easily picture the morning headlines: "Two Young Teens Robbed and Murdered in North Philly." Hopefully our demise wouldn't spark another riot.

Painting on his irresistible smile, Tommy flashed the wad of mostly ones at the woman in the booth. "Yes, ma'am, four of the best seats available for the fourteenth. That's Valentine's Day, you know."

Shaking her gray head, she punched up the tickets. "Lord a' mighty, I've seen it all! That'll be $8, please."

Back on the subway, Tommy grinned. "You see my man, when it comes down to it, people are all the same. The only color that matters is green!"

Valentine's Day 1965 was cold, with light, intermittent snowfall. Meeting at the shopping center, the four of us boarded a SEPTA bus and headed to the terminal at 69th Street. The weather, and the fact that it was Sunday, meant ridership on the subway would be light. It didn't matter. Through years of travel with my mom and aunt I'd developed my game face for riding public transportation. Throughout the years, no matter where I traveled, or at what time, I had never encountered a single problem. I told myself no one wanted to mess with me. The reality was that people are just people, whoever they may be, wherever they may be. If you treat them with respect and dignity, you'll receive the same.

The four of us encountered no problems at all. Our eight bucks got us tenth-row center seats for the show of the year. Tommy and Connie and Amy and I cheered and applauded and sang and danced in the aisles with the rest of the capacity crowd. The lineup included the Marvelettes, Martha and the Vandellas, Marvin Gaye, Tami Terrell, Kim Weston, Mary Wells, the Temptations, Stevie Wonder, and Junior Walker and his band.

Afterward, at the White Castle, Amy kissed me passionately, saying it was the best day she'd ever spent. She was right. The four of us had had a wonderful, memorable time together. None of us realized our good times and friendships would soon be ending.

ᴄ⁄ᴐChapter Twenty-Three◌ᴐ

T o no one's surprise, Lyndon Johnson was re-elected president. Bored and unable to sleep, I listened to the '64 election returns on my transistor radio throughout the night. The Johnson-Humphrey ticket carried forty-four states, collecting 43,129,484 votes to Goldwater/Miller's 27,178,188. The showing was strong enough to earn 486 of 538 electoral votes. Although Johnson was only fifty-five years old when he took office, to me and rest of the gang, as well as most of the country's younger population, he represented a return of power to the older establishment.

Johnson made strong efforts to continue Kennedy's unfinished agenda, including persuading Congress to pass legislation on civil rights, tax cuts, and medical care. After the 1964 election, he did his best to fight for desegregation and African American rights, including the 24th Amendment outlawing poll taxes and the 1965 Voting Rights Act, which eliminated literacy tests and other registration requirements designed to keep blacks from exercising their right to vote. Other milestones for our thirty-sixth president included the Civil Rights Acts of 1964 and 1968; the Elementary and Secondary Education Act; the Medicare Act of 1965; and 1966's Minimum Wage Act.

On June 13, 1967, President Johnson appointed Thurgood Marshall to succeed Justice Tom Clark on the Supreme Court. Marshall was sworn in on October 2, becoming the first African American to serve on the nation's highest court. At St. Pius X, Johnson's domestic victories were sometimes discussed; his international policies, including Vietnam, were never mentioned.

During his inaugural address, Johnson proposed new legislation for his Great Society program. While for one brief, shining moment Camelot existed, Johnson's Great Society never got off the ground. To many, his plan to revitalize and rebuild America was a failure, mired down in over-expenditures and lost to a country at odds over civil rights and an unpopular war.

Taking office, Lyndon Johnson inherited a growing problem in Southeast Asia. President Kennedy had sent military advisers to politically torn South Vietnam, pledging continued support against communist aggression from the north. As the internal struggle escalated, additional supplies and military personnel were deployed. But the official U.S. position remained advisory and one of non-involvement unless directly fired upon. 1964's Gulf of Tonkin Resolution changed all of that. The act found overwhelming support in both houses and placed almost unlimited power to fight communist aggression directly into the president's hands.

On February 8, 1965, a Viet Cong raid on a base in Pleiku, South Vietnam, killed several U.S. servicemen. The following day, under the president's direct orders, U.S. jets struck Viet Cong bases at Don Hoi. By the Feb. 11, air strikes against North Vietnam expanded in retaliation for guerilla attacks on American military bases in South Vietnam. On June 8, as American casualties mounted, Johnson authorized his commanders to commit U.S. ground forces to combat. In his 1966 State of the Union address, the president stated that American involvement in Southeast Asia would continue as long as aggression continued.

From 1961 through November 1965, more than one thousand American troops lost their lives in Vietnam. A year later, the number had grown to almost seven thousand. The unpopular and undeclared war, combined with growing civil rights unrest, would be the undoing of the Johnson administration and, ultimately, the Democratic Party's control. On March 31, 1968, a weary and worn Johnson announced to the country that he would not seek re-election.

It was nearly impossible to turn on my radio without hearing of the war America was now fighting. Even WIBG began broadcasting regular hourly newscasts. Tommy and I and the others would sometimes discuss the far-off war. While we weren't sure of all the details, most of us knew guys from the neighborhood who were in the Army. On weekends we'd sit around our wooded hideaway passing a bottle, smoking, and getting high. We talked about the future and the possibility of being drafted. But by school's end, politics and current events were forgotten as summer jobs and vacations filled our time.

While Johnson increasingly turned his attention to the problems in Southeast Asia, the civil rights movement once again turned violent. In June 1964, three young volunteers participating in a voter registration drive were murdered in Mississippi. Race-related violence would continue to be the top news story coming from my transistor throughout the summer. This time the often deadly confrontations were not confined to the South, as riots broke out in Harlem, Philadelphia, and other major cities.

Then, on February 1, 1965, Martin Luther King, Jr., and 770 of his followers were arrested in Selma, Alabama. The group had been protesting voter discrimination. The following month, 4,000 federal troops were sent to protect Reverend King and 3,000 demonstrators as they marched from Montgomery to Selma.

Race riots in large cities would again break out during the summer of 1965, including Chicago's West Side. In the predominantly black Watts section of Los Angeles, a clash between the California Highway Patrol and two black youths touched off six days of violence and looting. The struggle for integration and civil rights would continue to follow a violent path, culminating in the murder of the Reverend Martin Luther King, Jr., on April 4, 1968.

After nearly winning the National League pennant, my Phillies posted a mediocre season in 1965. With an 85–76 record, they ended up in sixth place, eleven and a half games behind Los Angeles. The Dodgers captured the National League pennant on the strength of an outstanding bullpen that included Cy Young winner Sandy Koufax. The young and talented southpaw had pitched a perfect game for LA on September 9. The Dodgers would go on to win the World Series in seven games against the Minnesota Twins. In Philadelphia, there was little to cheer about. The year's few highlights included pitcher Jim Bunning winning 19 games, and a 13 to 3 rout of the Dodgers in August.

I managed to talk Dad into attending a couple of baseball games in the spring. But increasing racial tensions on Philly's north side spelled an end to our father-son ballpark outings. I contented myself with listening to the games on my radio.

April 9 brought about more changes. The Major Leagues began a new era as baseball moved indoors. In an exhibition game in the newly built Astrodome between the Houston Astros and the New York Yankees, Mickey Mantle hit the first indoor home run. As the regular season got underway, San Francisco's Willie Mays hit his 512th home run to break Mel Ott's record. The Say Hey Kid finished a banner year with a sparkling .317 batting average. But as San Francisco Chronicle sportswriter Harry Jupiter put it, "As a player, Willie Mays could never be captured by mere statistics."

There would be more changes throughout the year, and many more throughout my life. My beloved transistor would lead me through many of them. On July 25, folk singer Bob Dylan was booed as he took the stage at the Newport Folk Festival with an electric guitar. His electrified Highway 61 Revisited LP would become one of the most acclaimed recordings of the rock era. A month earlier, the Byrds had established folk rock as a major musical genre, reaching the top of Billboard's pop charts with their amplified twelve-string version of Dylan's "Mr. Tambourine Man."

Psychedelic rock was born on August 15, when the Jefferson Airplane took to the stage for the first time. The next day Sonny and Cher's "I Got You Babe" hit number one. Soon San Francisco's Haight- Ashbury section would become ground zero for the hippie counter-culture.

In 1965, the gang and I were just getting used to the British Invasion sound when it abruptly changed gears. On August 11 the Beatles' second movie, *Help,* opened in New York. The original soundtrack, different from anything the band had previously released, shot to the top of the charts. Then, at year's end, the Fab Four announced they would stop touring to concentrate on studio recording. But the Beatles faced strong competition from fellow countrymen the Rolling Stones. On July 10, Britain's bad boys of rock displaced the Four Tops' "I Can't Help Myself" at number one with their groundbreaking hit "Satisfaction."

Sunday, December 12, I awoke to the tragic news that Sam Cooke was dead. Through an unfortunate string of misunderstandings, the immensely popular and talented singer had been shot to death by a motel manager in Los Angeles. Again, someone important to me had been taken. Again I turned to my radio for information and comfort.

For a while longer, my little transistor would be my constant companion. My father's unassuming and thoughtful Christmas present helped me to understand and accept the changing world around me. But soon even that would change.

Our last monthly party was a late-afternoon back yard blowout in May of '65. Sherry's mom laid out a large spread on the picnic tables, while her father grilled hamburgers and hot dogs. Sizing us up as he lit the brick barbecue grill, he smiled warmly.

"You guys have gotten much too big for me to take on!"

For most of us, the event was bittersweet. In just a couple of weeks we'd be ninth graders, free of St. Pius X forever. Marlena chose the get-together to announce that she was moving. With the growing needs of the war in Vietnam, her father, an executive at Boeing, was being transferred. In July her family would be leaving for Seattle. September would find Marianne at a well-known private finishing school. And I of course was headed to Paxon Hollow Junior High for ninth grade. Then it would be on to Marple Newtown Senior High. The rest of the gang would be going to Cardinal O'Hara Catholic High School.

That afternoon we ate and talked and danced, keeping to our best behavior. Even Tommy had left his flask at home. As the sun began to set, the mood and tone of the party shifted. Instead of pairing off to dance or get close, we found ourselves gathered together as a group on the freshly mowed back lawn. The same thoughts seemed to be on everybody's minds.

Finally Bob spoke up. "This sucks."

Nine heads nodded in solemn agreement.

"Are you going to Wildwood this year, Amy?" Marlena asked.

"Yes, but not until the middle of June. We'll be staying through Labor Day this year." She turned to me. I could read the pain in her beautiful eyes. "I'm sorry. I should have told you sooner."

I wrapped my arm around her shoulder, pulling her close. "It's okay."

Connie did her best to change the subject and ease the tension. "Well, this really is nice, isn't it? I mean the party and all. What are your plans for the summer, Frankie?"

"Dad's making me work. I got a job as a life guard."

"Oh, that's nice."

He shook his head. "It's at a lake over in Jersey. I'll be gone almost all the time."

"Well... we'll see each other in September, right? And Cardinal O'Hara shouldn't be too bad."

"Shit!" Nick looked up, glancing around the circle. "Sorry, but the damn place might as well be a reform school."

"What do you mean?"

"Don't you know? It's like two separate schools in one. The girls attend one side and the boys are restricted to the other."

Sherry voiced what everyone was thinking. "But that means we won't ever get to see one another."

"Yeah, how 'bout that?" Tommy said softly. "And you know they canceled the back-to-school carnival this year, don't you?"

"Yeah, I heard the merchants were complaining. That dick at the drug store says the carnies bring in a bad element," Bob added.

We looked at each other and laughed. "What the hell do they think we are?" I replied. The comment brought on more laughter and one of Amy's stinging right hooks to my shoulder.

The conversation waned as the last fingers of daylight faded from yellow to gold to pink and finally to a sad, inky blue. So that was it. We wouldn't even have a last summer together. By mid-June the gang would be no more.

Latter I clung tightly to the lovely girl with whom I'd spent the previous four years of my life. We'd been through so much together; we'd grown and laughed and cried and more. I didn't want to let her go. I found myself wishing I could close my eyes, and when I opened them it'd be first Wednesday of fifth grade again, and we could start all over. I didn't want to go back and change anything; it had been too wonderful a time. I just didn't want anything to end—or to change. Amy and I might not be moving away, but we were both moving on.

On the record player, the Flamingos sweetly harmonized the feelings I couldn't put into words:

" *'though we must part/there's no reason to cry/just say so long/because Lovers Never Say Goodbye* "

It was the last time Amy and I danced together.

On a warm afternoon in August, I hopped aboard a SEPTA bus and headed over to the WIBG studios. I found Hy Lit and Joe Niagara in the station's DJ lounge, an area affectionately known as the Bull Pen. Over Pepsi and pizza, my mentors encouraged me to pursue a career in broadcasting, saying that I was a natural and would make a great DJ. They suggested I take speech and even acting classes in high school and continue to keep up with the ever-changing music industry.

"It's a crazy, crazy business, Billy," Hy cautioned, "but you should already know that by now. You have to be a bit crazy yourself in order to survive."

"I think he'll do just fine," Joe added with a smile. He pointed the ever-present Cheroot at me. "Just don't let your head get too big for your head phones!"

I loved these guys. They were full-grown adults with the enthusiasm and unspoiled innocence and optimism of teenagers. Their wisdom came directly from personal experience. I was certain I would have found JFK to be the same.

That evening I wandered up to the Little League ball field. I watched the last game of the season, wondering about Ronnie. Perhaps since we were now in the same school, I would be able to see more of her. On my first day at Paxon Hollow Junior High, one of her friends told me she had moved to Florida at the end of eighth grade. A few nights later I ran into Larry Cartelli, Joe Capone, and Johnny Mancuso. A bottle was passed and the Beatles were bad-mouthed, and a few old doo-wop tunes were sung. Then they had me hot wire a car, and we went for a joy ride. I started to realize there were certain things that never changed.

My sister Mary graduated from West Chester State College, taught high school English, married, and had two beautiful daughters, Sarah and Jessica. After my parents divorced, Mom continued with her acting career. She retired in 1990 and moved to Seattle to be with her daughter and granddaughters. Mom passed away quietly in 2004. She still surprises me with unexpected visits from time to time via an old movie or TV show. After her death, a nice write-up appeared in *Variety Magazine* about the popular 4' 10" character actress from Philadelphia. I know she would have liked that. As of this writing, my ninety-something dad is still alive and doing well, although the years have tempered his conservative and practical nature.

After high school and a short tour in the Army, I returned to Philly to pursue a career in radio. When disco became king, my experience spinning records at hops and dances paid off. Joe and Hy had taught me well. For over thirty years I crisscrossed the country, living on the air "from town to town, up and down the dial." I masked the pain and loneliness with women, alcohol, and the unforgiving glow of the spotlight. Through God's good graces, I managed to survive.

When you are a boy of eleven you know everything; everything you need to know, everything you want to know, and a lot of stuff you don't care about. By the time you turn fifteen, your young world has flipped more times than a Willie Mc Covey baseball card in a hot game of match. Black has become white, and you find the ice cream has all melted. It's not the end of the world for the boy of fifteen, just the end of boyhood. There's a lot more yet to learn, a lot more to explore, find, and do. But the familiar sheltering innocence has fled, scattered to the winds by the realities of the world in which he lives. He awakens and finds the dreams of Camelot faded, replaced by the faltering realities of a society striving vainly towards a distant, amorphous greatness.

All this is true. I know. I was a fifteen-year-old boy. I lived in Camelot and ate the ice cream before it all melted, all twenty-seven flavors.

Last Wednesday of St. Pius X was warm and sunny. For the first time in nine years, the classroom's plastic wall clock seemed to speed up. Before I knew it we were wishing Sister Joanne adieu, leaving finely wrapped boxes of white linen handkerchiefs on her desk. Tradition at St. Pius held that the senior class be dismissed last, allowed to leave the building on their own, freed from the regiment of orderly lines. I found myself lagging behind, casually walking through the familiar halls for the last time. I was in no hurry. Amy was already on her bus headed home.

As I pedaled my big, black Columbia two-wheeler up the long driveway one final time, the last nine years of my academic life passed before me. That day I took the long route home, cruising down Sussex Boulevard and up North Central, enjoying the movie playing over in my mind. It had been a good time, a crazy, corybantic unforgettable time in my life. One, I decided, I wouldn't have traded for anything. Later I rode over to Amy's house. Oddly, I left my transistor radio sitting on the desk in my bedroom. There would be no sound track to our last day together. Perhaps it was appropriate.

Mrs. Johns' smile and friendly hug felt a bit too final. Conversation over chocolate ice cream was labored and difficult. Reluctantly we revisited the last four years. It was nice to talk over old times, but the tone reminded me of a wake.

In the back yard play fort, Amy and I awkwardly clung together. There didn't seem much for us to say. For some reason my friend Chris came to mind.

"Life's a bitch, Daddy-o. You'll never get out of it alive."

Amy smiled. "Chris."

"Yeah…"

"I miss him."

"So do I."

"I'm gonna miss you the most, Delinquent."

I looked into Amy's beautiful hazel eyes for the last time. "Me too, Bulldog. Me too."

She took the silver friendship ring from around her neck and slipped it into my jeans pocket. I still have it today.

I never saw Amy again.

The cruel reality of being young is that you have no real concept of time. You believe there will always be a tomorrow, always time for the things you want to do. I honestly don't know why I never tried to see Amy again. I spent the summer of '65 mostly alone, keeping to myself. In July, Tommy and Nick and Bob and I got together for a party at our hide-a-way in the woods behind Tommy's house. We shared a bottle, and smoked, and talked; laughed, and got high, and set off some fireworks. It was fun, but it wasn't the same. We were all too painfully aware that our moment was over. It was time to move on. I never sniffed glue again, but I carried my alcohol dependence with me well into adulthood.

I never saw any of the gang again either. In a town as small as Broomall, you'd think we would run into each other on occasion, pumping gas or shopping for groceries. We didn't. It's just another one of life's cruel little ironies. I've often been asked why I never tried to contact any of the old gang, especially now, as I write this memoir. I'm not sure I fully understand the reasons myself.

I was working on the air in Houston in the early eighties, when my mom decided it was time to sell the house. She and Dad had long since divorced, and she was moving back to her native Philadelphia. In the fall of 1989 I attended my twentieth high school class reunion. As I drove past the old house on North Central Boulevard, I thought of knocking on the door and asking if I could come in and look around. I didn't. It was their home now, filled with their personalities and their memories. I wanted my memories of my childhood home to be as I remembered them, when I lived there

It's the same with the gang.

Sure, it would be great to catch up and discover everyone's personal story. Perhaps someday I will. But I'd rather remember Tommy and Connie, and Nick and Marianne, and Bob and Marlena, and Frankie and Sherry as they were on that last Saturday evening, at our last party. And for now I prefer to remember Amy as my beautiful, hazel-eyed first girlfriend who smelled of oranges and wore a cute, pink knit stocking cap with a pink pom-pom. To me, she'll always be the girl with whom I shared my ice cream, and my days in Camelot.

The End

⌒About the Author⌒

B
J Neblett is the author of the highly acclaimed literary fiction romantic adventure Elysian Dreams.

His short stories and poetry have been featured in magazines and anthologies.

Raised in and around the city of Philadelphia, BJ began writing at an early age. For BJ, writing was a way to order his thoughts and to, "Make some sense of the world." That world was the 1960's where BJ discovered more than just childhood pleasures and boyhood adventures. He also discovered irony, an irony that seemed to escape those around him. And so BJ wrote. Starting with simple compositions in grade school, he quickly moved on to short stories. With Ray Bradbury and the Twilight Zone and Saturday afternoon matinees as his mentors, BJ wrote about space and friendly aliens and not so friendly things that go bump in the night. Soon discovering the opposite sex, BJ did what any smitten young man would do, he began to write poetry, his work appearing in a national anthology while he was still in high school. And so it continued: during service in the Army; throughout a thirty year career as a radio DJ and a stint working as a for hire cooperate softball gun; while on an extended cross country odyssey of self-discovery, and culminating as a master audio-video tech. BJ has seen and done it all. Today, recalling his corybantic life, BJ is still writing. With one successful novel under his belt, plus several published stories and poems, BJ is hard at work on a sequel to Elysian Dreams; a collection of Fantastic Literature stories; a follow up to Ice Cream Camelot, his historical memoir; and as always, more short stories. When not writing, BJ can always be found on the soft ball mound; kicking back around town with friends; tinkering with his old cars; listening to his extensive record collection, or just relaxing in his Seattle home with one of his vintage guitars.

BJ Neblett's on line persona:

Web Site: www.bjneblett.com

Blog: http: www.bjneblett.blogspot.com

Poetry: www.hereforaseason.blogspot.com

Books:

Elysian Dreams: www.elysiandreamsbook.webs.com

Ice Cream Camelot: www.icecreamcamelot.webs.com

Special Thanks To:

Stephen Plotkin, Reference Archivist, John F. Kennedy Presidential Library

Lynsey Sczechowicz, Laurie Austin, Audiovisual Archives, John F. Kennedy Presidential Library

Lynita Hines, Delaware County Daily Times Newspaper

The Marple Historical Society (Marple Township, Pennsylvania)

Sources and Further Readings:

Books/Publications:

Smith, Carter. Presidents, All You Need to Know. Hylas Publishing, 2004.

Kaplan, Fred. 1959, The Year Everything Changed. John Wiley & Sons, Inc., 2009.

Black, Allida. The First Ladies of the United States of America. The White House Historical Association, 2009.

Hill, Clint. Mrs. Kennedy and Me. Gallery Books, Simon and Schuster, 2012.

Kennedy, Robert F. and Arthur M. Schlesinger, Jr. Thirteen Days: A Memoir of the Cuban Missile Crisis. W. W. Norton & Company, 1999.

Lewis, Brenda and Rupert Mathews. The Historical Atlas of the World at War. Cartographica Ltd., 2009.

Brinkley, Alan. American History: A Survey, Volume 2: Since 1865. Alfred A. Knopf Inc., 1983.

The World Book Year Book 1963, The World Book Encyclopedia. Field Enterprises Educational Corporation, 1963.

The Baseball Encyclopedia: Tenth Edition. Macmillan General Reference, Simon and Schuster, 1996.

Bolander, Donald O., B.S., M.A. Instant Quotation Dictionary. Career Institute Inc., 1969.

Websites:

http://www.jfklibrary.org/

http://en.wikipedia.org/wiki/Jacqueline_Kennedy_Onassis# As_First_Lady

http://www.whitehouse.gov/about/first-ladies/jacquelinekennedy

http://www.presidentialtimeline.org/

http://battleshipcove.com/news-boarding-marucla.htm

http://timelines.com/topics/cuban-missile-crisis

http://en.wikipedia.org/wiki/Cuban_Missile_Crisis

www.infoplease.com/spot/civilrightstimeline1.html

www.infoplease.com/spot/marchonwashington.html

http://www.historyplace.com/kennedy/gallery.htm

http://kennedy-photos.blogspot.com/

http://en.wikipedia.org/wiki/Timeline_of_the_John_F._Kennedy_assassination

http://www.baseball-almanac.com/

http://www.networker.www3.50megs.com/index.html (JFK The Presidency)

http://www.marplehistoricalsociety.org/

http://en.wikipedia.org/wiki/Ernie_Kovacs

http://www.imdb.com/title/tt0055614/fullcredits (West Side Story)

http://timelines.ws/20thcent/1959.HTML

http://timelines.ws/20thcent/1960.HTML

http://timelines.ws/20thcent/1961.HTML

http://timelines.ws/20thcent/1962.HTML

http://timelines.ws/20thcent/1963.HTML

http://timelines.ws/20thcent/1964.HTML

http://www.vpcalendar.net/perpetual-calendars.html

http://en.wikipedia.org/wiki/1960%E2%80%9361_United_
States_network_television_schedule

http://en.wikipedia.org/wiki/1961%E2%80%9362_United_
States_network_television_schedule

http://en.wikipedia.org/wiki/1962%E2%80%9363_United_
States_network_television_schedule

http://en.wikipedia.org/wiki/1963%E2%80%9364_United_
States_network_television_schedule

http://en.wikipedia.org/wiki/1964%E2%80%9365_United_
States_network_television_schedule

CPSIA information can be obtained
at www.ICGtesting.com
Printed in the USA
LVHW090006041120
670652LV00032B/184